Nelson George is the author of twelve nonfiction books on African American culture and of five novels. He has received two ASCAP-Deems Taylor Awards, a Grammy, and the American Book Award from the Before Columbus Foundation for *Hip Hop America* and *Elevating the Game: Black Men and Basketball*. *Hip Hop America* and *The Death of Rhythm & Blues* were also nominated for National Book Critics Circle Awards. He has written for national magazines, including *Playboy, Billboard, Esquire, Spin, Essence,* and *The Village Voice,* and has written and produced several television programs as well as three feature films. He was born in Brooklyn, New York, where he still lives. He can be reached at www.NelsonGeorge.com

THE DEATH OF RHYTHM & BLUES

NELSON GEORGE

PENGUIN BOOKS

For Robert Ford, Jr.,
Robert Christgau, and Adam White

PENGUIN BOOKS
Published by the Penguin Group
Penguin Group (USA) Inc., 375 Hudson Street, New York, New York 10014, U.S.A.
Penguin Books Ltd, 80 Strand, London WC2R 0RL, England
Penguin Books Australia Ltd, 250 Camberwell Road, Camberwell, Victoria 3124, Australia
Penguin Books Canada Ltd, 10 Alcorn Avenue, Toronto, Ontario, Canada M4V 3B2
Penguin Books India (P) Ltd, 11 Community Centre,
Panchsheel Park, New Delhi – 110 017, India
Penguin Books (N.Z.) Ltd, Cnr Rosedale and Airborne Roads,
Albany, Auckland, New Zealand
Penguin Books (South Africa) (Pty) Ltd, 24 Sturdee Avenue,
Rosebank, Johannesburg 2196, South Africa

Penguin Books Ltd, Registered Offices:
80 Strand, London WC2R 0RL, England

First published in the United States of America by Pantheon Books,
a division of Random House, Inc. 1988
Published by Plume, an imprint of Dutton Signet,
a division of Penguin Books USA Inc. 1991
Published in Penguin Books 2004

1   3   5   7   9   10   8   6   4   2

Copyright © Nelson George, 1988
All rights reserved

ISBN 0-452-26697-1 (Plume edition)
ISBN 0 14 20.0408 1 (Penguin edition)

Printed in the United States of America
Designed by Chris Welch

CONTENTS

Acknowledgments **vii**

Introduction: A Meditation on the Meaning of "Death" **ix**

O N E

Philosophy, Money, and Music (1900–30) **3**

T W O

Dark Voices in the Night (1930–50) **15**

T H R E E

The New Negro (1950–65) **59**

F O U R

Black Beauty, Black Confusion (1965–70)   **95**

F I V E

Redemption Songs in the Age of Corporations (1971–75)   **121**

S I X

Crossover: The Death of Rhythm & Blues (1975–79)   **147**

S E V E N

Assimilation Triumphs, Retronuevo Rises (1980–87)   **171**

Epilogue   **199**

Notes   **203**

Index   **207**

Photographs follow pages **80** and **144.**

ACKNOWLEDGMENTS

This book draws on the hundreds of interviews and stories I've been involved in since my journalistic career began at the *Amsterdam News* in 1978. The first entertainment piece I ever wrote was a heavily edited story on Natalie Cole, which I hope is lost forever in the *Am News*'s yellowed files. Between then and now several people have been crucial to my education in the ways and means of rhythm & blues. Robert Ford, Jr., former roommate, surrogate older brother, and unappreciated five-star chef, taught me the record business from the ground up and is responsible for any flashes of absurdist humor in my prose. Adam White, during my two tours of duty at *Billboard*, hipped me to the British perspective on black music and gave me a chance to express myself in that magazine's pages. Robert Christgau's rigorous editing and intellectual demands at the *Village Voice* gave me the confidence to pursue my ideas and taught me that criticism is not a popularity contest.

There are many other people I should thank for their contributions, direct and indirect, to this enterprise, so here goes: my agent Sarah Lazin sold it; Wendy Goldwyn understood it the first time I mentioned it on the phone and, even better, bought it for Pantheon; Patty Romanowski, that ever helpful book lady, structured it; Wendy Wolf and her co-conspirator Tony Borden beat it into shape; Sharon Lopez and Antonette Dailey word-processed it. The research of Steve Ivory and Jeff Hannusch aided me as did the pioneering R&B scholarship of Portia Maultsby. Alan Leeds, a man of two eras, and Russell Simmons, a man of vision and bravado, remain active symbols of R&B; Andre Harrell, Warrington and Reggie Hudlin, and Richard Wesley are members of the Uptown Crew; Lydia Hannibal, Sylvia Greene, and Charlotte Hunter were friends through thick and a bit of thin; Spike Lee's *She's Gotta Have It*, August Wilson's *Fences* and *Joe Turner's Come and Gone*, and Charles Fuller's *Soldier's Story* provided artistic inspiration.

Periodicals that I referred to in writing this book include (in no particular order): *Billboard*, *Village Voice*, *Jack the Rapper*, *Black Radio Exclusive*, *Black Enterprise*, *Essence*, *Ebony*, *Jet*, *Players*, *New Music Express*, *Spin*, *Rolling Stone*, *Musician*, *Soho Weekly News*, *Goldmine*, *New York Times*, *Washington Post*, *Interview*, *Atlantic Monthly*, *Crisis*, *Wavelength*, *Soul Survivor*, and the dear departed *Record World*.

It would be great to thank individually all those folks in and out of the music biz whose insights helped shape this book, but the list would be too damn long and I'd hate to leave anyone out. I do, however, have to acknowledge the crucial input of musician-philosopher James Mtume, who injected some strong opinions during a few lengthy Brooklyn to East Orange phone calls. Many books were used as references, but three were essential to this book as technical, intellectual, and spiritual guides: *Mystery Train* by Greil Marcus, *Blues People* by Leroi Jones, and *Crisis of the Negro Intellectual* by Harold Cruse.

A MEDITATION ON THE MEANING OF "DEATH"

From the Manhattan window of the black record executive's office I could see tourists and office workers seeking ice cream, hot dogs, and an open space in the shadow of Rockefeller Center. We sat inside, the walls lined with framed posters of Coltrane and Diz and Bird and Miles. I was surprised there were no gold records hanging there, since in his two decades as a record retailer, promotion man, and now vice-president of black music for a major corporate label, the executive had been involved in the sale of millions of records, tapes, CDs, and, when they made them, eight-track tapes. We were talking about "crossover"—an industry term for shifting the sales base of black performers to the larger white audience—and its effect on black music. He was remarking how so much of today's music lacked what he called "that intangible something."

Somewhere in the middle of those comments he volunteered that he regretted "never making a big effort to expose my children to black life." Over the past fifteen years he'd used his steadily increasing income to raise two kids in the San Fernando Valley and later in a New Jersey bedroom community. He now found that despite the jazz reissues he brought home and the exposure to all the black pop artists his career gave them, his kids thought Phil Collins was as funky as Cameo and that hanging out in malls was a lot more fun than visiting relatives in Uptown, U.S.A.

He made no apologies for providing the best he could for his family. Nor should he. Integrated schools, the Topsider life-style, and the promise of college and a meaningful career were what it was supposed to be all about. Yet as his kids grew older, it was clear they didn't feel the same way about things. To his ears, nothing from affirmative action to soul food, from the welfare state to James Brown, was understood or appreciated. He wondered aloud whether he'd done something wrong and, if he had, what could he have done differently?

I have given this book a deliberately provocative title, but one that epitomizes the perspective of this work on post–World War II black popular music and black culture in general. Something died. It may come back in some form. In fact, I'm sure it will. But only by studying its death can we understand how that intangible "something" can be revived and sustained.

First of all, what is rhythm & blues? For the purpose of this work it has two meanings, one musical and one socioeconomic. The term originated in the 1940s as a description of a synthesis of black musical genres—gospel, big-band swing, blues—that, along with new technology, specifically the popularization of the electric bass, produced a propulsive, spirited brand of popular music. A decade later it would be called rock & roll to camouflage its black roots, and subsequently soul, funk, disco, rap, and other offspring would arise from these roots. Throughout this book I'll often use the term "rhythm & blues" in conjunction with those other terms because they are so strongly linked historically, and because crucial elements in the music have never changed.

But the "rhythm & blues world" means something extramusical as well. R&B—and music in general—have been an integral part of (and, to me, a powerful symbol for) a black community forged by common political, economic, and geographic conditions. When members of black families fled the fields of the South for the factories of the North, they brought with them valises of clothes, stories from their childhoods, music from their churches, and hopes about a fresh start in the new cities. While cities did offer them new business opportunities, and a break with their rural past, along with these positive changes came a whole new set of roadblocks—cramped, overcrowded housing, the cyclical scarcity of jobs, and the hard lesson that the basic inequalities of black life in America would not be solved by a change of scenery.

Today we're all too aware of the devastating sights of black (and other urban ethnic) slums, decimated by crime, poverty, joblessness, drugs. What we've forgotten is that these neighborhoods were once vibrant and richly diversified, home not just to street gangs but to doctors, attorneys, and hard-working folks of every profession. Though the distinctions between the haves and have-nots were always clear, the interaction between this wide range of people made for real, living culture. And the music, and the way it was bought and sold, reflected the communal, city life.

The response of the black communities to the prospects after World War II was to attempt to move forward—be it by turning to *Ebony* magazine or to the Nation of Islam, both of which were born out of the optimism and despair of Chicago's South Side. Though these institutions may have fundamentally disagreed on tactics, both served as catalysts for black political and economic aspirations. Supporting these institutions and others like them around the country was the full complement of city life: barbershops and beauty parlors, grocers and theaters, street corners and record shops, where blacks of all ages gathered and worked, often for white employers, though unified black protest would increase black ownership eventually.

The thing that pulled this whole community together, at least for a time, was that despite their many and sometimes conflicting agendas, its members had a common desire to achieve equality under the law, end overt and covert racism, and acquire firm power both inside and outside their own circles. On these points the black community stood united. And, to the amazement of just about everyone, this sense of purpose (which was the essence of the R&B world) would eventually help break down doors and push through much critical legislation in the 1950s and 1960s. And when "freedom" came, some black people found it to be as tangible as money in the bank, which in the American value system is about as real as it gets. The black record executive and others of his generation found desegregated America a place of unexpected creature comforts that his parents never would have imagined.

But there was a problem. The very causes and energy that once pulled that world together began to pull it apart, and here it is not just instructive but, to me, essential that we look at what it all meant for the music. Like that record executive, I can't shake off the feeling that in the enormous groundswell of change in the black community since World War II, something crucial *has* been lost. In the twenty years since the Great Society, which marked a high point in R&B music, the community that inspired both social change and artistic creativity has become a sad shell of itself: unhappily, while the drive behind the movement for social change was the greatest inspiration for the music, the very success of the movement spelled the end of the R&B world. One of the underlying assumptions of integration was that a solid education among whites would produce blacks qualified intellectually and socially to fit into middle-class, white-collar, corporate America. But rarely, except by those outside the civil-rights orthodoxy, was there any discussion about what kind of people, morally and spiritually, this "progress" would produce. The truth is that since white values were held up as primary role models, many blacks, through no fault of their own, lost contact with the uniqueness of their people, and with their own heritage. The sixties battle cry, "Black is Beautiful," has been answered in the eighties with nose jobs and blue contact lenses. Pursuing an anglicized self-image, these "transformed" black people, with their belief that anything can be sacrificed to generate more capital, are one of the disturbing triumphs of assimilation. Interestingly, many second- and third-generation European immigrants have experienced the same cultural isolation.

As a result of these broad social changes, black culture, and especially R&B music, has atrophied. The music is just not as gutsy or spirited or tuned into the needs of its core audience as it once was. Compare the early Aretha Franklin to Whitney Houston. Franklin's music always relied heavily on the black inner-city experience, and especially on the black church. When she forgets that, she stumbles. Houston is extremely talented, but most of her music is so "color-blind," such a product of eighties crossover marketing, that in her commercial triumph is a hollowness of spirit that mocks her own gospel roots.

And while many blacks have prospered financially, recent years in particular have brought heightened economic disparities within the black community. In fact, the critical community diversity, so key to the culture, has in large part been lost because now the doctors—as well as the record execs—are likely to live far from their audience and clients. Again, the music world gives the best (or worst) possible examples of this, because of the vastly complicated network of people who are involved in the marketing of a song. Musicians, of course, have been caught up in the "flight" syndrome, but so have salesmen, concert promoters, record-store owners, and, most crucially, deejays and their employers. This gets to one of the key elements in my story: radio has historically been so intimately connected with the consciousness of blacks that it remained their primary source of entertainment and information well into the age of television. Even in today's VCR- and CD-filled era, black radio plays a huge role in shaping black taste and opinion—when it remembers its black audience. As I'll explain, black radio increasingly chooses to forget or ignore that audience. It's a choice with dire consequences for the R&B world.

As you read on, keep in mind that this is not a definitive or comprehensive history of rhythm & blues music, nor was it ever intended to be one. First of all, I don't believe it's possible to write such a story. "Definitive" is a term for critics who forget that history has as much to do with perspective as with facts. You won't find an encyclopedia of life stories here. The people profiled in this book were selected because they were personal heroes, had some telling understanding of black music history, or because they—sometimes negatively, sometimes inadvertently—affected the direction or the character of the R&B world.

I wanted to write a book that would slice through the many layers of the R&B world, and perhaps expose some of the areas that have been unfairly neglected both by academics and by journalists. Black radio is the most important of these, in my opinion, which is why I've chosen to concentrate so heavily on its history. By linking the evolution of black radio to the growth of the independent labels, the development of retail outlets, and the structure of today's record companies, I hope both to fill a gap in the critical imagination and to tell a story that is the *essence* of R&B. All those factors and actors, *along* with performers' creativity and talent, interact to determine which artists are deemed important and which aren't—who will become today's stars, and where to look for tomorrow's. That's why I spend as much time looking at businessmen as I do at musicians; my experience as a journalist and my instincts as a critic tell me that's where the story lies.

But I have an agenda that goes beyond an argument about music. As I suggested at the beginning, there is something missing in black America, and symptoms of the illness are in its music. But I don't want this book to be just a eulogy. If one idea could be said to inspire *The Death of Rhythm & Blues*, it is: "You can tell where black people are at any given point in history by our music." I've heard black people say this countless times, but my "beef" was that they never really thought about the state of blacks. They were just spouting a nice piece of rhetoric. I took that rhetoric to heart. Thinking about the present and the future, I went looking through the past. *The Death of Rhythm & Blues* is what I found.

Nelson George
Brooklyn

THE DEATH OF RHYTHM & BLUES

PHILOSOPHY,

MONEY, AND

MUSIC

(1900—30)

A great many Americans, spoon fed words of democracy like "brotherhood" and "divided we fall" since childhood, are uncomfortable with the idea that an ethnic or racial group needs to band together and have goals that clearly and purposefully set them apart from the rest of the country. Yet racial, national, and religious power blocs have always been integral to how power is wielded in this nation.

Because of the disenfranchisement of blacks, it has been hard for them to assume power positions in America. Since we were introduced to the country as slaves, we've occupied a uniquely isolated part of this "melting pot" nation. Yet the idea of racial unification, of establishing a black agenda and sticking with it—as the Jews, Italians, and Irish have so often done—has never been fully realized. Assimilation or self-sufficiency? Within the realities of the American system both are necessary for advancement but only assimilation, the strategy that dilutes the racial power bloc in exchange for an American identity of dubious rewards, has dominated the thinking of most black Americans. We can see the roots of this debate in the contrasting philosophies of Booker T. Washington and W. E. B. Du Bois, the dominant black leaders of the early twentieth century.

From his base on the campus of Alabama's Tuskegee Institute, Washington amassed a vast network of supporters, from President Theodore Roosevelt to the heads of the black media. The industrialist Andrew Carnegie once gave the college $60,000 in bonds from U.S. Steel on the condition that $15,000 of it be utilized to serve the personal needs of Washington and his family. With friends like these the ex-slave garnered enough influence to become the quasi-official leader of U.S. blacks. It was said that he had veto power over federal appointments in the South not only of blacks but of a great many whites and that he had enough connections to in some way get back at any black institution that opposed him.

Washington gained this intimidating power by advocating for his people not equality and education but vocational training in areas of manual labor. (Tuskegee for example became one of the finest agricultural colleges in the South.) His practical vision determined that black people should survive and function in America as skilled workers capable of running their own operations in a segregated company. It was implicit in his thinking that blacks would ultimately become so skilled that the white businessmen's desire for quality workers would overcome racism. As Washington wrote in the early 1900s in response to calls for civil-rights legislation, "Brains, property and character of the Negro will settle the question of civil rights. The best course to pursue in regard to a civil rights bill in the South is to let it alone: let it alone and it will settle itself. Good school teachers and plenty of money to pay them will be more potent in settling the race question than any civil rights bills and investigative committees."

Unfortunately he has been seen by many blacks, then as now, as an Uncle Tom. As an unembarrassed member of the ruling establishment, he refused to vigorously attack lynching, to defend the rights of Southern blacks to vote, or otherwise to be a verbal warrior in the tradition of Frederick Douglass, the black leader who preceded him.

Washington was a paradox. He wouldn't champion the need for expanded black political power, yet he sought and captured more clout in the nation's capital than all but a handful of elected officials and business moguls. He could argue in a speech that a black man had invited his own lynching, yet several times he endangered the Tuskegee operation by hiding would-be victims on the campus.

His philosophy of pragmatic capitalism and backslapping politics were viciously attacked by members of the Northern black elite. They resented his leadership and, because of his political clout, the limitations it imposed on them. Maybe some accommodation could have been worked out if Washington hadn't been so dogmatic, but he viewed any deviation from his program as a betrayal. So in 1903, when young historian-activist W. E. B. Du Bois skewered Washington in *The Souls of Black Folk*, lambasting his policies and offering a new agenda, an all-out philosophical war was on. Du Bois, supported by even more militant anti-Washingtonians like William Monroe Trotter, put politics first, seeing the keys to black liberation in gaining an education and the power of the vote. Then they could force whites to live up to the words of the Constitution.

What Du Bois labeled the "talented tenth," the privileged, educated black elite, would provide leadership. (That Du Bois clearly saw himself as part of this tenth is of no little import, as we shall see.) It was from Du Bois's fertile mind that the idea for the National Association for the Advancement of Colored People was spawned, inspiring the use in the civil-rights movement of successful blacks as role models for the race. And the black drive (aided by liberal whites) for integration emerged.

Washington saw black America as a pyramid, with himself on top; his appointees and allies in the middle; and at the bottom, on their farms, in factories, and in small businesses, most other blacks. Du Bois envisioned a pyramid filled at the top with educated, polished (and lighter-skinned) blacks, and below, a mass of blacks following them. Unfortunately, neither leader could imagine these pyramids existing in harmony. As black essayist James Weldon Johnson wrote in 1933, "One not familiar with this phase of Negro life in the 12- or 14-year period following 1903 . . . cannot imagine the bitterness of the antagonism between the two wings."

Washington's advocacy of marketable skills and hard work, was, I think, admirable as a practical, economically sound way not simply to mobilize blacks but to feed and employ them (though not to the exclusion of Du Bois and his fellow activists). But Washington and his philosophy fell into disrepute, partly through a backlash against his authoritarianism, and partly because he had no heir strong enough to continue articulating his stance and maintain his network of contacts.

Ultimately, though, his decline came about because the black intellectual elite found Du Bois's vision infinitely more appealing, in no small measure out of self-interest. The rejection of Washington and the rise of the NAACP meant that the drive to assimilation became the dominant item on the black agenda. Du Bois's victory is demonstrable today. Any poll of black Americans would reveal a strong desire to be more completely accepted into the white American mainstream.

Only a minority of blacks would openly agitate for more self-sufficiency. I find myself among that minority, not because I dislike whites or disdain the American dream—at least in both cases not entirely—but because I see the assimilationist's triumph, in the 1980s as it was in the 1920s, of little material value in improving the lives of most Afro-Americans.

Those who find Washington backward on the broader question of racial equality find much fuel for their argument in the specifics of his economic program, with its orientation toward agriculture. But this focus was only due to the fact that at the time most blacks lived in the unindustrialized South. There is no reason to believe that Washington would not have adapted his strategies to the technological opportunities this century has provided.

Such groundless critiques, however, have contributed to the perception of Washington as a Neanderthal man. A typical example of Washington-bashing from the popular arts is Moses Gunn's portrayal of him in the film *Ragtime*. There is irony in that, because it was in the area of the arts that Washington had one of his finest, though unfulfilled, insights. The introduction and failure of this project provide a good idea of why a separate black economic agenda has always been stifled.

In the spring of 1915, the release of *Birth of a Nation*, a film by D. W. Griffith based on Thomas Dixon's novel *The Clansman*, sent waves of celebration and horror across the land. In a year that marked the fiftieth anniversary of the end of the Civil War, Griffith's epic testified to every racist and reactionary instinct in the nation, rewriting the history of the war and Reconstruction through eyes that saw only the bestiality of blacks, the corruption of Northern abolitionists, and patriotism behind the Ku Klux Klan's campaign of terror. That Griffith employed all the latest technological innovations of cinema in creating these hate-filled images of black evil and white purity is typical of America's track record of mating brilliant technique with destructive imagery.

Blacks felt outrage. But how should they express it? Protest was widespread but ineffective in either surpressing the film or sapping its box-office appeal. Du Bois, editor of the NAACP's house organ, *Crisis*, articulated the need for blacks to make a rebuttal and coauthored an outline that NAACP executives took to the president of Universal Studios, Carl Laemmle. The movie mogul agreed to make the film if the NAACP put up half the money. The organization's monied white members declined.

Down at Tuskegee, Washington and his secretary, Emmett J. Scott, began searching for a way to make their own film. After some unsatisfactory dealings with white companies, Washington and Scott decided that they should make the film themselves. They explored purchasing film stock, acquired projection equipment, explored the cost for shooting on campus, and wrote a script based on Washington's propagandistic autobiography, *Up from Slavery*. They negotiated with a black Chicagoan, Edwin Barker of the Advance Motion Picture Company, to handle production, promising the cooperation not only of themselves but of the six hundred chapters of the National Negro Business League and the black press in raising funds and publicizing the project. It seemed like a formula for a real large-scale black-run attempt at not just refuting *Birth* but building a film studio with the blessing of the strongest black institution in existence.

But on November 14, 1915, before the deal with Barker was set, Washington died at Tuskegee. Scott was determined to continue with the film, however, and a month later signed with Barker. A great many whites and blacks of good faith invested time and money into *Birth of a Race*, but without Washington's influence the film slipped into the hands of con men, swindlers, and incompetents, not the least of whom turned out to be Barker himself. At one point Barker told *Variety* that the film wasn't about blacks at all. It opened in Chicago in November 1918, and it was, by all accounts, a travesty of Washington's and Scott's efforts.

If Washington had lived to see the project through there is no doubt in my mind that *Birth of a Race* would have achieved its goal of forcefully rebutting Griffith. (Of course, that doesn't mean it would necessarily have been a good film since political leaders are rarely good artists.) The film aside, who knows what the project might have inspired? For its core was an independent production company—Washington's view of economic separation realized. And black culture could have benefitted tremendously. Despite this failure, others would embrace the concept of an independent black cinema or, at least, the concept that the black audience desired more varied images of itself than Hollywood offered.

But their efforts were similarly hampered by the difficulty of raising money and the studios' monopoly over theaters, held into the 1950s.

There are few historical references to Washington's taste in music and, given the intensity of his efforts in other areas, he probably didn't give music much serious thought. Washington, a product of the prim, structured world of black colleges like Virginia's Hampton Institute and his own Tuskegee Institute, apparently looked down on the blues-shouting and banjo-picking that was popular throughout the South while he was building his empire. Around the turn of the century, the choral style called jubilee singing, in praise of a Christian god, was the favored music of the black elite. It was clean-cut, respectable, staid—what Washington thought the hard-working masses would find motivating.

The black educator's indifference to music is a shame, since Washington and his contemporaries among the black elite would have been well advised to pay more attention to an incipient industry that could have been a potent weapon in the struggle for the soul of black America. In fact, this ignorance of the importance of music, not as an entertainment force but as a social and economic tool, was a weakness later disciples of both Washington and Du Bois suffered from, seeing the music and its milieu as vulgar.

SELLING RACE

The record industry began as a stepchild of the sheet-music business, since popular tunes originally were consumed primarily through the sale of sheet music. From World War I through the mid-1920s, advances in technology permitted an explosion in record sales, causing music industry historians to dub this period the "golden age." Ragtime, highly syncopated piano-based music that sprang from the innovations of black composers such as Scott Joplin, was the most popular "pop" style of the first two decades, and it would be utilized profitably by any number of white composers. (Irving Berlin, for example, wrote "Alexander's Ragtime Band" in 1911.) When newspapers labeled ragtime "vulgar, filthy, and suggestive" because of its vibrant, sexual danceability, the black elite, who were highly sensitive to what whites thought of them, agreed, implying that such overt displays of the "African spirit" hindered the advancement of the race.

However, the makers of recorded music didn't let concerns of class or racism deny them a profit. Starting with the sale of ten thousand copies of Mamie Smith's "Crazy Blues" in 1920 on the Okeh label (then an offshoot of the General Phonograph Company), black talent performing black music was an integral part of the business. Black bands from New Orleans, like trumpeter Louis Armstrong's Hot Five, large ensembles such as the orchestras of Duke Ellington and Jimmy Lunceford, and "social bands" that played the Elk's Halls or Masonic Temples were big favorites.

It was during the early days of recorded music that economics and semantics embraced each other for the first time, to the detriment of blacks. The origins of the term "jazz" have always been debated, but it most likely came from black slang. Whites, however, popularized the term in print, defining it as a music that, unlike ragtime or spirituals, put great emphasis on improvisation. Primarily because of its appeal as dance music, this style became so popular among whites, and white bands began playing it in such large numbers, that from the 1920s to the 1940s, jazz was seen as white music. In retrospect, critics would point out how ridiculous it was to dub pale 1920s bandleader Paul Whiteman the "King of Jazz." Indeed, at a time when lynching in the South reached this century's peak, F. Scott Fitzgerald used "the Jazz Age," to describe a period of white indulgence—an indulgence that led them to explore, more for amusement than edification, the "primitive" artistic expression of blacks. The beauty of American capitalism is that it can assimilate anything into its production machine, package it, and sell it as if it were a new item. For much of the first half of the century, jazz as a music and as a social expression was so merchandised.

While the term "jazz" gave Whiteman equal weight with Ellington, and Bix Beiderbecke comparable standing with Louis Armstrong, the term "race" was applied to forms of black music—primarily blues—that whites and, again, the black elite disdained. Some writers in recent years have attacked the use of the phrase "race music," as record labels of the period called blues, but as Albert Murray wrote in *Stomping the Blues* (1976), "race" was commonly used by blacks themselves in the early part of this century to define themselves. "The fact remains—oblivious as certain critics may be to it—that in the black press of the 1920s the most prominent Negro leaders and spokesmen referred to themselves as race spokesmen and race leaders . . . the indignation over the race terminology as applied to records has been misguided at best."

In fact, I think the appeal of this working-class, rural black music is very well described as race music. The blues, either in the wailing voice of Bessie Smith or Ma Rainey, or in the demonic songs and guitar licks of Delta blues legend Robert Johnson, spoke to the gut feelings of the masses of unassimilated blacks who frequented juke joints and barrel-houses. This is not to say it couldn't be adulterated. One of the worst offenders was black middle-class composer W. C. Handy, who is called the father of the blues only because he was one of the first to commit it to sheet music. Again, it was clear even before World War II that semantics could be as important to the history of American music as creativity—and when it came to assigning credit, it could be more important.

It is also crucial to note that an aesthetic schism between high-brow, more assimilated black styles and working-class, grass-roots sounds existed in the community, a schism that would be stretched, bent, or closed depending on the mood of the times.

Handy, though hardly the blues' daddy, was demonstrably insightful about the economic value of blues in a way most of his middle-class peers were not. Aside from claiming as his own a slew of traditional blues melodies he arranged but didn't compose, Handy financed one of the first black record labels, Black Swan, in 1921. Handy emphasized that fact in his advertising. On the sleeve to Trixie Smith's "Trixie's Blues," the jacket copy boasts, "The only records made entirely by colored people," and "The only records using exclusively Negro voices." Trixie Smith was a "classic" blues artist in the tradition of Bessie Smith and Ma Rainey, but Handy, an educated man, also reached out to satisfy the market for more urbane black music. The innovative black band leader Fletcher Henderson was hired as Black Swan's musical director, and Ethel Waters, a woman whose brillance as a pop singer was overshadowed by her later acting achievements, was his most prominent catch. I use the phrase "pop" in reference to Waters not to distance her from the blues but to distinguish her smooth, nonethnic timbre, which made her a star on Broadway. Waters had what years later would be labeled crossover potential. As another Black Swan ad suggests, Handy was attempting to show the diversity of black talent: "Only bonafide Racial Company making talking machine records. All stockholders are Colored, all artists are Colored, all employees are Colored. Only company using Racial Artists in recording high-class song records. This company makes the only Grand Opera Records ever made by Negroes. All others confine this end of their work to blues, rags, comedy numbers, etc."

It was a nice try, a necessary try, but one that ultimately failed. In 1924 Handy sold Black Swan to the Paramount Recording Company, a subsidiary of the powerful film studio. There were other early attempts at black-owned labels, but most, like Black Swan, failed in competition with larger white-owned operations. In a general sense, of course, racism hurt Handy and his counterparts, but so did chaotic distribution. The bigger black bands, under the banner of swing, could be sold through regular record stores; race music had no such entree. And even where an outlet could be found, the companies could seldom afford any kind of manager to monitor sales. As a result the records were often distributed and accounts payable were collected in a haphazard manner. The Pullman porters, the black men in white jackets and black caps who served in the railway cars, made up a black underground communications network, traveling across the country bringing news from one black community to the next, by word of mouth, and by selling black newspapers like the *Chicago Daily Defender* and records they brought from Chicago, New Orleans, and St. Louis. By the time they hit Tennessee, Mississippi, or Florida, the porters, a great many of whom were shrewd businessmen, had marked up the prices considerably. But they were under no pressure to let their distributors in the North know by how much. Race records could sometimes be found in an extremely well-stocked general store; even a furniture store might have them next to a Victrola in order to increase sales of the new technology. In either case, the gap between the record-makers and the actual sale could be large. Another factor that hurt the race labels was that much of their core audience—rural blacks—lived in areas that wouldn't be electrified for several decades.

THE FIRST WAVES

Radio broadcasts were rarely used to promote grittier forms of music. If you liked swing in the 1920s and 1930s you could pick up live broadcasts of Duke Ellington at the Cotton Club and Chick Webb at the Savoy in Harlem, Earl (Fatha) Hines from Chicago's Grand Terrace, or maybe a late set from some California band from the West Coast Cotton Club. Significantly, these broadcasts weren't aimed at blacks. Broadcasters and advertisers were simply meeting America's demand for big-band music. These bands just happened to be black and popular.

The first programming to utilize race music was aimed at attracting black listeners to a particular product. Sponsors, starting in the 1930s, bought blocks of air time, day or night, to promote pork chops, chitlins, secondhand furniture, patent medicine, and anything else thought to appeal to blacks. A representative example is the "King Biscuit Time," broadcast in the early 1940s from the teeming little metropolis of Helena, Mississippi, deep in the heavily black Delta region. At noon, singer-harmonica player Rice (Sonny Boy Williamson) Miller and guitarist Robert Lockwood brought listeners fifteen minutes of blues and greetings from the makers of King Biscuit flour. At one point the broadcast became so popular that a line of Sonny Boy cornmeal was introduced. These broadcasts did sell some 78 RPM records, but they were more valuable both as advertising for selling cornmeal and for enhancing the performers' value as live attractions.

But in general, those seeking unpolished blues wouldn't find it on records or the radio. These items weren't essential to the leisure time of poor and working-class blacks, and to entrepreneurs interested in targeting this market they clearly were not very attractive investments. Instead many black and white businessmen, aware of the growing economic weight of the concentrated black communities, would have pinpointed black baseball as the way to go. Black-owned teams had operated as far back as 1885. One Long Island–based squad tried to disguise itself, playing under the name Cuban Giants.

In the 1920s there were two significant leagues, the Negro National Baseball League and the Mutual Association of Eastern Baseball Clubs, and a number of independent teams that barnstormed, touring throughout a region challenging other local teams. Gangsters, bootleggers, numbers-runners, and a great many entertainers owned teams. For example, in 1931 Louis Armstrong gave his name to and partially financed a seventeen-member New Orleans team named Armstrong's Secret Nine. The strongest advocate for black baseball was Andrew (Rube) Foster, a black businessman and former pitcher who became the unofficial commissioner of the seven-team Negro National League. He believed that black baseball could be more profitable and exciting if it was better organized. Over the next twenty-four years, his league, despite many shifts in titles, cities, and ownership, combined with leagues run by a number of other blacks to fulfill Foster's ambition of satisfying the craving of blacks for athletic entertainment while providing employment, on and off the field, for blacks in a Jim Crow world. Besides a raft of legendary ballplayers, including pitcher Satchell Page, outfielder Cool Papa Bell, and catcher Josh Gibson, the Negro Leagues gave rise to black businessmen-managers such as Cumberland Possey of the

Homestead Grays and W. A. (Gus) Greenlee of the Philadelphia Craw-fords, men who excelled in the front office and in the dugout.

In big-city ballparks like New York's Yankee Stadium or Chicago's Comiskey Park, as well as on country diamonds around the South, black baseball—one of the few public displays of black competence—became an integral part of black social life. The fans filled the stands wearing their Sunday best, enthusiastically commenting on the action and eating food from well-filled baskets. Live music, played before and after games, and even between innings, enhanced the festive atmosphere.

To my mind black baseball was, at its best, an extension of Washington's idea of black self-sufficiency. Of course not all the owners or officials were black. Nor did its existence in any way satisfy the craving of blacks for integration into the white leagues. But the Negro Leagues did create black stars, train black managers, and employ blacks in support positions. And black baseball shouted, to those who listened properly, that, in the tradition of other ethnic groups, some form of intragroup solidarity could produce economic and social benefits.

The assimilationist–versus–self-sufficiency debate and the semantic revisionism of black music would grow more intense through World War II. New elements that would affect black philosophies and music were on the way. Much of the change would develop out of the ever-restless currents of black creativity. But equally important would be a mating of technology and commerce that spawned new music, new aesthetics, and a generation of very lively talkers.

DARK VOICES

IN THE

NIGHT

(1930–50)

Blacks remained loyal to the Republican Party from the end of the Civil War until the presidential election of 1932, when they finally had to abandon the party of Lincoln, the Emancipation Proclamation, and Reconstruction. That romance, tested and found wanting through Jim Crow and the unremitting acts of physical and psychological terrorism against blacks, had finally ended with Franklin Delano Roosevelt's New Deal. As the poorest of a troubled nation, blacks had the most to gain from the introduction of Social Security, a minimum wage, and public-works programs that created jobs and constructed pools, parks, and libraries in their communities. New Deal programs also gave many black artists a chance to develop their craft. Two of the most prominent writers of the postwar period, Richard Wright and Ralph Ellison, helped make ends meet by working for the Federal Writers Workshop.

The political shifts in black allegiances and the relief programs of the New Deal may have helped blacks in bread-and-butter ways, and certainly in the more rarefied world of art, but no one—not even the broad-minded Roosevelts—contemplated a more radical program to promote economic incentives *within* the black community, or to address the very fundamental disenfranchisement of blacks socially and politically. The president was no fan of sharecropping, but the notion that there could be a separate realm of black economic activity—even something as simple as aid to help blacks purchase their own land—challenged too many assumptions about the way things were supposed to operate, at least in the 1930s. Whites were unable to consider the idea that black productivity could actually benefit the broader economy, while the top priority for blacks remained getting full access to the white world.

Perhaps suspecting that this New Deal would mean much of the same for blacks, in 1934 W. E. B. Du Bois made a historic and, in light of his past battles with Booker T. Washington, a most amazing argument in the pages of *Crisis*: he advocated segregation. Feeling that the highest levels of the NAACP were dominated by whites and blacks too committed to an integrationist policy to aggressively pursue a truly black agenda, Du Bois had decided that only a black-directed organization, one that encouraged racial solidarity, could really create black power. The separate-but-equal implications of his essay shocked the NAACP leadership, who sent the sixty-six-year-old scholar from the *Crisis* to the presidency of Atlanta University—the organization's equivalent of a gold watch. His recognition of the inherent problems of an integrated organization fighting for black equality and his advocacy of self-sufficiency was a remarkable shift at the end of a life directed in other ways. It suggests that a person who truly analyzes the mechanisms of power in America will realize how confining unbridled assimilation can be for blacks.

The NAACP rejected its founder but not his assertion that some change of direction was necessary in the organization. Du Bois's outrage sparked an aggressive campaign of lawsuits against Jim Crow that would build momentum for major court decisions against discrimination and bolster the career of a young attorney named Thurgood Marshall. In 1935, when Marshall won a case allowing Donald Murray to attend the University of Maryland's law school, no one would have believed what this incipient legal campaign would achieve in just twenty years.

While civil-rights legal activism developed, those in the black music world found a way to operate within the confines of a segregated society. They helped build what would become the postwar R&B world, and in the process they also nurtured a sense of black community and pride that would be essential to the civil-rights movement. Two crucial figures in laying this foundation were Dave Clark, a businessman with a hustler's guile, and Louis Jordan, a saxophonist with a unique vision. First on the scene was Clark.

DAVE CLARK

Dave Clark, thin, wiry, honey-colored, began his career as a utility man playing both reed and brass instruments in Jimmy Lunceford's big band after graduating in the mid-1930s from college in Jackson, Tennessee, with a music degree. The course of Clark's life was altered by Lunceford's road manager, Harold Oxley, who suggested that the young musician become an advance man, a job that required Clark to travel to cities ahead of the band and stir up enthusiasm for the performer by putting up posters, placing advertisements in the black press, and getting Lunceford's latest recording in the local jukeboxes. "This was before there was really any black radio," says Clark, "so this was the only way to expose your music. In fact, when the jukebox operators began putting them in every little joint in the city, it sparked the recording of more black acts, because if the boxes didn't have good swing or blues, blacks wouldn't play them." As an advance man Clark often introduced new records to a city. "Since it took so long for music to travel across the country, a hot record could be big for a year or two."

Clark's reputation grew quickly. Moe Gale and Joe Glaser, the rival owners of New York's two biggest booking agencies, both engaged him to do advance work, bringing Clark into contact with Louis Armstrong and Billie Holiday, among others. Most of the acts Clark worked with recorded for Decca Records, a large company that had a monopoly on the big black stars of the swing era. One white Decca staffer offered Clark a job, realizing that his efforts were beneficial to Decca's bottom line. But the offer fell through, Clark says, because "the boss upstairs wasn't too keen on hiring blacks"—despite the many blacks who recorded for the company. So Clark was made a consultant, a 1930s version of what is now called an independent promotion man.

That is why one night in 1938 Clark walked into the lobby of a radio station in New York City wearing a chauffeur's uniform. Martin Block was doing his nightly broadcast of "Make Believe Ballroom," a show composed of recorded music. This was a revolutionary programming concept that had been introduced a few years before in Los Angeles, but it was Block who made the format work. His embrace of recorded music over live performances would eventually lead to a shift in the role of records on radio. Block definitely had vision, but he wasn't a total visionary. His playlist included such tame white acts as Paul Whiteman, Tommy Dorsey, and Glenn Miller, but excluded Duke Ellington, Count Basie, Jimmy Lunceford, and the period's other magnificent black big bands. It was a condition Dave Clark wanted to correct.

He was carrying with him a 78 RPM recording of Lunceford's "St. Paul's Walking Through Heaven with You," a good but undistinguished swing tune. Blacks weren't allowed in WNEW's offices in 1938, but it wasn't unusual for a black chauffeur to drop off a message with the doorman. Clark explained that the station's owner had sent him over with a record for Block to play. He added menacingly that the boss would be home listening for it. The doorman "went right up there and [Block] played that record right off," says Clark proudly of his magic moment. Black music historian Portia Maultsby asserts that this makes Clark the record industry's first promotion man—the first person to entice a deejay to play a record in an effort to sell more recordings. The relationship between recorded music and radio would be crucial for the evolution of rhythm & blues, since it was to be the first major American musical style to emerge through the playing of its records on the air. Clark, in the years to come, would play an active role in encouraging this symbiotic relationship.

Black radio in the 1930s had progressed little from its sponsored-show origins. There were still no stations aimed exclusively at blacks and no stations that specialized in forms of black music besides swing. There were, however, a growing number of black announcers, most notably Jack Cooper, whose career began in 1929. By 1935, through the sale of airtime to sponsors, he was heard a combined five and a half hours a day over several Chicago radio stations. He even called one of his daily broadcasts "The Negro Hour," though Cooper still went after white listeners and a middle-class black audience. While Cooper and his few peers utilized some black vernacular in their presentation, they worked hard to blend in with the blander white announcers. As Norman Spaulding, a black announcer of the era, observed, most black announcers then "were not Southern born, or left the South at an early age and had no trace of a Southern accent. With their race pride . . . [they] did not want to sound like Amos and Andy or Stepin Fetchit." This meant that while professing race pride, Cooper and company were motivated by a real snobbishness against the rawer modes of black expression, in music and in language. To a degree, this bias echoed the Southern-Northern subtext of the Washington-Du Bois conflict and would recur in different guises in the seemingly unending debates over black image versus black reality.

LOUIS JORDAN

One artist who was able to bridge this gap made his solo debut in 1938 on the same Decca label Clark toiled for. His name was Louis Jordan, a tenor saxophonist and singer with a sly, ingratiating approach who had played with Chick Webb's big band until the swing drummer's death earlier that year. Jordan immediately started up a band of his own, which originally consisted of eight players, later stripped down to six, before the addition of a guitarist brought the regular lineup to seven. So while his band became famous as the Tympany Five, Jordan never had a combo that small. The success of the Tympany Five standardized the size of the postwar black dance band—to seven. Fewer horns made the rhythm more pronounced, partly because there was more space in the arrangements and partly because of Jordan's lean, emphatic beat in 2/4 time that he dubbed the "shuffle boogie." In the years before World War II folks said Jordan was "jumpin' the blues," and the style was known for a time as "jump blues."

Like rural and classic blues, Jordan's material was steeped in black vernacular and the "hep-cat" slang of the day. But, in a significant step along the road from blues to rhythm & blues, the song selection was part of a formal marketing strategy. With considerable input from white staff producer Milt Gabler, Jordan's material was commissioned and then shaped into an urbane yet rootsy mold. It didn't necessarily express Jordan's experience but was thought to mirror that of big-city blacks often not one generation removed from life in the rural South. The titles "Beans and Cornbread," "Saturday Night Fishfry," and "Ain't Nobody Here But Us Chickens" suggest country life, yet the subject of each is really a city scene. In "Chickens," for instance, the central image is of chickens in a coop having a party that's keeping the farmer from sleeping. But clearly the bird bash is just a metaphor for a black house party that the farmer—perhaps the landlord, maybe the police—wants to quiet. Jordan's vocal, sassy and spirited, spiced with funny spoken asides, is as buoyant as its shuffling groove. His flamboyant humor made some compare him to Cab Calloway, a swing-era bandleader known for his baggy zoot suits, jive talk, and greasy hair, which he would fling around. But Jordan had just as much in common with Jack Benny's sidekick Eddie (Rochester) Anderson, whose harried expression and gravelly voice made him a film and radio star in the 1930s and 1940s. He was an everyman, like Jordan, with black and white appeal.

Jordan was a natural crossover artist. He was so skilled an entertainer and so progressive a musician that his talent leaped over the walls of segregation. "I made just as much money off white people as I did colored," he boasted proudly. "I could play a white joint this week and a colored next." During his peak years, 1938 to 1946, Jordan enjoyed five million-selling 78s, due in some degree to his popularity on Nickelodeons—jukeboxes with a screen and tape loop—on which pre-MTV music shorts appeared. Clips of Jordan singing hits like "Caledonia Boogie" perfectly captured the fun of his live shows, and sold records. (The clips, instigated by Jordan and Gabler, were also shown along with black independent films in black neighborhoods.) In differing ways Marshall, Clark, and Jordan would serve as links between the pre- and postwar black experience. Their innovations would develop with time. But for the next few years all that would be overshadowed by the war against Adolph Hitler to save the world for democracy and brotherhood.

World War II was a time of heroism and pain. It was also a time of opportunity for blacks. The war, straining America's resources, meant its largely untapped supply of blacks (and white women) were given a chance to prove their loyalty to a nation that had discriminated against them for nearly three hundred years.

During the war years, most black soldiers and their families looked ahead to a new American reality, hoping that the call to arms would force this nation to begin to live up to the sentiments in the Constitution. For many, the start of the new era was symbolized by Marion Anderson's Easter Sunday concert in 1939, held in front of the Lincoln Memorial in Washington. Seventy-five thousand Americans of every color and class attended the performance after the great classical diva was blocked from appearing at Constitution Hall by the Daughters of the American Revolution. It was a triumph of dignity over racism and surely a harbinger of the future. A year later Richard Wright's *Native Son* was published to overwhelming critical acclaim, showing whites for one of the first times in print the violent reality of the everyday war at home.

In the early days of the war effort, the government tried to hold the line against black advancement, but often, due to political pressure and manpower shortages, it had to reverse itself. On October 9, 1940, the

White House announced that it was government policy not to "inter-
mingle colored and white enlisted personnel in the same regimental
organizations." Just seven days later, Benjamin O. Davis was named
the first black general in the regular army. On January 15, 1941, Yancey
Williams, fresh out of Howard University, went to federal court to get
the secretary of war to consider his application for enlistment in the
Army Air Corps as a flying cadet. A day later the War Department and
the army announced the formation of a squadron for black cadets. By
July the black air school was opened in Tuskegee under the watchful
eye of Booker T. Washington's operation there, which, even after his
death, wielded some clout in black affairs.

A number of individuals also distinguished themselves, opening opportunities for other blacks. One example is Dr. Charles Drew. After
organizing a pioneering blood-plasma bank in New York City in 1940,
he was appointed medical director of Great Britain's blood-plasma project, creating a model for mass production of plasma that would be an
essential tool of mercy on the shores of Europe over the next four years.
Labor leader A. Philip Randolph, who organized the Brotherhood of
Sleeping Car Porters and scared Roosevelt with talk of a march on
Washington, agitated for more black jobs in defense plants. With men
and women like Anderson, Davis, Drew, and Randolph, blacks made
waves during the war.

This sense of pride, which in some black GIs manifested itself in
justifiable impatience, led to many bloody confrontations. Black soldiers
and white MPs in North Carolina shot it out in August 1941 after an
argument over where blacks could sit in a military bus. A black private
and white MP were killed. Racial confrontations between black fighting
men and army security forces were so common that one could seriously
question just whom the MPs were policing, all soldiers or just the dark
ones.

After the war, black GIs came home with opened eyes and hearts full
of pride. Those who had served in Europe had picked through the ruins
of that continent's great nations, seen the respect and awe their skin
inspired, and had proved, in ways they weren't allowed to in World
War I, that blacks could fight for America as well as the next man. In
Asia, battling against men with yellow skin, it was clear that one's
complexion didn't determine one's ingenuity or bravery. It was also
apparent to black soldiers that the racist taunts used by Americans to
inflame emotion against the Japanese weren't very different from the
curses shouted at them back home. Only a true Uncle Tom—and this

generation had its share—didn't see bigotry as a weapon of U.S. policy. It was also clear that if you really broke it down, whites didn't instinctively hate differently shaded humans; they were just as brainwashed as any kamikaze pilot. All that had to be done, some blacks thought, was to show whites what they were made of—and, yeah, be a credit to the race—and, God willing, they'd make it through.

It is crucial to the story that the practical examples of change cited here were ordered by the federal government. By executive order and changes of policy, Washington would, for the next twenty-five years, be increasingly sensitive to the desire of blacks for social change. Private industry, however, remained relatively immune to these decrees after the war, though tokenism flourished. And the idea of government support for black business was foreign then to whites as well as black leaders, who were blind to anything outside their integrationist goals.

Ironically, it was at this time, when the dream of an integrated postwar America began to flower, that the son of an Arkansas sharecropper founded a remarkable business based on serving the very special needs of segregated blacks. In 1942, John Johnson started a little magazine in Chicago, *Negro Digest*, that was well enough received to make him consider starting a black version of *Life*: a publication full of pictures that would present the many success stories in the national black community that whites found inconsequential. In November 1945, he inaugurated *Ebony*. The magazine sold for a quarter, and his black audience loved it. But advertisers were skeptical. The racist truism that blacks don't read was widely believed—as it is today by many editors in book publishing.

In *Ebony* lore, one key to the magazine's survival was a meeting between Johnson and Zenith president Eugene McDonald. The publisher sought the meeting after an informal survey of black Chicagoans, including his mother, revealed that most blacks who owned a radio had a Zenith. Johnson flattered McDonald with an autographed copy of black explorer Matthew Henson's account of Admiral Robert Peary's journeys to the North Pole. He knew McDonald had traveled on one expedition with Peary. The ploy worked. At a crucial time in *Ebony*'s history, Johnson obtained ads from Zenith, both immediately enriching the magazine's bank account and stimulating other major advertisers to consider *Ebony* as a sales tool.

It could not have been more appropriate that radio ads started appearing in *Ebony* in the late 1940s. If you had electricity then—and a good many rural blacks didn't yet—a radio, Zenith or otherwise, was the gateway to a world of rhythm & rhyme, blues and jokes, that had previously existed only in juke joints and barrelhouses, where local emcees and comics amused customers. Moreover, radio would be a catalyst for a major upheaval in the promotion, sales, and distribution of all popular music. Much was happening, all of it at the same time, all events affecting each other, all of it manifestations of the rhythm & blues world.

GOING THROUGH CHANGES

To see how the R&B world began, we need to double back a bit to the war years to see the profound affect they had on the record industry.

Following Japan's attack on Pearl Harbor in 1941, the government halted the manufacture of record players, radios, and other consumer products requiring electronic components, as the war effort took priority. Shellac, the key ingredient in record manufacturing at the time, came from Japanese-controlled Singapore, so there wasn't much around. Yet the misery of the war increased Americans' desire to be entertained, and the music business, like the movie industry, boomed. In 1941, record sales were $50 million. By 1945, they reached $109 million, even though the quality of the pressings had deteriorated, since old records were being scrapped and then reused to satisfy the demand.

This rise was amazing in light of a deep philosophical and economic dispute in the industry. The American Federation of Musicians, the musicians' union, was rightfully fearful that the increasing use of records on radio would eventually put many members out of work, particularly since big bands relied on live broadcasts for so much of their revenue. On August 1, 1942, AFM president James C. Petrillo, in a desperate move, tried to stop progress. He ordered a recording ban, demanded that the record labels give musicians a royalty to compensate for lost revenues from recorded music, and pressured nightclubs to stop using jukeboxes. Records cut prior to the ban, plus some primarily vocal recordings and scattered bootleg sessions (falsely said to have been recorded before the ban), made up the bulk of record releases during the next two years. Decca gave in first, signing a royalty agreement in 1943. Capitol settled soon after, but the big boys, Columbia and Victor (aka RCA), held out until 1944. So Petrillo won . . . sort of.

He could strike and get concessions. He couldn't, however, hold back the forces of economics and technology; nor could he channel audiences' changing enthusiasms. The big-band era and the dominance of swing was over. For lonely GIs and equally lonely women at home, the sentimentality of Frank Sinatra, Peggy Lee, Perry Como, and Nat King Cole was preferred to the frantic rhythms of Gene Krupa and the blasting trumpets of Harry James. Tastes had changed. During the strike, the big-band singers rose to prominence, overshadowing the bandleaders who first exposed them and establishing string-laden vocal recordings as the sound of white pop in the 1950s.

The big bands ran into other economic barriers as well. After the war everything cost more: gasoline, buses, hotel accommodations, and musicians' salaries. And the musicians themselves were changing. During the war those who'd avoided the service grew comfortable, lazy, and, according to accounts from the period, sloppy. Together these factors conspired to make many big-band leaders call it quits in 1946, including Benny Goodman, Woody Herman, Benny Carter, Tommy Dorsey, Les Brown, and Jack Teagarden. Some would later come back in some form to join the remarkably stable organizations of Ellington and Basie as caretakers for the once-vibrant sound of swing.

Creativity in improvisational music had moved in another direction, one that ensured exciting experiments and, ironically, one that enabled rhythm & blues to become the dominant dance music of postwar America.

Like Louis Jordan, a number of ambitious young musicians, including trumpeter Dizzy Gillespie, saxophonist Charlie Parker, and pianist Thelonious Monk, were all big-band refugees. Congregating at Harlem's Minton's Playhouse and other uptown after-hours spots for jam sessions, they were quite consciously creating a new music known, in hep-cat lingo, as bebop. In its purest form, bebop is a complex, rapidly shifting small-group music (two horns, bass, drum, piano) that turned pop melodies into slivers of chords and rhythmic phrases. The rhythm didn't ride on the tom-tom or snare drum, where even poor dancers could find it, but flowed through every instrument. Sure, the drummer kept time, but usually only with a tense, jingling pattern on the cymbals that was impossible for most dancers to follow. This sound made bebop as much a listeners' music as anything heard at Carnegie Hall. Bebop differed from swing and rhythm & blues not just musically but in the players' attitude toward their audience. Cool, self-assured, and, despite widespread drug use among its stars, often dignified in appearance, beboppers made it plain they really didn't care if people—black squares as well as white—understood what they were playing. This was musicians' music, first and foremost. Only those who pledged allegiance to the musicians' brilliance, mesmerized by daredevil improvisations, were welcome.

The most extroverted bebop pioneer was Gillespie, who, with his beret, goatee, constant hep talk, and puffed cheeks when blowing, cut a slyly comic figure. He often clowned onstage, but unlike another great trumpeter, Louis Armstrong, Gillespie escaped an Uncle Tom tag by his ability to simultaneously laugh at his jokes yet maintain his dignity. Despite his humor, Gillespie, like Parker, Monk, and the others, took his music seriously and considered it art as high-minded and elitist as the Western classical music he both envied and despised. The bebop attitude overrode any lingering connection to the black show-business tradition that turned any cultural expression into a potentially lucrative career (though eventually that would happen to the beboppers as well). At this juncture in bebop history, its adherents found it a higher calling than mere entertainment. These musicians were less secular stars than quasi-religious figures, and their fans often referred to them with godly reverence.

For the masses of blacks, after bebop's emergence, jazz was respected, but in times of leisure and relaxation they turned to Louis Jordan and a blend of blues, jump blues, ballads, gospel, and a slew of sax-led instruments and fading black swing orchestras. General black taste in the 1940s can be sampled in Broadcast Music Inc.'s rhythm & blues awards. Decca's Jordan far outdistanced the competition, with one song in 1943 ("Five Guys Named Joe"), one in 1944 ("GI Jive"), two in 1945 ("Caledonia Boogie," "Mop Hop"), six, at the height of his popularity, in 1946 ("Beware Brother Beware," "Buzz Me," "Choo Choo Ch'Boogie," "Don't Worry 'Bout That Mule," "Let the Good Times Roll," and "Stone Cold Dead in the Market," with Ella Fitzgerald), and four in 1947 ("Ain't Nobody Here But Us Chickens," "Boogie Woogie Blue Plate," "Early in the Morning," "Jack You're Dead"). In 1943 and 1944, large black orchestras led by instrumentalists showed strength (vibraphonist Lionel Hampton, saxmen Erskine Hawkins and Buddy Johnson, trumpeter Cootie Williams), while Nat King Cole, a singer with a crooning big-band vocal style, debuted. Change was quite evident from 1945 to 1947. The orchestras disappeared, replaced first by the rough, gravelly rural voices of Arthur (Big Boy) Crudup and Roosevelt Sykes, then by bluesmen with followings among newly arrived big-city blacks, and finally by smooth, blues-influenced crooners like Private Cecil Gant, Charles Brown, and Ivory Joe Hunter, as well as the astringent tone of Dinah Washington. To some degree that last group of male singers was the black equivalent of the white ex-big-band vocalists (Gant was promoted as "the sepia Sinatra"), though they drew much more overtly on the blues than their white counterparts.

But in 1948 and 1949, there were no white equivalents of Wynonie Harris's "Good Rockin' Tonight" and "All She Wants to Do Is Rock" on King, two churning, driving records on which Harris was as brash and ballsy as a horny bull. There was no white equivalent of the Ravens' "Bye Bye Baby Blues" on Savoy, with its harmonies and lead-to-chorus interplay that embraced gospel call-and-response in a way the Mills Brothers and Ink Spots, the black harmony stars of the swing era, rarely attempted. There was no white equivalent of the half-crazed shouts, unintelligible words, and stomping beat of John Lee Hooker's "Boogie Chillen" and "Crawling Kingsnake" on Modern. And there was no white equivalent of the honking, stuttering tenor-sax-led hits of Big Jay McNeely ("Deacon's Hop") and Paul Williams ("The Hucklebuck") on Savoy, or the honky-tonk piano-based hits of Amos Milburn on Aladdin (five made the BMI list in 1949, including the raunchy "Chicken Shack Boogie"). The words were bluesy in tone and subject matter, but the rhythms and voices were fresh and new.

So were the labels that recorded, promoted, and distributed these records. Jordan, Cole, and the big bands recorded for large, nationally distributed companies such as Decca, Victor, and Capitol. However, all the new artists were signed to independent labels that began appearing during the war and would proliferate in the next seven years. While the majors had problems identifying the new music—MGM called it "ebony," Decca and Capitol prefered "sepia"—the new labels were rhythm & blues from the start, though bebop, country, electric blues, and gospel were all recorded by the new labels. In 1949, when *Billboard* changed the name of its black pop-music chart from "race" to "rhythm & blues," it wasn't setting a trend, but responding to a phrase and a feeling the independent labels had already made part of the vocabulary.

The biggest surprise on the indies list (see pp. 27–28) is that Los Angeles produced the largest number of significant R&B labels. Of the thirty companies, nine called Los Angeles home, including all those inaugurated in 1945. This resulted from an influx of blacks in Southern California, as GIs just back from Asia stayed on and Southern blacks, particularly those from Louisiana, Texas, and Oklahoma, found in sunny California a climate, both atmospherically and socially, more temperate than existed back home. In total about half a million blacks moved to

LABEL	OWNER	CITY
1942		
Savoy	Herman Lubinsky	Newark
Excelsior (became Exclusive in 1944)	Leon and Otis Rene	Los Angeles
1943		
Apollo	Ike and Bess Berman	New York
1944		
National	Al Greene	New York
Gulf-Gold Star	Bill Quinn	Houston
King	Syd Nathan	Cincinnati
1945		
Modern	Jules, Joe, and Saul Bihari	Los Angeles
Philco-Aladdin	Ed and Leo Mesner	Los Angeles
Bronze	Leroy Hurte	Los Angeles
Four Star	Richard Nelson	Los Angeles
Super Disc	Irving Feld, Viola Marsham	Los Angeles
1946		
Bulleit	Jim Bulleit	Nashville
Specialty	Art Rupe	Los Angeles
Mercury	Irving Green (president)	Chicago
1947		
Atlantic	Herb Abramson, Ahmet Ertegun	New York
Aristocrat-Chess	Leonard and Phil Chess	Chicago
1949		
Freedom	Saul Kaul	Houston
Macy's	Macy Lela Wood	Houston
Peacock	Don Robey	Houston
Imperial	Lew Chudd	Los Angeles

1950

Trumpet	Willard and Lillian McMurry	Jackson, Mississippi

1951

Dot	Randy Wood, Gene Nobles	Gallatin, Tennessee
Red Robin	Bobby Robinson	New York
Nashboro-Ernie Y	Ernie Young	Nashville

1952

Duke	James Mattias	Memphis
Sun	Sam Phillips	Memphis
Meteor	Lester Bihari	Los Angeles– Memphis
Vee-Jay	James and Vivian Bracken, Calvin Carter	Chicago– Gary, Indiana

Los Angeles and adjacent cities like Compton during the war years. Their presence made the area a rhythm & blues hot spot, though much of the music released on the Los Angeles indies came from those fertile musical tributaries, New Orleans and Memphis.

I wish it were surprising—but it isn't—that only one of the two Harlem-based labels, Bobby Robinson's Red Robin, was black-owned. Most indies were started by whites, many of them Jewish; blacks weren't the only people kept out of the American business mainstream by discrimination. Unwelcome on Wall Street, many Jewish businessmen looked for places where there were fewer barriers to entrepreneurship. They often turned to black neighborhoods—in some ways paralleling blacks' discovery that their avenues for advancement were less barricaded in the world of entertainment. Only two of the black labels on my list, Don Robey's Peacock and family-owned Vee-Jay, would be major forces in the black market, and Vee-Jay was the only one to have a significant impact on the white market.

None of these companies would have had any impact whatsoever without the maturation of black radio. In St. Louis (KXLW), Atlanta (WERD), Louisville (WLOU), Memphis (WDIA), Los Angeles (KRKD), New Orleans, (WYLD), Miami (WMBM), and Nashville

(WLAC), stations that programmed rhythm & blues, with additional shows catering to blues, gospel, and jazz depending on where they were located, began broadcasting. In addition, there were many programs in the late 1940s still being broadcast on the purchase deals of the past, with powerful deejays still working on two or three stations in a market, though that practice was fading. What was growing, however, was the impact of the deejays, some of whom were as exciting as the performers they promoted. As with the R&B labels, the overwhelming majority of black-oriented stations were white-owned (Atlanta's WERD was one important exception), but the deejays, not the owners, defined the stations and made them profitable. As we'll see, they were paid little relative to the revenues generated, and so they developed a host of hustles, from concert promotion to talent management to payola (pay-for-play). In the rhythm & blues world payola was as common as tacking posters to telephone poles to announce upcoming shows.

What was also accepted, and quite enthusiastically, was the presence of white deejays. Integration would have many unexpected side effects, one of which was the development of a group of whites who, like many in the Jazz Age, were fascinated with black music and black style. Unlike the contemporaries of Fitzgerald, these new Negrophiles embraced black culture to the point that they became "honorary" blacks and, in some cases, subject to the same discrimination as their dark role models. Johnny Otis, a Los Angeles resident of Greek descent, was one of the first of this breed. As a bandleader, songwriter, and talent scout, Otis was a real force in the Los Angeles scene. And in terms of promoting rhythm & blues, these black voices behind white faces would be more important than any single musician.

What follows are detailed discussions of the independent rhythm & blues labels, the black radio stations and the voices that made them, along with the mom-and-pop retail stores and live shows that combined to form the core of the rhythm & blues world.

R&B INDIES

Willard and Lillian McMurry were selling furniture in the late 1940s when Willard bought out a rival store in their hometown of Jackson, Mississippi. He asked his wife to sell off the merchandise while he decided what to do with the storefront. Inside she found a record player and some old 78s. One of them was by Wynonie Harris. Lillian decided to give it a listen. "It had a great beat and the vocal was the most unusual, sincere, solid sound I'd ever heard," she told *Living Blues* years later. Selling Harris's jump blues, and spirituals by Mahalia Jackson and Sister Rosetta Tharpe, Lillian found the records went quickly and that her customers were asking for more.

On a trip to New Orleans she bought three hundred country, spiritual, and rhythm & blues recordings and they also sold out quickly. Admittedly bitten by the "phonorecord bug," Lillian got her husband to let her turn the storefront into a combination furniture store and record shop called Record Mart. Her father built shelves down one side of the store, and she began ordering from distributors in New Orleans and Memphis. Then she bought three hours of radio time a day on WRBC radio with "Ole Hep Cat," which was evidently the most listened-to-show in Jackson. "We advertised the package deals, played the records, had guest artists, and sent out catalogues of records in our shop." The McMurrys also purchased time and provided free records to deejays on WSLI, WJXN, and WOKJ, all around Jackson. As a result, "mail orders [and] our over-the-counter business were booming and sometimes our helpers needed a pair of skates to wait on customers."

Eventually the McMurrys moved from selling music to recording it, and again, Lillian's curiosity led the way. One day she became fascinated by the sound of a black teen harmonizing in the listening booth along with a record by a vocal group. That was the beginning of Trumpet Records, a label that existed from only 1950 to 1955 but was the home of Elmore James's original version of the blues classic "Dust My Broom" and Sonny Boy Williamson's first recordings. Though Lillian expresses exasperation with the record industry—primarily because of the bootlegs from her catalogue that appeared around the world—the company's reputation for honest accounting and the fact that it continues to pay royalties to artists' heirs makes it one of the few indies whose integrity isn't questioned today.

The McMurrys and their contemporaries, men and women who often moved into music by accident, are part of the mythology of the industry. Their bright ideas and bad judgments are the standards by which the record industry still rates its progress and practices. The McMurrys dropped out early. Most of the other R&B indie founders of the early forties and fifties kept their hand in at least until the seventies, when the industry was reshaped by larger hands. Still, the music they commissioned and distributed would eventually change what America thought popular music should sound like.

The relationship between the artists and these capitalists was as complicated as any love affair between a couple of different color and class. The artists, who could be characterized as naïve country types or smart-ass city kids, saw in these embryonic record-makers a way to escape the "line syndrome" that confined black dreams: assembly line, picket line or unemployment line. There was no question in their minds that making records was the ticket to red Cadillacs, long, tall ladies (or lean, cool gents), and diamond pinky rings—the symbols of the ghetto hustler.

Blacks who knew better were rarely involved in show business and certainly with nothing as rough and uncultivated as the bluesy shouters, street-corner singers, and chugging rhythm sections of R&B. And the record-company owners knew better than to let on that things like song publishing or record royalties could produce long-term earnings. At first some owners didn't know it themselves. And who knew then that these songs "by niggers for niggers" would come to have a catalogue value as great as those of the Tin Pan Alley tunesmiths, that the refurbished blues and gospel music of the 1950s would live on and generate money decades into the future?

What they found out in the short term was that controlling the publishing rights of a song generated lots of money if white groups covered black hits. (This formula worked increasingly well as the decade went on; Pat Boone's Little Richard covers are only the most notorious. Neither label owners nor the artists had any sense of the future. All they knew was that a black market existed, and if you had the right singer and the right arranger and got it to the right deejay, you couldn't lose. It didn't have to last. It probably wouldn't. No one cared about longevity. All it had to do was sell. Most of these record men were white, but in no way all. One of the things that defined the R&B world, one that separated it from most other American businesses, was the ability of blacks to form businesses and profit from a product their own people created. Of course, not all of them were on the level, and even Booker T. Washington would have admitted that some black businessmen were dishonest or even incompetent. The stories of two very different black record men are representative of the period's attitude toward artists, music, and the business.

In his autobiography, Little Richard recalls complaining to Don Robey, the black founder and president of Duke-Peacock Records, about some unsatisfactorily small royalty payments. Instead of receiving a pack of lies—the usual answer from record men—he claims that Robey, a big, burly, light-skinned bear of a man, reared back and punched him in the chest so hard Richard sustained a hernia. Even in the world of rhythm & blues, it was highly unusual for a label owner to attack a performer. Yet no one who knew the man disputes that Robey might well have knocked down the self-proclaimed king of rock & roll.

Robey wouldn't have struck him because of the thievery accusation but because the singer cursed him. Don Robey was not a man you cursed in person. In fact, most folks avoided disputes with him. Suspected of all manner of wrongdoing (prostitution, numbers-running, gambling), Robey's reputation usually preceded him. "He was just like a character out of *Guys and Dolls*," an engineer told *Rolling Stone*. "He'd have a bunch of heavy guards around him all the time, carrying pistols and that kind of stuff, like a czar of the Negro underworld."

Gangster or not, Robey was a major presence in the world of black Houston. He ran a taxi company, owned the Bronze Peacock Club, which boasted one of the largest showrooms in the Southwest, and as a result, got involved in talent management, tour-booking, and record-manufacturing. A decade before Berry Gordy's ascendence in Detroit, Robey was a successful black record executive, though his road to success was quite different.

In 1949 Robey opened Peacock Records to record Clarence (Gatemouth) Brown, a blues singer and guitarist, after Robey objected to contract terms offered by the Los Angeles–based Aladdin label. In 1952, Robey bought Duke Records from Memphis deejay James Mattias. Together the combined labels would be important homes for gospel and rhythm & blues into the 1970s, recording the Five Blind Boys and Dixie Hummingbirds for churchgoers and seminal R&B stars Willie Mae (Big Mama) Thornton, Johnny Ace, and Bobby (Blue) Bland for sinners. Through his affiliation with Buffalo Booking Agency, he would also become a potent booking agent as well, dominating the business in the Southwest.

To Dave Clark, who'd worked for Robey as a staff promotion man in 1952, he was someone to be idolized. Robey, after all, bought Clark his first $500 suit. "He was one of the greatest black record manufacturers who ever lived," says Clark. "A lot of black companies went out of business, a lot of label presidents ended up poor. Don Robey ended his life a very rich man."

Given the tales of rip-offs by rhythm & blues entrepreneurs, white and black, some might consider Dave's comments more condemnation than praise. Robey was a pioneer who gave black talent a shot, a black surviving in a racist industry. Robey, like the Chess Brothers in Chicago,

Herman Lubinsky at Savoy, and others, took the economic risks. They took the gamble. They deserved to benefit. No question.

But did they benefit to the detriment of their artists? Clark's comments about artists reflect an attitude held by Robey and many other label owners. "Some of the artists didn't tend to be too smart; some of them were so smart they outsmarted themselves. Back in those days a guy would go out and make him a record. First thing you know he wanted a Cadillac. Don Robey said, 'All right, I'll get the Cadillac, but you got to pay me just like you got to pay the Man.' And when royalty time came, you ain't made enough money out of the record to pay for your Cadillac. Guys would come get $4,000 to $5,000 at a time. You see, all the artists wanted to be big shots. They all wanted big cars. They all wanted fine clothes and everything that went with it."

No one ever accused Robey's operation of sentiment. After Johnny Ace's death by Russian roulette backstage at a Dallas auditorium in 1954, Robey, in a practice standard in the industry, released a number of posthumous singles, including the million-selling "Pledging My Love." The last of these, "Still Love You So," was advertised in the trade press in 1956 with the debut of a singer named, quite suspiciously, Buddy Ace. The ad copy read, "Complete your collection with his last record of the late great Johnny Ace. Start your collection with the first record release of this up and coming artist." Clearly the artist was some poor guy Robey had cajoled into recording as "Buddy Ace" to exploit Johnny Ace's continuing popularity. Under the name of Deadric Malone, Robey "wrote" hundreds of songs, recorded by his artists, though it is more likely Robey purchased the songs. His creativity lay more in finance than melody. "Shit, Robey didn't write any of them," Bobby Bland told Peter Guralnick in *Lost Highway*. "He got them from—well, there used to be a lot of writers who went through there. No, he didn't steal them! They always got what they asked for"—probably small cash advances.

Despite an unsavory reputation, Robey was a businessman of considerable foresight. Dave Clark was a crucial cog in his operation. So was musical director Joe Scott, who supervised Bland's great recordings. His chief lieutenant at Duke-Peacock, however, was a black woman named Evelyn Johnson. Their agency, Buffalo Booking, was registered with the American Federation of Musicians in her name, and when it came to day-to-day operations at the offices, it was Johnson, not Robey, who made decisions. She'd had to pass on her ambition to become an X-ray technician when Texas state officials refused to let her take the state boards. Instead she became a jack-of-all-trades. She supervised the building of one of Houston's first recording studios and one of the nation's first black-owned record-pressing plants. Throughout the next two decades, she ran Buffalo Booking, organizing national tours for its clients. With the combination of Robey, Johnson, and Clark, whose expertise in this area was extensive, if you even smelled like a hit, Buffalo Booking would get to work. From St. Louis over to Atlanta, down the coast to Miami and New Orleans, back over to Atlanta and down the coast to Miami and New Orleans again, and then back over to Houston, Buffalo Booking dominated the Southern wing of the chitlin circuit. Consistent sellers like Bland and B. B. King easily did over three hundred dates a year.

Robey's domain extended deeply into gospel. In the early fifties, Peacock's recording of the Five Blind Boys' "Our Father" was one of the first gospel recordings to find its way onto jukeboxes. In a 1973 *Record World* interview Robey took credit for "putting the beat in religious records. I was highly criticized when I started it, but I put in the first beat. Then after the public started to buy the beat, why, then I put a drum into it. Then a guitar, then a trombone." Whether or not you believe Robey's claim, it is true that his label released records that led gospel music closer to its secular cousins.

Don Robey built an empire worth millions in a city far removed from the main line of entertainment. Yet his geographical location worked in his favor. Robey was a big fish in a pond that hadn't held any that big before. He released music—bluesy rhythm & blues (Ace, Bland) and gospel (Blind Boys, Inez Andrews)—that had its strongest following in the states nearest his operations, while his holdings in records, clubs, and booking fed off each other, insuring a steady cash flow.

Meanwhile Harlem, home of the Apollo Theater and so many young creative talents, the magnet for Afro-America's brightest talents, never had a black-owned operation of comparable stature, though one man might have built one. Bobby Robinson was Harlem's best-known record-store owner, as well as musical entrepreneur. A small man with sad, sleepy eyes and a slippery way with English, at one time or another he had Gladys Knight and the Pips and King Curtis under contract; a fruitful relationship with New Orleans's greatest writer-producer, Allen Toussaint; involvement with several number-one pop and black hits as a producer-writer; and the respect of so many of his competitors that pilgrimages to his Harlem record store were almost mandatory for any trip to New York. Yet one can't help but view Robinson as a man who missed opportunities. Disliking the Little Richard–style vocal of young Otis Redding, Robinson passed on "Shout Bamalama." A year later Redding was a star. In the eighties, Robinson recorded Grandmaster Flash and the Furious Five before the breakthrough hits "Freedom" and "The Message" on Sugar Hill.

Despite his Harlem location and hyperactive career, expectation outstripped his accomplishments. Central to Robinson's story is his role as a record-store owner. In 1946 he opened Bobby's Records, on 125th Street near the corner of St. Nicholas Avenue, a location that put him between the Apollo and the entertainment-business hangout Frank's Place. His store quickly became the place entertainers and record executives stopped in to monitor sales and get an early hearing of competing cuts. In 1951 he formed his first label, Red Robin, and over the next ten years it would be joined by Enjoy, Everlast, Fire, and Fury. Wilbert Harrison's "Kansas City" in 1959, Lee Dorsey's "Ya Ya," and Gladys Knight and the Pips' "Every Beat of My Heart" were Robinson's best-known releases.

Perhaps most emblematic of what Robinson tried to accomplish were his doo-wop recordings, beginning in 1951. "I gathered what little information I could and began producing doo-wop groups," he told David Toop. "There were a couple of groups out there at the time—the Orioles and the Ravens. The Ravens were a jump-type rhythm & blues thing. They were the forerunners of the doo wops. I got some groups together. We didn't have anyplace to rehearse, so what I did was close the record store early, at 11 AM, lock the door, and rehearse right inside. The first group was the Mellow Moods—a standard tune, 'Where Are You Now That I Need You.' I started to get very good success immediately. Once you start, everybody starts to run to you, so then followed the Vocaleers, the Scarlets, the Teenchords. Altogether I introduced about thirteen or fourteen groups in that category."

There are few more romantic images in popular culture than that of a group of young black teenagers, gathered on a corner under a streetlight, in the hallway of a tenement building, or in the entrance to a subway, working on sugary harmonies balanced by a low strident bass. Then, after a tryout in the office of a neighborhood record company, they slide nervously into a studio to make a record. . . . Like the frenzied rhythms of bebop and the rambling, rapid-fire exhortations of the R&B deejays, doo wop was a unique outgrowth of postwar black America. But without the arrogance of the jazzmen or the salesmanship of the announcers, doo wop represented a form of innovative innocence. There were flashes of urban anger in it—sometimes the sweet tenor lead and the rumbling bass support bounced off each other in sardonic commentary on the sentimentality of the music's ultraromantic lyrics. But by and large doo wop projected the warmth and optimism of its young singers. To this day the sound of a doo-wop record from this period, be it an acknowledged classic or some obscure oldie, connotes vivid and remarkably unsullied images of urban adolescence.

Just think of the names. As Britain's *New Music Express* remarked, "The bird groups multiplied like rabbits, soon to be joined by insects, flowers, and automobiles." Penguins, Flamingos, Crows, Ravens, Orioles, Clovers, and Gladiolas met Cadillacs, El Doradoes, Edsels, Impalas, Fleetwoods, Cardinals; tons more made records as memorable as your first kiss and then disappeared from the scene.

The Vocaleers, signed to Robinson's Red Robin label, are a typical doo-wop tale of here and gone. They came from 145th Street between Lenox and Seventh avenues, had a number-eight rhythm & blues hit with "Is It a Dream?" in 1953, and cut a doo-wop collector's favorite called "Be True." Robinson first heard the Vocaleers when they came in second at the Apollo amateur night. Street-corner historians say the group was as popular in Harlem then as Jackie Robinson and Willie Mays. Yet not a year after their hit the Vocaleers were no more—split up over ego problems and lead-vocal duties, whatever magic they possessed gleaned today only from dusty 45s and the memories (or myths) of doo-wop fanatics.

Neither Robinson nor any of the doo-wop capitalists, such as George Goldner in New York, Rainbow's Eddie Heller in Washington, or Dootone's Dootsie Williams in Los Angeles, considered artist development. All they thought about was capturing the moment. They recorded singers at a pace that suggested the market was going to evaporate the next day. For Robinson this inability—or was it unwillingness?—to invest in an artist for the long term dogged his career. No enduring stars did their best work under any of his logos. It was sad, but certainly typical for R&B business people. Robinson simply didn't realize the durability of his products. This failure is a reason one man who once asked him for advice came to overshadow Robinson on his own turf.

INNOVATIVE ATLANTIC

Ahmet Ertegun, originally with Herb and Miriam Abramson, brother Nesuhi, and later Jerry Wexler, made Atlantic Records one of the class acts of rhythm & blues. They paid royalties, though offering notoriously low advances. They were loyal. (For example, after Ruth Brown signed with them in 1949 she was seriously injured in an auto accident and was unable to record anything for almost a year. Yet wisely their interest in her didn't fade.)

By and large, during its years as one of R&B's most important labels (roughly from 1950 into the mid-1970s), Atlantic was extremely sensitive to shifts in black musical taste. In fact, this white-owned company was often on the cutting edge of new directions. The owners, particularly Ertegun in the 1950s and Wexler in the 1960s, would be given—and readily accepted—credit for the creative vision behind Atlantic's sound and success. Yet it was never that simple there or at any of the other prominent black-oriented indies. Leonard Chess of Chess Records could claim he knew everything about the blues, but it was bassist Willie Dixon whose musical judgments would be crucial to the recordings of Chuck Berry, Bo Diddley, and Muddy Waters. At Duke-Peacock, Don Robey, one way or another, supplied the material, but if you ask Bland, it was trombonist and house arranger Joe Scott who gave his music its haunting pathos. At King Records in Cincinnati, everybody knew about Syd Nathan and his cigars but few recognized that arranger Henry Glover was critical to actually making the music happen in the studio.

At Atlantic, the man to remember during the 1950s was Jesse Stone, together with a great house band that gave the green, red, and white label its first aural identity. Stone was no kid seeking a break when he began working with Atlantic in 1947, but a seasoned show-biz veteran. At age four Stone had put on a dog act; he sang and played violin and the dogs jumped around his feet. The teenaged Stone hung around the wide-open Kansas City of corrupt Democratic boss Tom Pendergast in the 1920s, an era that spawned the swinging Southwest big bands. As a pianist and vocalist, he organized a band backed by a female vocal group, the Rhythm Debs. At a Detroit gig, Duke Ellington took a liking to Stone and got him booked at the Cotton Club. Hanging around New York, Stone landed a $15-a-week job as a musical handyman at the Apollo, helping Pigmeat Markum add songs and on occasion even jokes to his routine, while updating the house band's book of arrangements.

He cut some swing sides in the 1930s, and then met Cole Porter just before the war. The famous songwriter advised him to purchase a rhyming dictionary, noting, "If you're gonna dig a ditch, you use a shovel, don't you?" Stone, a good friend of Louis Jordan, was one of those who encouraged him to form his own band, even before Chick Webb's death in 1938.

In 1942 Stone's composition "Idaho" became a national hit when Benny Goodman recorded it for Columbia. With Herb Abramson, Stone worked for Al Greene's National Records in 1945. Both felt Greene didn't understand blacks or their music enough to market it properly. So they left to start their own label. However, it wasn't until they ran into Ertegun and his money that they were able to realize their ambitions. (Or at least Abramson did, since he was made a partner, while Stone was put on salary.)

In fact, the music needed Stone or someone like him to understand its innovations and give it form. The crucial period for Stone and Atlantic was apparently a 1947 trip down South by Ertegun, Abramson, and Stone to study the taste their previous New York–created recordings weren't reaching. It was a trip that established the tradition of Atlantic looking to the South for talent and direction. "The kids were looking for something to dance to," Stone told Nick Tosches. "I listened to the stuff that was being done by those thrown-together bands in the joints, what was missin' from the stuff we were recording was the rhythm. All we needed was a bass line." Stone's "doo, da-doo, dum; doo, da-doo, dum" became associated with Atlantic and rocking rhythm blues. Moreover, Stone's observation that bass lines were key in changing the face of black music ties in with the coming of electric bass guitars.

In the hands of master swing bassists such as Oscar Pettiford or Count Basie's Walter Page, the bass line was a gentle stream that flowed well under the ensemble brass and reed lines that dominated the big-band style. But when Leo Fender gave Monk Montgomery a prototype for his bass guitar in 1953, he more than improved the basic sound. The electric bass forever altered the relationship between the rhythm section, the horns, and other melodic instruments. To Quincy Jones, who at the time was splitting his arranging skills between big band, jazz, and pop, "It really changed the sound of music because it ate up so much space. Its sound was so imposing in comparison to the upright bass, so it couldn't have the same function. You couldn't just have it playing 4/4 lines because it had too much personality. Before the electric bass and the electric guitar, the rhythm section was the support section, backing up the horns and piano. But when they were introduced, everything upstairs had to take a back seat. The rhythm section became the stars. All because of this technological development. The old style didn't work anymore and it created a new language"—a language first spoken by a bassist in a black dance band.

When Lionel Hampton's rocking band played, a raunchy aggregation like Jordan's Tympany Five, they jumped the blues into a frenzy. The electric bass had a punchy, dynamic range that would become identified with rhythm & blues. Moreover R&B musicians' willingness to integrate new technology into their vision would make their sound, despite its many detractors, as consistently innovative as any genre of American music in the coming years. The patterns of Stone and others, in conjunction with the increased use of the electric bass in the fifties, would turn this country's ears around.

The first artist Stone cites as recording with the new rhythm pattern was saxophonist Frank Culley, on a tune called "Cole Slaw" (Stone claims it was actually an adaptation of his 1942 composition "Sorgham Switch"). Culley's instrumental version didn't hit, but Louis Jordan, after adding some suitably humorous lyrics, made "Cole Slaw" a hit in 1949. Stone even cut a version himself for RCA/Victor. Culley, saxophonist Sam (the Man) Taylor, and, later, King Curtis, along with pianist Harry Van Walls and drummer Panama Francis (both of whom played on "Cole Slaw"), would become the backbone of Atlantic's house band. Under Ertegun's guidance and Stone's intimate direction, these players appeared on the label's first series of rhythm & blues hits. The Drifters' "Money Honey," the Clovers' "Your Cash Ain't Nothing But Trash," Joe Turner's "Shake, Rattle and Roll"—some of the best were Stone compositions. Ertegun and company deserve the acclaim they've received for surviving into the corporate era. But the men in the studios always need to be given the utmost respect for the ideas and spirit they injected into the grooves.

BLACK RADIO

In 1950, for keeping the Arabs and Jews from killing each other in Palestine, Ralph Bunche won the Nobel Prize, the first black so honored. That same year poet Gwendolyn Brooks won the Pulitzer Prize for her collection *Annie Allen*, the first time that award was given to a black writer. It seemed like the word "Negro" couldn't be used in the news without the word "first" being attached to it. Blacks were making strides in quieter ways as well. The research of black sociologist E. Franklin Frazier revealed that in 1953 blacks owned one-third of their dwellings—an increase of two-thirds over 1940, while 74,526 blacks attended universities, up from 17,880 in 1930. Tuskegee Institute reported that 1952 was the first time in seventy-one years of tabulation that there were no lynchings.

Yet behind the positive news items were reports that showed racial violence had hardly disappeared. Illinois governor Adlai Stevenson called out the National Guard to the Chicago suburb of Cicero, where 3,500 or so blazing rednecks tried to stop (and lynch?) a black family with the guts to believe they could live anywhere they pleased. It wasn't called lynching when Harry T. Moore of the Florida NAACP was killed and his wife injured after someone left a bomb in their home—but damned if he wasn't still dead. It didn't make headlines in the white press or the news breaks of black radio, but the old evils of sharecropping, Jim Crow, and dependency on whites were giving way in the postwar years to new ones: welfare, drug addiction, and urban police brutality. This demographic shift to the cities brought one more big change, which would become essential to the development of R&B. Now Negroes, the people once invisible to white America as so artfully depicted in Ralph Ellison's 1952 masterpiece, *Invisible Man*, became objects of attention and, in the eyes of manufacturers, a market worth exploiting.

In the mid-1950s, *Harper's* ran an article on "Negro radio," cowritten by a then-unknown black writer named Alex Haley, that bought black radio's impact, culturally and economically, into focus. The future best-selling author made four points: radio helped black as well as white businesses reach potential buyers; helped blacks know where they could shop without fear of harassment; provided prestigious jobs for blacks; and provided outlets for community service announcements by civic and church groups. Points one and two can be illustrated by sampling trade advertising from the period.

Coinciding with the emergence of a vast number of indie labels was the growth of black radio. "Serving and selling 328,000 Negroes in the St. Louis area since 1947," proclaimed WXLW in the early 1950s. At the same time, WOKJ of Jackson, Mississippi, let everybody know: "The ONLY way to the 107,000 Negroes" of that community was the "nation's highest Hooper-rated Negro station." The sales staff of Memphis's powerful 50,000-watt WDIA weren't shy about the fact that they reached 1,237,686 Negroes (10 percent of all black Americans) and that Negroes constitute 40 percent of the Memphis market.

In December 1947, *Ebony* found only sixteen blacks employed as deejays out of an estimated three thousand around the country. "Most of the sepia spielers who operate on twenty-one stations from coast to coast are relative neophytes, catching the crest of a boom that has skyrocketed the chatter chaps to a new peak," the magazine reported. "Hired in recent months because they're good business, colored jockeys have been catching on fast, drawing flocks of fan mail and getting better sponsors. They have been as popular as the records they play—and no small number are by Negro artists." Eight had a show-business background, and nine were college graduates. *Ebony* made it a point to note that few can be "identified as Negro on the air, even getting anti-Negro notes assuming them to be white. . . . Discovery that a voice has no color has opened new vistas to Negroes in radio." Following the model of Jack Cooper, these announcers passing for whites tended to be conservative in their programming choices, leaning as heavily on Count Basie and Sarah Vaughan as on their vowels.

One man *Ebony* mentioned, but only in passing, would become one of the most influential black deejays of all time. But it shouldn't be surprising that *Ebony* made little note of Al Benson's style, since he was just the sort of character any self-respecting upwardly mobile black would view as a discredit to the race. "His distressing grappling with words over two syllables once brought laughs of derision from many, but they could not laugh away his ability to reach out across the air and win vast audiences of listening Negro women and teenage girls," wrote one black publication in the fifties. "Even today one of the big questions in Chicago radio circles is: 'How does that Al Benson continue to get away with it?' "

At his peak Benson, aka the Midnight Gambler, hosted five shows and twenty hours of programming a week, earning as much as $100,000 a year in the process. Eddie O'Jay, a young deejay in the early fifties in Milwaukee, recalls, "Benson killed the King's English and I don't know if he did it on purpose or not. Everybody had to see Al if they wanted to sell to the black market in Chicago, whether it was beer or rugs or Nu Nile hair cream. . . . He wasn't pretending to be white. He sounded black. They knew he was and most of us were proud of the fact. 'Here's a black voice coming out of my little radio and we know it's him.' "

The lessons Benson taught about the appeal and profitability of his "black everyman" style were adopted all over the country, ushering in the era of the "personality deejays."

By 1955 there were over five hundred of Benson's children floating across the country on transistorized clouds, hawking records from far-away stores, along with stuff to make your wife two or three shades lighter, even if she looked good to you already. The ads never distracted listeners from the music but could sound as wild and greasy and cool as the platters played alongside. From Mexico to Canada, on little stations that went off at dusk to 50,000-watters, these cats rocked right through the static.

A listener up on his black history might have realized that these nighttime motor mouths were very much the inheritors of the black oral tradition that spawned Br'er Rabbit, Mr. Mojo, and the other rural tricksters created by Afro-Americans during their forced vacation in the "New World." Yet for all the cornpone some laid on listeners, they were often as urban as the corner of Lenox and 125th Street. With music as their inspiration, personas and rhymes were concocted with a smile and endless ingenuity. For many, bebop, because of its rhythmic instinct and rebellious style, was a verbal starting point.

Lavada Durst, who surely with great happiness called himself Dr. Hep Cat while at Austin's KVET, made the bebop-deejay connection with this couplet:

If you want to hip to the tip and bop to the top,
You get some made threads that just won't stop.

As I said earlier, it became clear early on that bebop wasn't a dancing (or mass-radio listening) style, yet there are many examples of deejays who played lots of rhythm & blues embracing its polysyllabic beauty. For example, New York's Jocko Henderson, aka the Ace from Space, often referred to bebop during on-air raps on his "1280 Rocket" broadcast:

Be bebop
This is your Jock
Back on the scene
With a record machine,
Saying "Hoo-popsie-doo, How do you do?"
When you up, you up,

And when you down, you down
And when you mess with Jock,
You upside down.

Coining phrases was an integral part of the mystique of the rhythm &
blues deejays. The resourceful Henderson came up with, "Great gugga
mugga shooga booga," which became part of New York slang.

It was the deejays' roles as trendsetters and salesmen, both of themselves and of the music, that made them essential to the growth of
rhythm & blues. Gary Byrd, a current radio and television announcer,
remembers watching veteran deejay Wild Bill Curtis as he pushed a
now-forgotten Drifters' single, "We Gotta Sing." Byrd says:

> First he'd be playing the music and he'd slow everything down and
> start talking. And he'd tell the story of how this record came into
> his hands. And he would go into a story about these guys who he
> had met sometime ago back in the days they were unknown and
> the guys turned out to be the Drifters and . . . blah, blah, blah, their
> new record and boom, boom, boom, first in the world to play their
> record. The record would come on. Well, as the record is playing,
> he'd be punctuating it with an "Ohh" at all the critical points where
> the excitement was. Then when he'd finish it, he'd go into this
> whole thing of "It's so bad, it's so bad. Oh, I just don't believe it."
> While he's talking he's recuing the record. At the end when he's
> finished he says, "And then one more time." Ironically it was kind
> of like a forerunner of the whole idea of extending the record which
> occurred later, on the disco trip. He was just extending the groove.
> And then the phones would start lighting up and people were
> saying, "What is that record? Can I get it?" And the record stores
> would be calling because people are calling them asking, "Do they
> have this record that was just played on WUFO by the Drifters?"

A bunch of these flashy pioneers dubbed themselves the Original 13,
forming the core of an old-boy network capable of making or breaking
hits. Jockey Jack Gibson, Jack (the Bell Boy) Lorenz, Larry Dean, Ed
Cook, Bill Powell, Ken Knight, Gene Potts, Hot Rod Hulbert, John
(Honey Boy) Hardy, Jimmy Woods, Hal Jackson, Tommy (Dr. Jive)
Smalls, and Spider Burke are usually remembered as the charter members, though Ed Castleberry's name is sometimes included. While the
original lineup grows more elusive with time, these men, black and

white, constituted the core of the first wave of great rhythm & blues deejays to follow Benson.

By looking at the career of one, Jack Gibson, we'll get a flavor of the attitude and life-style of these men. Light-skinned, quick-witted, and strong-willed, Gibson was the son of a Chicago physician and, as such, benefited from a quality education and stable family background. Gibson's introduction to radio came at all-black Lincoln University in Pennsylvania, where, at his father's urging, he was preparing for a degree in medicine. Gibson thought he wanted to be a gynecologist.

Then he met a clever classmate who'd devised a small transmitter capable of broadcasting to the Lincoln dorms. He asked the outgoing Gibson if he wanted to be an announcer. When Gibson quickly realized how much he enjoyed life behind the microphone (and the attention it generated), his medical ambitions faded. Upon graduation in 1944, he moved back to Chicago, seeking work as an actor. Radio dramas then still dominated the American imagination and offered black actors a unique opportunity to work in a medium where color was not an obstacle. Gibson landed steady work on pre-TV soap operas like "Young Widow Brown" and "Ma Perkins," as well as "Here Comes Tomorrow," a radio drama about the black Redmon family that was a liberal attempt to humanize blacks for white listeners. Looking back Gibson says, "I played a postman one day, a teacher the next, or maybe a bank clerk. Whatever the author wrote and sometimes things he did not." He was a natural ad-libber, a gift that troubled his superiors but would be the key to his future. A representative of Auto Dealers Outlet, a Chicago used-car operation and regular advertiser on the Windy City's CBS affiliate, WBBM, was in the studio's green room and happened to hear Gibson satirically imitating the commercial pitch of another announcer over an open mike. The auto dealer was keen on reaching South Side blacks, and in Gibson he heard an effective pitchman. Between two later stars of television, Gary Moore and Dave Garroway, Gibson hosted an hour long program for $65 a week, playing swing, jump blues, and bebop when not pushing "no money down, pay later" specials.

Jack's work in Chicago led a group of black Atlanta businessmen to contact him in 1949 when they raised the money to start WERD, the country's first black-owned radio station. He boasts, "I'm proud to have been the jock who flipped the switch at 6 AM on a brisk October morning in 1949 and greeted the day with a hearty 'Good morning, Atlanta! We are here! . . . We are here!' . . . We really didn't know what the hell we were doing, but we were doing it! I would plunk down my nickel every day for the Atlanta *Daily World*, the black newspaper there, and during our newsbreak at noon, I would read all of the stories that pertained to Atlanta. We had no format, so to speak, and we would listen to a white station in Atlanta and copy their format. Whatever they did on Monday we did, in our own soulful way, on Tuesday, and so on and so on. We even had a Sunday afternoon symphony. I hosted it because I was the only one who could pronounce the names of most of the classical artists that we played."

Jack moved to Louisville's WLOU in 1951, and there he made his contribution to R&B deejay lore. Inspired by his proximity to the Kentucky Derby and the city's devotion to horse racing, Gibson had the jockey outfitter Giuseppe make him some custom jockey silks. Working alone or occasionally with a female jock known as Louisville Lou, Gibson gained a national reputation and a loyal local listenership. He signed on with a bugle blast while shouting, "My father wasn't a jockey, but he sure taught me how to ride. He said in the middle, then from side to side. Ride, Jockey Jack, ride." His sign-off was: "The white rug is down and I'm getting ready to split. You be cool till I get back in with you tigers tomorrow." Then he'd growl.

In 1952 Gibson moved up the ladder and farther South when he was named program director of Miami's new WMBM. He was elated by the title, the extra money it meant, and the opportunity it offered to hang around the pool at the Lord Calvert Hotel—the only class hotel in town to register blacks—interviewing visiting stars like Nat King Cole, Billie Holiday, and Sammy Davis, Jr. He recalled gleefully to Lee Ivory, "I would interview stars who fed me drinks until I couldn't see the hand in front of my face. I ad-libbed most of the commercials because there was no way that I could read the copy.

"I had a chance to make an extra $25 a week promoting a beer product in the days when you could give away anything on radio. Ballantine Ale distributors had dropped off ten cases of the stuff at the station and I was on the air rapping to beat Billy about what joyous partying would be available if you came and picked up an absolutely free case of Ballantine, the three-ring beer that's right for you. Man, the causeway was jammed in both directions. People of all races and ethnic origins in cars and trucks of every make you can imagine were clogging arterial streets in an effort to get to the WMBM office to pick up their ale. It took the police almost an hour to get from the main highway to the station door where in less than ten minutes they were handcuffing me and WMBM's station manager, who was white, and taking our asses to the slammer for creating a public disturbance. Busted my ass right on the air."

Gibson was lured back to WERD in 1954 as program director, where, with the approval of the station's management, he became a community activist. "In Atlanta I was so involved that I became close friends with the chief of police," he says. "Anytime they had a disturbance in the ghetto he would call me. I would get on the air and tell them to stop or sure as hell the police would come in to whip some heads. Soon as my airtime was over I'd come into the neighborhood and act as a mediator to help settle the problem. As I went through the neighborhood a woman might holler out, 'I got your favorite meal, butter beans.' I'd go on up there and break bread with her family. Any of the personality jocks could have done the same thing in their community. If you're going to be successful in black radio you must belong to the community. You couldn't stay hidden. You couldn't be just a voice."

During Gibson's second stint in Atlanta, until 1958, Dr. Martin Luther King, Jr., emerged out of the shadows of his father at the Ebenezer Baptist Church to become a national leader. The offices of King's Southern Christian Leadership Conference (SCLC) were located downstairs from WERD and, according to Gibson, King "would holler upstairs to me when he had an important or timely announcement to make. I would lower the microphone out of my window and down to his office so he could make his statement. Afterward I'd pull the mike back upstairs, add my two-cents worth of commentary to the importance of Dr. King's work, then return to my programming."

Because of the deejays' visibility, young musicians also flocked to Gibson and company. The deejays' willingness to search out new talent—for financial renumeration, of course—was an essential part of their contribution to the music. Zenas (Daddy) Sears, the popular white rhythm & blues deejay on Atlanta's WGST, started a series of weekly talent contests in 1946 in conjunction with his broadcast. A soft-spoken, hard-drinking local singer-songwriter named Chuck Willis emerged as the star of these shows. The deejay, along with a local record-store owner, brought Willis to Columbia's black-oriented Okeh subsidiary, where he would record forty sides over the next five years. During that time Sears acted as Willis's manager and, through his broadcast connections, got the singer his own television show in Atlanta where, according to Sears, "we did little dramatic things: I would write the show with a little story and Chuck would do five or six numbers every week." At the suggestion of the flamboyant Screamin' Jay Hawkins, who often started his show by leaping out of a coffin, Willis wore a turban on stage, adding a touch of flash to a prematurely balding entertainer who Sears admits was a better songwriter than performer. "Don't Deceive Me," "I Feel So Bad," "It's Too Late," and "Hang Up My Rock & Roll Shoes" are among his best known compositions, songs that Elvis Presley, Buddy Holly, Otis Redding, the Band, and Charlie Rich have since recorded. However, Sears's discovery didn't enjoy his biggest hit until he'd left the deejay's management, signed with Atlantic, and recorded the old Ma Rainey blues standard "C. C. Rider" in 1957. That year on "American Bandstand," Dick Clark used Willis's recording to spotlight a new dance called the stroll. Instantly he became the king of the stroll. A year later Willis was killed in a car crash just outside Atlanta.

Roy Hamilton, a big-voiced baritone, became a popular rhythm & blues crooner when he convinced black Newark deejay Bill Cook to handle his career. In 1953 Cook broadcast nightly over WAAT from 10 PM to 1 AM from a night spot called the Caravan Club. In *Soul Survivor* magazine, Cook gave a colorful account of their first meeting. It shows how self-important the deejays became and how, when monetarily motivated, they utilized their clout:

> One night, sitting there in the Caravan Club with a bunch of ladies, both black and white, and trying to be impressive—sometimes you get to play the big shot when you become number one in your field—I saw this big tall boy come walking in, with his off-color shoes, off-color tie, suspenders that buttoned on the outside of his pants—a peculiar thing to behold. But he was handsome and very broad shouldered. He stood there for a long time and I asked him what he wanted. He said he was a singer and he'd like to do a song for me. The ladies were looking at his big broad shoulders, he was so young and full of vinegar. I asked him what kind of songs he knew and he said he knew some popular songs. Believe it or not, he only had two or three songs he knew other than spirituals.

Hamilton did know a pop standard called "You'll Never Walk Alone," but it wasn't until the ladies kept paying attention to him and "he wouldn't go away" that Cook got the house band to back him. Hamilton opened his mouth and, Cook recalls, "it was a libido thrill. So exciting.

He didn't need a band, his voice was so booming big that he had to move away from the microphone."

Duly impressed, Cook used some favors owed him to get Epic Records, a Columbia sister label, to sign Hamilton with the stipulation that he, not the label, would pick the release date for the first single. Cook chose January 4, 1954, eleven days before the traditional influx of records to start a new year. Tapping into his radio contacts Cook was able to create real excitement for "You'll Never Walk Alone" in the New York area. He told *Soul Survivor*:

> WNHR in Union, New Jersey, had just come into being, and I went out there and asked the program director, George Hudson, if he would agree to interview Roy Hamilton and play the record every hour on the hour. He heard it and agreed, and the fellows out there played Roy Hamilton every hour on the hour. When they went off the air in the evening, I picked it up on my program. I played it every half hour and interviewed him. Then, on WHOM in New York, Willie Bryant agreed to pick it up on his "Willie and Ray Show" at two in the morning, and we rushed over there by car so that we could go on during their last hour, from two to three. Finally, there was this station WOV that broadcast from the Palm Cafe with Sugar Ray Robinson's sister on a show called "Daybreak" and she played him every half hour until daybreak."

It is not surprising then that Hamilton's first single was a hit, establishing him as a recording artist and starting a career that lasted into the sixties.

Pulling together all these strains of rhythm & blues radio—its flamboyance, ability to make hits, and community involvement—was Memphis's WDIA, one of the seminal postwar black broadcast outlets. It came on the air in 1948, after a year-old country station failed on the same frequency. Apparently at 250 watts the country station didn't have the reach to compete with the powerful clear-channel country broadcasters out of Nashville. But when WDIA was starting up, there were no comparable rhythm & blues stations in the city, just bluesman Sonny Boy Williamson, who did a daily fifteen-minute blues broadcast on West Memphis's otherwise white KWEM, sponsored by Hadacol tonic. So white businessmen Bert Ferguson and John R. Pepper decided to tap the city's burgeoning black community, and they hit an unexpected jackpot. Within four years, WDIA would be known throughout the South as the "Mother Station of the Negroes."

The new format was inaugurated October 25, 1948, by Professor Nat
D. Williams, aka Nat Dee, a former history teacher at Booker T. Washington High School, who until 1940 had hosted the Palace Theater's
amateur night. Williams's late afternoon broadcast, "Tan Town Jam-
boree," and his sunrise show, "Tan Town Coffee," became the building
blocks of WDIA. Legend has it that when the engineer cued him for
that first broadcast, the otherwise loquacious Williams went blank. He
started laughing at his sudden stage fright, and that laugh—not a line
of jive—became Nat Dee's trademark. And that was only fitting. College-
educated and schooled in black culture, Williams's more urbane style
was characteristic of many of the early black deejays.

In total contrast to Williams was Maurice (Hot Rod) Hulbert, known
for his fast talk and jive phrasing. Hulbert worked several shifts a day,
displaying a remarkable versatility in the process. Mornings he became
Maurice Hulbert, Jr., host of the gospel program "Tan Town Jubilee,"
where he read scripture and played music in his role as secular minister.
Then at 10 AM he took off his minister's robes—figuratively speaking—
and slipped into a silk suit, becoming Maurice the Mood Man for "Sweet
Talkin' Time," a program aimed at black housewives that emphasized
mellow talk and sexy ballads. The remarkable aspect of Hulbert's morning metamorphosis was that many in Memphis didn't realize that the
soul-stirring deejay and the love man were the same person.

After a well-deserved rest Hulbert returned in the evenings as Hot
Rod, head cheerleader of the "Sepia Swing Club." A classic joke has it
that Hulbert talked so fast one day he struck himself in the eye with his
tongue. Like a bebop saxophonist, Hulbert played with the melody of
real words, turning them into a new rhythmic language, as in his creation of the phrase, "O-ble-doo-ba-blah-blah-doo-lay-a-way," which
was his artful mispronunciation of an ad for the E-Z Credit Layaway
Company.

A number of these deejays, clearly as entertaining as the music they
played, also harbored musical ambitions. The classic example is Riley
B. King, sometime deejay and blues guitarist, better known as B. B.
King. He had walked into the lobby of WDIA, spotted Nat Dee, and
began playing. It wasn't unusual for itinerant musicians to walk into a
radio station and begin jamming in hopes of attracting attention. The
technique had worked for King at KWEM, where he'd so impressed
Sonny Boy Williamson that the blues vet asked the rookie to fill in for
him at some local club dates.

King won again, this time because WDIA co-owner Ferguson happened to be walking by at the time and saw in him the perfect vehicle for a new program being sponsored by an all-purpose tonic called Pepticon. The fifteen-minute daily broadcast was designed to compete with Williamson's Hadacol show, and Ferguson signed King on as host. So before he was B. B., Riley King was known around Memphis as the Pepticon Boy, who sang the following jingle on WDIA and on the back of flatbed trucks around Memphis:

Pepticon, Pepticon, sure is good,
You can get it anywhere in your neighborhood.

And that's how legends are made.

Though WDIA pocketed the Pepticon money, King was allowed to advertise his local appearances—not that King was making any big money. Despite his regular club gigs, King still performed at the Palace Theater on amateur nights, treasuring the $1 every contestant received. This was even after he began hosting the nightly Heebie Jeebies show on WDIA, another indication of the low salaries paid to black deejays. Luckily for King, his reputation as a musician grew, and the station's management nicknamed him Beale Street Boy—an echo of his Pepticon title—which became B. B.

In 1950 King's local appeal led to the formation of the singer-deejay's first band, which included a fine vocalist-pianist named James Alexander. They recorded several local hits, often right in WDIA's studios. The key record was the 1951 "3 O'Clock Blues," a national hit that led King to sign with the New York–based agency Universal Attractions for appearances at the jewels of the chitlin circuit: the Howard in Washington, the Royal in Baltimore, and the Apollo in New York, all backed by the Tiny Bradshaw Band. Three things happened as a result, each having an impact on the history of R&B. First, King began the initial leg of his professional musical career as a star exclusively for black audiences. Second, Alexander would take over King's crack local band and record with them under the flashy stage name Johnny Ace. Third, and most important for Memphis radio, King's spot on WDIA was filled by another deejay with a flair for music, Rufus Thomas.

Thomas's colorful history began years before with the tent shows that traveled the South bringing entertainment to rural areas. As a teenager, Rufus was a tap dancer during the summers with the Rabbit Foot Minstrels and the Royal Americans, playing one-night stands in little towns where blacks and whites sat show after show separated by a narrow aisle. For Rufus this was a crash course in race relations and show business. He learned that the laughter generated by his steps and stage patter could charm the reddest neck.

In 1940 Thomas replaced Nat Dee at the Palace amateur night, and when King left WDIA, Nat Dee brought Thomas on board. Between working a textile plant and cutting the occasional 45—his "Bear Cat" on Sam Phillips's local Sun label was the thematic antecedent of his sixties Stax Records hits "Walking the Dog" and "Funky Chicken"— Thomas hosted the "Hoot 'n' Holler" show from 9:30 to 11 PM. He filled the Memphis night with wonderfully dirty rhymes, such as:

> *I'm young and loose and full of juice,*
> *I got the goose, so what's the use?*
> *We're bright and gay but we ain't got a dollar!*
> *Rufus is here, so let's hoot 'n' holler!*

With Nat Dee, Hot Rod Hulbert, and Rufus building listenership, Ferguson and Pepper plowed money into the station, buying a 50,000-watt transmitter that reached all of Tennessee and parts of Arkansas and Mississippi. With that additional power, WDIA became a twenty-four-hour station in 1954. For promotion Ferguson had some 40,000 flyers distributed to mailboxes in black Memphis, the kind of aggressive image-development never before seen on behalf of a station catering to blacks. However, the station's best promotion was its interplay with the city's black residents. WDIA became a verbal bulletin board; announcements for lost relatives, children, and pets were slipped in among the ads, the music, and the platter chatter. Anything happening in black Memphis, be it a big charity dance or a flophouse fire, reached WDIA's airwaves. Each institution of black Memphis—the Palace and Handy theaters, Lansky Brothers Clothes on Beale Street, the local black churches—had a business or social relationship with the station and its staff. The deejays often appeared at important functions as hosts or even promoters. The station, through its deejays, came to symbolize and help stimulate the segregated economy of Memphis.

It was a phenomenon that didn't go unnoticed by local white businessmen. White station owners faced with sagging advertising schedules or saddled with weak positions on the far right end of the AM dial moved into R&B radio after the pioneers had proved its viability. Significantly, many of these stations leaned on white deejays to capture the black audience. Memphis's chief exponent of broadcast blackface was Dewey Phillips of WHBG. Starting in 1950, Phillips's mix of raunchy blues and spirited rhythm & blues, along with his manic personality, made him a Memphis institution. He was so well established with young white fans of rhythm & blues, as well as with blacks, that Sam Phillips had Dewey debut Elvis Presley's first single. Dewey Phillips is interesting not just because he played black music but also because he had more intimate public contact with blacks than was generally accepted by Southern whites at the time. Even if, as music historians have reported, his on-air raps carried some veiled contempt for blacks, Phillips's dee-jaying made him as much a part of the rhythm & blues world as Nat Dee, B. B. King, or Rufus Thomas. To some of the unsympathetic souls who knew Phillips was white playing black music, the man was surely a "nigger lover."

White deejays' desire to sound black resulted in some bizarre situations. Case in point was the twisted tale of a black announcer named Vernon Winslow. After graduating from Chicago's Art Institute with a degree in design, Winslow traveled to New Orleans to teach at Dillard University. For ten years he lived in the city, listening to jazz on the radio and compiling an impressive record collection. One day Winslow called his favorite station, WJBW, to compliment an announcer on his knowledge of jazz. The announcer, a white man who in reality knew very little about blacks, asked to meet him. During the meeting, Winslow had to field some surprisingly stupid questions, such as, "Why do blacks wear zoot suits and talk jive?" He began to realize just how much he knew, and began to think about being an announcer himself.

A year later Winslow, tired of teaching, decided to give announcing a try, and he wrote letters to several local stations. One replied that black programming was still years away for them. But WJMR did respond, "See they didn't know if I was white or black, but they assumed I was white from talking to me on the phone, because I didn't sound like most blacks in New Orleans," Winslow told Jeff Hannusch. WJMR's offices were in the Jung Hotel, a place blacks usually were not welcome, but Winslow's olive skin and straight hair got him past the front desk and, for a while, befuddled his interviewer. Finally he asked Winslow, "By the way, are you a nigger?"

Winslow was then told that there was no way they could let a black man on the air. Instead they offered him another position: training a white deejay to sound black. This was blackface broadcasting in the extreme. Winslow wrote, chose the records, and gave the deejay a name, Poppa Stoppa, based on local slang. Phrases like "Look at the gold tooth,

Ruth," and "Wham, bam, thank you, ma'am," flowed from the lips of
a white deejay to whom Winslow constantly fed the latest trends in
black speech. For a few months the charade worked (and the show was
a smash). Then, one night when his white surrogate left the studio,
Winslow read part of his own script on the air. He was fired on the
spot. Winslow went back to Dillard while WJMR kept the Poppa Stoppa
name and continued using white announcers in the role.

Six months after his dismissal from WJMR, Winslow received a tel-
egram from an advertising agency offering the writer of the Poppa Stoppa
show a job as an advertising consultant. As Winslow told Hannusch,
"It just blew my mind! Apparently the Fitzgerald Advertising firm and
the Jackson Brewing Company had heard the Poppa Stoppa show and
it was just what they were looking for. They had completed a study
about the black population's market potential and they just went wild."
They asked Winslow to write some more scripts and come up with
another name. As he recalled, " 'Doc' was a name you called everybody
then—'Hey, doc, you got a match?' 'Hey, doc, can I buy you a drink?'
Then the term came out 'Daddy-O.' I'd heard Louis Jordan use it at the
auditorium. I put the two together and they went for it."

Vernon Winslow was now Dr. Daddy-O with a radio show called
"Jivin' with Jax," broadcast from the New Orleans Hotel every Sunday
and sponsored by Jax Beer. But the ride wasn't so smooth for Dr.
Daddy-O. He was, after all, still black. To get to his broadcast location
he was forced to take the freight elevator. He then moved his operation
to New Orleans's famous J&M Studios, first sending tapes over to the
hotel for broadcast and later broadcasting live from the studio with Dave
Bartholomew's house band providing background music. A real black
man talking real black slang excited the city, and Dr. Daddy-O became
a ubiquitous presence either in the voices of his many colorfully named
local imitators (Ernie the Whip, Jack the Cat, Okey-Dokey, Momma
Stoppa) or in his weekly column in the black Louisiana *Weekly* paid for
by Jax Beer.

Historians of New Orleans's fertile music scene credit Dr. Daddy-O
with leading local radio away from swing jazz to the rocking sound of
rhythm & blues that became in the fifties, along with gumbo, the city's
most popular local delicacy. The breakthrough record was local singer
Roy Brown's "Good Rockin' Tonight' in 1947. Dr. Daddy-O played it
"loud and long," occasionally as often as three times in twenty minutes.
This play was crucial in making it a national hit by the next year, opening
the gates for a music community that would spawn Lloyd Price, Fats

Domino, Little Richard, Smiley Lewis, Allen Toussaint, and a slew of other singers and musicians.

Despite the parodistic elements in Dewey Phillips and the racism behind the white Poppa Stoppas, the majority of white R&B deejays loved the life-style that working with black audiences afforded them. One of the best loved white deejays of this period was Bill (Hoss) Allen, a gentle, deep-voiced man who, with slicked-back hair and pencil-thin mustache, could have passed for a light-skinned black. After serving in the army in the war, he attended Vanderbilt, that bastion of Southern education, before venturing up to Massachusetts, where he worked as an acting apprentice at the Priscilla Beach Theater, a move that displeased his family ("My mother didn't like playacting"). In 1948 he moved back South to his hometown of Gallatin, Tennessee, and landed an announcing job at WHIN, a new 1,000-watt station there, where from 3 PM to evening sign-off he hosted a jazz show called "Harlem Hop." Through letters and phone calls, listeners began asking for Bull Moose Jackson, Cecil Gant, Wynonie Harris, and the whole new generation of postwar entertainers.

In September of that year, in a move crucial to the growth of rhythm & blues, Gallatin record-store owner Randy Wood decided to sponsor Gene Nobles's program on Nashville's nearby WLAC, which had a powerful 50,000-watt, clear-channel transmitter. That fall Allen auditioned at WLAC and was given a noon spot on which Wood bought a minute of airtime. At WLAC Allen found again that his listeners craved the new sounds. Returning GIs were particularly demanding, often bringing records to the station for Allen and Nobles to play. As a result of this new music, letters would arrive at WLAC and, equally important, Wood would receive orders. What no one at the station knew was that WLAC was heard clear from border to border as well as in the Caribbean and, via shortwave radio, in Europe and northern Africa too.

This positive response encouraged Wood to experiment. He had about two thousand ten- and twelve-inch 78 RPM blues records in his storeroom. Buying time on Nobles's show at the rate of $6 a minute, Wood offered four records for $2.49 through the mail. For two weeks there was no response. Week three two huge sacks of mail arrived at WLAC. Wood borrowed money from a Gallatin bank to purchase fifteen minutes of time on Nobles's show. Soon the record shop sponsored both Nobles and Allen. Ernie's Record Mart in Memphis sponsored John (R.) Richbourg, and Herman Grizzard worked with Buckley's in Nashville. Wood founded Dot Records in 1951, eventually taking the money generated by black music and its fans to create a pop-oriented label with signees like Gale Storm, Tab Hunter, Lawrence Welk, and that reluctant psuedo–rock & roller Pat Boone. Randy Wood's record shop remained more important to R&B than his record company, however, for it stimulated the opening of more stores catering to this music.

One other key aspect of the radio-record relationship is payola. In the eighties it is still the source of as much controversy as it was in the late fifties. But you will not be able to understand its role in black radio in that early epoch or even today unless you realize that Al Benson's $100,000 salary was an anomaly and that most black deejays worked long hours and were grossly underpaid. Well into the late fifties $50 for broadcasting six-hour-plus shifts six to seven days a week was thought to be good money. "Union" was a dirty word. There were no contracts, no health insurance, and little opportunity for promotion into management. A black could be a program director—though that position didn't have the power it does now—but not an advertising or station manager. Deejays were told regularly by white management that the black janitor could be brought into the studio to replace them at a moment's notice. Their rapid-fire bravado masked economic and social insecurities. They were expected to solicit their own advertising, which encouraged the deejays to be hustlers as much as rappers, and then management took 90 percent. Most got no cut of national advertising that came in through the station's advertising staff, though the advertising was placed on their show due to their popularity.

These conditions created payola, the practice of deejays getting paid by record companies to play their product. Today payola is largely a tool major labels use to control the playlist of pop radio, spending small labels off the air. But for the deejays of rhythm & blues radio, it was a way to get a piece of the pie, a pie made sweet by their talents.

Dave Clark, who back in 1938 inaugurated the black radio-record connection, loved these deejays and will, with prodding, admit to having paid plenty of payola in his time. Before joining Duke-Peacock in 1954 Clark worked for Savoy, Apollo, King, United, Atlantic, and Chess records, usually for two or more at a time. "Unless you were a top jock, [you weren't] making no money," he asserts. "Hadn't been for payola they couldn't have survived. We wanted to help the men who reached the audience and knew the music. This wasn't evil. They knew who to collect from and who not to. They [the deejays] collected from the folks that made the money. Some people didn't make anything off [a label] because they knew that company had nothing to give them."

Not every record was promoted with payola, according to Clark. "When you got a record that you thought was going to do something, you put money behind it, just like you do today. Some of the deejays were so big and so strong they commanded a whole lot of money. Guys could get as much as $1,000 or more for playing one record. Some jocks, who were important but not earning much, you might give a little something every week, almost like salary. Not just to play any particular record but to alert you to new talent, let you know how your records were doing in the area, and listen to advances to let you know if a record was worth pushing. It was like an investment."

Money wasn't the only item traded for airplay. Plane tickets, groceries, clothes, and other nonmonetary "gifts" were part of the game as well. One Southern deejay remembers asking a New York label for money to help pay off his insurance. Instead the label offered to start a song publishing company in his name and give him a piece of the royalties on some of their records. Foolishly the deejay opted for cash, a one-time deal he still regrets. But other jocks of the period, notably white announcer Alan Freed, took money regularly. And, yes, these deals were usually made without the artists' permission or even knowledge.

I don't mean to whitewash payola in black radio, but unless one deals with the environment that spawned it, the one-sided conclusions of numerous payola investigations since the fifties define the discussion. Even Dave Clark would admit payola had its dark side. A veteran black deejay recalls that Clark, trying to woo a deejay who wouldn't play his records, bought the air personality a much-needed pair of shoes. "But still got no answer," the old record executive recalls. "Dave went up to that guy's station and finds the cat asleep in the studio with his feet on the control board with Dave's shoes right there. Dave snatched the shoes off the guy's feet. Well, as you can imagine, the deejay woke up. Dave says, 'I hope you'll play my records now.' "

So, on and off the level, R&B labels and black radio grew through the war and in the ten or so years after to become institutions and examples of "natural integration"—that is, the mix of whites and blacks it created shared genuine interests economically and musically. Moreover, if you consider these deejays as entrepreneurs—as I do—and not merely as employees, then in the midst of this integration (but not assimilation) it is clear the era produced a wealth of Washingtonian figures. They benefited by the power to entertain, and from the exploitation of black music, and were crucial to its growth. You might not like all their methods—Robey's "songwriting" is particularly objectionable. Still, as urban models for balancing black capitalism with the realities of a white-dominated society (whites of course even owned most of the black labels and stations), this "rhythm & blues world" had real merit.

A FORGOTTON OMEN

During these same years another model passed, one that hasn't come close to being replaced and whose demise was a sad omen for the shapers of the rhythm & blues world. Jackie Robinson's signing with the Brooklyn Dodgers in 1945 and his donning of their blue and white uniform in 1947 is hailed, quite rightly, as a major event in the integration of America. It now lies at the heart of this nation's popular culture. Unfortunately, not too many people cared that it meant the end of Negro baseball and the demise of a "naturally integrated" black institution. Ask an older black man about it and you'll be told sagely, "That is the price you have to pay for entry into the game. Look at the number of black players who dominate Major League Baseball, making millions and becoming role models for the nation." Yet if, following the advice of Bob Woodward and Carl Bernstein's Deep Throat, we follow the money, we see that this trade-off, while on the surface great for blacks, was in reality an economic steal for baseball's owners.

The Negro Leagues didn't die without flair. In the late forties the Cleveland Buckeyes, competing with the newly integrated Cleveland Indians, introduced simultaneous television and radio broadcast that predated the Major League by a few years. In 1953 the Indianapolis Clowns signed a woman for second base named Toni Stone, making her one of the first female athletes ever to compete professionally against men. But by 1953 only four Negro League teams remained in existence, and by 1960 they were gone, the players dispersed, and many of the black business people associated with the game henceforth ignored by the chiefs of Major League Baseball. The leagues and their many participants ultimately reappeared on occasion as inductees into a special wing of the baseball Hall of Fame and as answers in black trivia games.

Robinson's arrival in Brooklyn forced this nation to take its Constitution seriously, a shattering event for many white Americans. But a look at the baseball business today shows that only a few steps in the journey to real integration have been taken. While there are black scouts in most organizations, there have only been three black managers since

1947—Frank Robinson, Maury Wills, and Larry Dobey—and none has lasted in the job more than two years. There has never been a black general manager, though Henry Aaron has been director of player personnel for the Atlanta Braves for many years. This only raises the question: "Is it necessary to break Babe Ruth's career home run record to qualify for top front-office jobs in baseball?" Answer: "It is if you're black."

Since the death of the Negro Leagues, there has only been one black owner on any level—fittingly, a radio-station owner who purchased a low-level St. Louis Cardinal farm team in Savannah, Georgia, in 1985 (and sold it in 1987). The major decision-making and crucial economic roles in baseball—positions that determine not just player selection but use of independent vendors and contractors—clearly exclude blacks. In the Negro Leagues there were black league presidents such as Rube Foster, who started and ran the Negro National League in the 1920s; team owners such as Robert A. Cole and Horace G. Hall, who owned the Chicago American Giants in the thirties, and Gus Greenlee, a team owner and league president from the thirties into the forties. In contrast it would take the National and American leagues, at the rate they are currently advancing black management, at least two more generations to produce black figures of equal stature.

Furthermore, precisely because of the struggles they endured, the black players had a wonderful spirit and little willingness to believe in their inferiority. As veteran sportswriter Robert Lipsyte wrote in 1983, "The Negro Leaguers were never as bitter about their exclusion from mainstream baseball as one might imagine; they lived better than most black men of their time, and the only difference between them and their heroes, the white Major Leaguers, was degree. They had thrilling games, money, an adoring public, and ladies in the lobby."

Since Robinson's debut, blacks have done the same thing in Major League Baseball that they have done in popular music: entertain, make large salaries, and generate money for businesses that funnel precious little of it back into black communities. They feed the dream machine that tells black youths that entertaining—on a stage or a ball field—is the surest way to leap racial barriers. But without access to power, blacks lost more than they gained economically from integrating Major League Baseball.

THE

NEW NEGRO

(1950—65)

here was a "new Negro" in America after World War II, one who was pushing against the barricades of racism and winning victories large and small. Evidence could now be found as readily in the courtroom as at the ballpark. Yes, the Supreme Court had spoken again. "With all deliberate speed," the justices had said in 1954, a phrase that echoed like a hymn or a fearful cry, depending on how you heard it. Many blacks felt some discomfort about the juxtaposition of "deliberate" and "speed," as if the nine wise men were themselves a little frightened at the social revolution their ruling was sure to accelerate.

But it was too late to turn back, and a healthy part of white America, albeit grudgingly, was starting to agree. Of course this was not without some prodding by Thurgood Marshall, who argued the NAACP's historic case for school desegregation before the High Court; by Representative Adam Clayton Powell, Jr., of Harlem, a former minister whose rapidly increasing seniority was as chilling to his more reactionary Democratic colleagues as Earl Warren's decisions; by Martin Luther King, Jr., the young preacher so eloquently leading Montgomery and the South against domestic apartheid; and by hundreds of other blacks and whites, men and women, exercising moral leadership around the country. Integration looked like the way to long-promised equality.

This social success would have a profound and unexpected effect on the nature of black leadership. Prior to this generation, most Afro-American leaders had stayed within the black community, their effectiveness measured by their contribution to the well-being of blacks within that community. That whites at least acknowledged them—mass white respect was too much to ask—was a plus, especially for a politician, but not essential to their importance to their black core constituency. For every Booker T. Washington, there were activists like Marcus Garvey, ministers like Adam Clayton Powell, Jr., and business people like cosmetics-maker Madame C. J. Walker, who became one of black America's first self-made millionaires through sales to blacks. In the mid-fifties that began to change.

Soon, it seemed, the fact that a potential black leader or celebrity could gain the attention and admiration of white America became more important than his or her tangible contribution to black well-being. Willie Mays was a good example of this. Arguably he was one of the most brilliant athletes, white or black, ever to play baseball. But in the eyes of all too many fans, it was some strange relationship between his bat, his glove, and his color that made him stand out—and made it easy for white commentators to turn him into a hero. His athletic ability, like that of so many other exceptional black performers, was interpreted by many whites not as a potent symbol of black excellence but as the latest evidence of an old stereotyped image: the black buck filled with animalistic vigor and virility. Of course he'd be a terrific athlete, commentators implied. Competing in the American dream game was just a natural course for a man like Mays. White Americans patted themselves on the back for having advanced such opportunities by integrating the Major Leagues. But as far as opening up neighborhoods or jobs to blacks, the effect of Mays's stardom was negligible. Perhaps more kids took batting practice more seriously after watching Willie, but did any fewer get lynched? In my mind, the first black policeman on a previously all-white force was probably a greater hero.

The message of racial competence a man like Mays might have sent got dangerously muddled in American minds with too many old notions of where blacks naturally excelled. If anything, Mays and other black sports stars contributed to a new kind of racist dichotomy, by which blacks were seen as either subhumans or superhumans, but never as normal people, average enough to be touched, felt, or lived with. This impression was further enhanced, in baseball as in other sports, by the elevation of only star-caliber blacks to the top levels. While journeymen whites filled out team rosters, blacks without the superstar potential of a Mays, Hank Aaron, or Roberto Clemente didn't last. Roaming centerfield at New York's Polo Grounds—his Southern grace and speed contained within but never confined by its walls—Mays was different things to three different constituencies. He was the pride and joy of every black person in the stands; he made great copy for sportswriters; and he became an object of romance for white liberals, who remade black players, musicians, and hustlers into ebony Uebermensch-types, invested with powers far beyond those of, say, your average white philosopher. Beatniks, poets, and sailors of hip cultural currents focused their own unease with Eisenhower's America through the prominent new blacks. Crystalizing these feelings was a youthful, pugnacious writer named Norman Mailer.

After the success of his best-selling first novel, *The Naked and the Dead*, and the failure of his second, *The Deer Park*, Mailer explored his fascination with the alternative world of black America. He decided to use his secondhand perception of that world to articulate his own fantasies of rebellion against the mainstream. Starting in the 1950s and through the next decade, Mailer and other white intellectuals like him turned this fascination into a strange, often unintentional rape of black ideas and styles. Ironically, this was committed by some of the very people who loved (or at least claimed to love) black creativity. In his 1957 essay "The White Negro," Mailer suggested that a new white social outlaw was wandering the landscape, a "hipster," a "philosophical psychopath," whose primary inspiration was the sexuality and music of Afro-Americans. Mailer wrote the seventeen-page piece, which originally appeared in Irving Howe's celebrated left journal, *Dissent*, in part because he felt that this cult of imitation was a protest against white fear of school integration, and because he believed these fears were directly linked to white anxiety over black male sexual superiority. Mailer may have hit on something here. That mythological threat— black male lust for pure white womanhood—has motivated the lynching and castration of thousands (maybe millions) of black men since the first slave was delivered to Virginia in 1619.

Yet in perpetuating the romance of blackness, supporting the notion that black jazzmen, for example, were in touch with some primal, sexual energy, Mailer was as guilty of stereotyping blacks as the rednecks and social mainstreamers his white Negro opposed. While liberals hailed and debated Mailer's provocative rhetoric, many working-class white teens were already living out the ideas Mailer articulated, infatuated as they were with black style and culture. But Mailer saw jazz as the crucial element in this new modern white personality; he had no real idea of what most Negroes, or their white teenage fans, were recording or buying.

If Mailer had done a little more homework, he might have cited first the white R&B deejays, and then a kid named Elvis Aaron Presley. Elvis had been recording professionally for three years by the time "The White Negro" was published, and it may be that Mailer's musings were at least in part inspired by the white public's perception of this country boy. Elvis's immersion in black culture, both the blues and gospel, was as deep as his white Mississippi background would allow. Aside from the music he heard on black radio (Memphis's WDIA and Nashville's WLAC were favorites), Elvis also utilized now-obscure bits of black culture to create the stylized look so integral to his mystique. Even before he'd made his first record, Elvis was wearing one of black America's favorite products, Royal Crown Pomade hair grease, used by hep cats to create the shiny, slick hairstyles of the day. The famous rockabilly cut, a style also sported by more flamboyant hipsters, was clearly his interpretation of the black "process," where blacks had their hair straightened and curled into curious shapes. Some charge that the process hairstyle was a black attempt to look white. So, in a typical pop music example of crosscultural collision, there was Elvis adapting black styles from blacks adapting white looks.

Again, even before he reached Sam Phillips's Sun Studio, Elvis would go shopping over on Memphis's notorious black sin strip, Beale Street, stopping at Lansky's Men's Clothing Store, where local blacks got "laid out." Elvis bought cool gabardine slacks with hot pink or lime green inlets to match his equally iridescent jackets and socks, plus Mr. B., low-collared shirts designed and marketed by the great jazz vocalist Billy Eckstine and essential to black style in the early 1950s. Elvis wore them with the collar turned up and all the attitude he could muster. Of course, Elvis's reverse integration was so complete that on stage he adopted the symbolic fornication blacks had unashamedly brought to American entertainment. Elvis was sexy; not clean-cut, wholesome, white-bread,

Hollywood sexy but sexy in the aggressive earthy manner associated by whites with black males. In fact, as a young man Presley came closer than any other rock & roll star to capturing the swaggering sexuality projected by so many R&B vocalists.

And, yeah, his voice. It was obvious from "Heartbreak Hotel," "Hound Dog," and "That's Alright Mama" that Elvis did more than listen to the records of Big Boy Crudup and Big Mama Thornton. He attempted, with amazing success on his early records, to inhale their passion into his soul. This sound, emanating from a white Southerner of all people, scared white parents and the guardians of separation just as if Presley were black. As the singer told one skeptical reporter, "The colored folk been singing it and playing it just the way I'm doin' now, man, for more years than I know. Nobody paid it no mind till I goosed it up." What Elvis didn't mention was that whites hadn't been bothered because this music was played across the tracks, not on national television.

What his manager, Colonel Tom Parker, knew (and none of the concerned authorities seemed to realize) was that Elvis was just a package, a performer with limited musical ambition and no real dedication to the black style that made him seem so dangerous. Presley, as his sad life later revealed, never put the time into developing his interpretation of blackness—the most important part of his appeal—in the way Mick Jagger has, for example. Where Jagger has consistently refreshed his appeal by keeping in contact with developments in black music and incorporating them into his own music, Presley proved a damned lazy student. Unlike Chuck Berry, the real genius of what we call rock & roll, whose guitar licks, humor, and storytelling skills produced a catalogue of intense, personal music, Presley was a mediocre interpretive artist who spent all of his career in Colonel Parker's grip. If Presley had stayed closer to the blues style of his Sun Records or had, for example, continued to mimic the work of black songwriter Otis Blackwell (who not only wrote "All Shook Up," "Don't Be Cruel," and other Presley hits but whose guide vocals were imitated by Presley), he might have produced twenty years of music equal to his myth.

Despite his many putrid recordings, Presley's power as a symbol of white Negroism thrived. Even during his Hollywood years, he still embodied the dangerous sexuality mainstream America saw in blacks. Lacking the political consciousness implicit in Mailer's essay, Presley still codified white youth rebellion. Alas, it was his sorry destiny to watch Englishmen like Jagger take the iconic image of the white Negro several steps past him, while his manager led him down the long road of schlock. It was bad music and movies that, as much as drugs, ultimately destroyed him.

Two more worthy and, in musical terms, more valuable "white Negroes" of the period were the songwriters Jerry Leiber and Mike Stoller. In their glory years, roughly 1952 to 1962, the duo did for white Negroes what Elvis was incapable of: mold an aesthetic in which Tin Pan Alley tunesmithing was as important a part of rhythm & blues as black skin, making it easier for whites (and middle-class blacks) to play an increasing role in the musical direction of R&B.

Unlike minstrel composer Stephen Foster, George Gershwin in his black-themed work (*Porgy and Bess*), and W. C. Handy (whose attitude toward the blues he transcribed was as patronizing as that of any white), Leiber and Stoller had the uncanny ability to write convincingly from the viewpoint of blacks. Their songs constituted the thinking white man's equivalent of Presley's gyrations. Other professional white Negroes—Johnny Otis, Ahmet Ertegun, and the Chess brothers among them—wrote rhythm & blues hits. But only Leiber and Stoller maintained a level of consistent professionalism that both made their work distinctive and increased the sophistication of all rhythm & blues. In a period when Broadway was boasting about its "integrated musicals"— shows such as *Oklahoma* with music and plot balanced to tell a story as well as entertain—Leiber and Stoller wrote "playlets," story songs of urban life told through black dialect and humor (e.g., the Coasters' "Shopping for Clothes," "Charlie Brown," and "Yakety Yak," tales of an unlucky brother bedeviled by big-city life). Like Langston Hughes's Jessie P. Semple tales of a hayseed in Harlem, Leiber and Stoller's songs were deft vignettes from everyday life, laced with social significance.

Crucial to this accomplishment was the fact that these two young Jewish men grew up around blacks. When Leiber was five his father died and his mother bought a candy store in Baltimore near a black neighborhood. The candy store grew into a grocery store, and Leiber found himself entering the homes of his black customers to deliver potatoes, canned foods, and coal. Years later Leiber told Robert Palmer, "I loved the dark rooms with the coal fires, the smells of cabbage and pork cooking—lots of kids to horse around with. A radio was always playing. Those radios were like magic boxes to me. They played music I never heard anywhere else. Sometimes they played Southern country music but mainly they played rhythm & blues."

Leiber flirted with gangs, hung out with blacks, and briefly took piano lessons before his family moved to Los Angeles in 1945. His older sister's marriage to songwriter Lew Porter made him decide, after considering an acting career, to pursue his interest in music. At sixteen, a job at a record store gave Leiber access to the flood of rhythm & blues appearing on Los Angeles indie labels and got him interested in writing lyrics.

A classmate at Fairfax High suggested he meet a pianist studying composition named Mike Stoller. Stoller was raised on Long Island by an engineer father and a mother who'd performed on Broadway in Gershwin's *Funny Face*. When he was eleven Stoller took piano lessons in Harlem with the aging stride pianist James P. Johnson. A passion for bebop led him, at fourteen, to sneak into the jazz clubs on 52nd Street. As a teen he even joined a social club on 124th Street in Harlem. Seeking the good life, the Stollers moved to Los Angeles in 1949. By then Mike, though insecure in his ability to improvise, dreamed of being a jazz musician. However, classical composition and Hollywood film-scoring seemed more attainable goals, so he studied under arranger Arthur Lange and composed for the Santa Monica Orchestra. Stoller still maintained his feel for the street, often hanging out with teens from a Mexican neighborhood near his home. Wearing chinos and Hawaiian shirts, Stoller was a most unusual looking classical composer-to-be at Los Angeles College.

When Leiber called Stoller, the composer was initially uncooperative. He associated songwriting with the pop fluff of the Hit Parade and wanted nothing to do with it. Leiber persisted, and showed up at Stoller's front door one day with a book full of lyrics. Stoller was still a reluctant partner until he realized Leiber was writing in a classic blues narrative style, repeating a refrain between verse couplets. Together they moved to a piano, and a songwriting team was born. Because Leiber had a strong voice, the pair toyed with the idea of recording him but felt, unlike Sam Phillips in Memphis, that it was inappropriate and perhaps impossible for a white man to sing black music authentically. That was just one example of the respect they had for blacks and their music. Writing R&B songs was part of their overall embrace of black life. They attended black dances, spent much time listening to the jump-blues band of Johnny Otis, and bought a lot of jazz records. "We found ourselves writing for black artists, because those were the voices and rhythms we loved," recalled Leiber. "By the fall of 1950 when both Mike and I were in City College, we had black girlfriends and were into a black life-style."

Lester Sill, a staff member of one of Los Angeles's top rhythm & blues labels, Modern, gave the duo their first shot in 1951. Sill brought them into Modern's offices, where the members of a local vocal group, the Robins, were gathered. Stoller played piano while Leiber sang "That's What the Good Book Says." The Robins liked it and said they'd do it. It was one of those storybook moments typical in R&B's loose business environment. From that start Leiber and Stoller went on from 1951 to 1956 to write songs rarely heard by whites. Big Mama Thornton's "Hound Dog" (later cut by Presley) and Wilbert Harrison's "Kansas City" were just two of their rhythm & blues hits. Ray Charles, Jimmy Witherspoon, Little Esther, Wynonie Harris, Joe Turner, James Brown, Ruth Brown, the Isley Brothers, Charles Brown, and Bull Moose Jackson all sang Leiber and Stoller for blacks only.

A shift to New York and a close relationship with Atlantic Records resulted in their work with the Coasters, as well as equally stellar, though less idiosyncratic, compositions for the Drifters. In *Baby, That Was Rock & Roll*, his book on Leiber and Stoller, Robert Palmer pinpoints an important change in the team's writing, one reflective of the impact another white Negro was having on the relationship between black music and white adolescents. "There is a definite progression in the Coasters records, from an in-group (black) humor to a more universal and teen-oriented sense of fun," he writes, also noting that their songs began depicting conflicts between "the young and their parents" and not between blacks and surrounding white culture.

Leiber and Stoller were undoubtedly influenced by the success of Alan Freed at New York's WINS and by a phrase, "rock & roll," that he'd popularized and that was affecting the perception of black music played by whites. At Cleveland's WJW in the early 1950s, Freed had become an unusually obsessive white rhythm & blues deejay, using the on-air handle Moon Dog, based on Todd Rhodes's instrumental "Blues for Moon Dog." For Freed, R&B was an acquired taste. WJW had been a MOR "good music" station when Freed, at the urging of local retailer Leo Mintz, began cautiously adding black music. The phone response was phenomenal. Freed saw a good thing and went after it.

Eddie O'Jay, then a deejay at black-oriented WMAZ, recalls that Freed imitated "every black artist you could think of. He didn't copy off any one black deejay, because there weren't any around that I knew of that he could sound like, but anything that was black he would say. Any slogans, he would say them. They [WJW] naturally had a clear-watt station and it would beam everywhere, so everybody knew him."

By applying the term "rock & roll" to what he played, a phrase that often appeared in black music as a euphemism for fucking, Freed tried, with some initial success, to disguise the blackness of the music. In the 1950s, "rhythm & blues," like "Negro," meant blacks. Calling it rock & roll didn't fool everybody, as Freed would ultimately find out, but it definitely dulled the racial identification and made the young white consumers of Cold War America feel more comfortable. If rhythm & blues was ghetto music, rock & roll, at least in name, was perceived to be a "universal music" (a key term in the history of black music's purchase by whites). That term made it acceptable for whites to play the music by removing the aura of inaccessibility that, for example, had kept Stoller from singing rhythm & blues. This is not to downplay the impact white covers of black material had on white teens and their attitude toward the music, but the term "rock & roll"—perhaps the perfect emblem of white Negroism—was in itself powerful enough to create a sensibility of its own.

Rock & roll—the words alone evoke notions of hedonism, romantic wandering (taken from the blues), and pseudo rebellion akin to the blues but without the mature battle of the sexes essential to that black expression. But as Freed knew, rock & roll wasn't a music but a marketing concept that evolved into a life-style. Years later critics and fans would search for the first rock & roll record, a quest Freed would probably have laughed at, since he never seemed to know what rock & roll was. The many recordings made under his name in the 1950s reflected a taste for big-band swing with bluesy sax breaks and covers of standard tunes (see, for example, "Sentimental Journey," on his *Rock & Roll Dance Party Vol. I* of 1956).

His albums show that if anything truly defined rock & roll for Freed, it wasn't any particular style of music. To Freed, it purely and simply meant money. Capitalizing on white teenage America's ready embrace of the varied kinds of music Freed placed under the rock banner (doo wop, solo ballads, up-tempo electric blues), he landed a job at New York's powerful WINS, promoted concerts at huge theaters, starred in a pack of bad movies, received more payola than any deejay of his time (he reportedly had his own bagman), and, as the 1978 film *American Hot Wax* suggests, even eventually came to believe that rock & roll meant more than a way to line his pockets. "I think Alan Freed got over," O'Jay says without rancor. "Bless his soul."

If rhythm & blues was the discovery of the black market, rock & roll was the exploitation of white teens, first by Freed and then by marketeers without his ingenuity. The records Fats Domino and Little Richard made before Freed's term gained national currency don't differ radically from what they made later. They were always after the same sound, except that for them, as for Leiber and Stoller, the audience changed from blacks of all ages to white teenagers. Cultural connection between audience and performer was all well and good, but cash paid the bills, and the white teens had the dough to spend.

It was another black performer who would truly articulate this sound of the young and restless, clearing the pimples off Freed's bastard child. Chuck Berry, once an aspiring beautician in St. Louis, invested the phrase with a mythic power it may not have previously deserved. More effectively than Jerry Lee Lewis or Elvis Presley or even Little Richard, he used his songs to tell tales, about the postwar teen experience. In a shorthand storytelling style adapted from the blues and Louis Jordan, Berry wrote of sexual frustration and liberation, adult repression, and teenage wanderlust, defining what has remained the basic text of all youth-oriented popular music. What Freed implied with "rock & roll," Berry described. His content was so bracing because its presentation was so elementally exciting. As rock & roll's first guitar hero, Berry, along with various rockabilly musicians, made that instrument the genre's dominant musical element, supplanting the sax of previous black stars. Simple to play, with a ringing anthemlike presence even when strummed crudely, the electric guitar captivated legions of white kids, sending them into air-guitar solos in front of mirrors across the nation. Berry's memorable riffs inspired several generations of white garage bands, giving many marginally gifted white teenagers a shot at stardom. As for Berry, he never disavowed his blackness (as in the underrated "Brown Eyed Handsome Man"). However, his white teen records "Rock and Roll Music," "Sweet Little Sixteen," "Johnny B. Goode") cut so deeply to the mood of the moment that Berry has been forever identified by blacks with what they perceived as the silly world of white teenagers.

The generational schism and teen-eye view that has always been the crux of the rock & roll ethos was mostly foreign to black consumers, young as well as old. That is not to say that all blacks rejected rock & roll, both as a business term or social attitude, but R&B made a connection to black listeners that was both musical and extramusical. Music made by the white bands was inevitably (and often deliberately) adolescent, addressed to adolescent ears about adolescent fears. Black teens might listen, but their heads were in different places, and R&B articulated that difference not just in vocal or aural effect but in attitude. Rock &

roll was young music; R&B managed to be young and old, filled both with references to the past and with fresh interpretations, all at the same time.

Furthermore, in the battle for self-awareness and black solidarity, rock & roll's concerns seemed frivolous indeed. The rise of the civil-rights movement had put black America at war with the racist ideology that had stopped their Reconstruction-era progress almost a century before. Blacks knew that every peaceful march and favorable court decision was being answered with acts of officially sanctioned violence. To a people engaged in such struggle it wasn't difficult to view Berry as a jive cat helping Freed pimp black music to white record-buyers (as payola, Freed got a songwriting credit on Berry's first hit, "Maybelline").

There was something else happening musically at that moment in the rhythm & blues world that had nothing to do with rock & roll and much to do with the mix of secular and spiritual energies brewed by the civil-rights movement. For all their clout behind the black barricades, church leaders had been content to protect their flock from white devilment but rarely to instigate social action in the street. (Adam Clayton Powell, Jr., had been an exception since the 1930s.) King and his religious aides were changing that in the 1950s. Working closely with the NAACP, the Congress of Racial Equality (CORE), and other secular crusaders, King was inspiring a new activist black clergy, bringing born-again citizens in close contact with elements of the black community (communists, Marxists, show-business figures) they would have assiduously avoided before.

While this spiritual-secular coalition was forming in the political sector, the music world was witnessing the breaking of a longstanding taboo, as gospel began to fuse with rhythm & blues. In one sense this should have caused no controversy. After all, the creator of gospel ("good news") music, the Reverend Thomas (Georgia Tom) Dorsey, had been a bluesman and brought many bluesy ideas to spiritual music in the 1920s. No matter. The split between the blues and the church had long been respected and accepted by most black music-makers. "There is, after all," wrote Albert Murray in *Stomping the Blues*, "a world of difference between the way you clap your hands and pat your feet in church and the way people snap their fingers in a ballroom, even when the rhythm, tempo, and even the beat are essentially the same."

The barriers were solid, but only until the mid-fifties. Some of Don Robey's Peacock gospel releases; some records by the Orioles ("Crying in the Chapel" in 1953) and Clyde McPhatter as a Domino, Drifter, and solo artist; the phrasing of another ex-Domino, Jackie Wilson; the spectacular career of Sam Cooke—all these were signposts of change. But it was a blind jazz pianist with a taste for the cool style of Nat King Cole who brought it all home.

CHARLES'S SOUL

Most rock & roll historians, with their characteristic bias toward youth rebellion, claim that the last two years of the fifties were a musically fallow period. But that claim only works if you're willing to ignore Ray Charles's brilliant work. In subject matter, the great "What'd I Say?" (1959) is rhythm & blues. In its use of piano, girl chorus, call-and-response structure, and plain old *feel*, it is devotional gospel. Though possibly disturbed by Charles's gospel borrowings, such as his 1956 single "Hallelujah, I Love Her So," the secular black audience loved the commitment of his vocals and the man-woman, love-conflict stories he told. This sound, not yet called soul, emphasized adult passion—the actions of people dealing with cars, kids, and sex. By breaking down the division between pulpit and bandstand, recharging blues concerns with transcendental fervor, unashamedly linking the spiritual and the sexual, Charles made pleasure (physical satisfaction) and joy (divine enlightment) seem the same thing. By doing so he brought the realities of the Saturday-night sinner and Sunday-morning worshipper—so often one and the same—into a raucous harmony. It was in this spirit that Charles's children began to multiply, begetting converts and boosting record sales. The sanctification of the chitlin circuit was in full swing, as lucrative career promises tempted gospel's finest out of choirs and into clubs. Over the next decade, musical alumni of the black church would replace street-corner singers as the prime movers in rhythm & blues—think of Lou Rawls's sweet ballads, Gladys Knight's stomping love songs, and the thundering preacher style of Solomon Burke. Even those performers with no legitimate church history claimed to have gospel roots, just to get that stamp of authenticity.

Just as crucial as Charles's bold musical move was the fact that his innovations were made available to a wide consumer audience. By their own admission, Wexler and Ertegun's greatest contribution to the birth of soul was simply their decision to put new records out when other labels were too timid. For example, when the Soul Stirrers' lead singer, Sam Cooke, at the urging of black adviser Bumps Blackwell and James

Woody (J. W.) Alexander, attempted to forsake gospel for pop with "You Send Me" in 1957, Specialty owner Art Rupe was outraged, not out of any real concern for the music but because a backlash by church-goers could endanger his company's gospel sales. The gospel catalogue was the backbone of his profit, and the last thing he wanted to do was anger a loyal audience (and proven source of income).

Atlantic, on the other hand, was basically an urbane R&B and jazz label, with no gospel catalogue or established market to protect—only a new, yet unknown one to win. Charles may have been a gamble but what a risk worth taking. With his own band, arrangements, and di-rection, Charles was the R&B world's first self-contained star. Where Jordan had relied heavily on outside material to fuel his hit machine, during this period Charles was an independent entity whose chief al-legiance was to his muse.

Musically this would change when he moved to the more corporate ABC in 1962. While cutting the classic *Modern Sounds in Country & Western, Vols. I* and *II*, Charles relied on material submitted by others and utilized many outside arrangers. But outside the studio, his control of Ray Charles as business commodity expanded. He opened his own label, Tangerine, basically managed himself, recorded other singers, and cut jazz instrumentals as well as soul-influenced records—as much for his own edification as for public consumption. With the creation of soul as a musical genre, Charles, despite his well-publicized arrests for heroin possession, became a folk hero and, as noted before, was regarded as "a genius"—the first time that overused tag would be applied to a rhythm & blues musician. Charles's subsequent status as "an American institution" has obscured just how much he was a musical prototype at this time.

Charles's moves toward economic independence reflected an aware-ness on the part of many forces in the black community that they needed some form of black self-sufficiency. Now, Charles was never a Muslim—the pianist has never followed much but his own idiosyncratic sense of what is right for Ray Charles and what isn't. But economically (if not spiritually), Charles's desire to control his own fate and the Muslims' advocacy of black economic self-determination made them somewhat philosophically compatible. In the same neighborhoods where Charles's music, on his own ABC-distributed Tangerine label, blared out of open windows, the minions of Elijah Muhammad were spreading their mes-sage through *Muhammad Speaks* and the oratory of ex-pimp Malcolm Little, aka Malcolm X. Even those turned off by all the Muslims' "blue-eyed devil" rhetoric had to be impressed by the fresh fish and baked goods offered at the well-organized mosques.

Black self-sufficiency was a radical concept in the last few years of the fifties. The integrationist pull toward the white mainstream had a subtext that said white institutions, be they stores or schools, were automatically superior to their black counterparts. "Separate but equal" was not a goal the average black of the fifties was interested in or thought was even attainable. The Muslims' administrative competence and discipline attacked this concept by showing the ability of blacks—of course when guided by the proper ideology (theirs)—to match whites. It contradicted the integrationists by suggesting that black control could solve the community's economic and social ills. On some level, even old Booker T. Washington, by now viewed as the ultimate Uncle Tom by many black activists, would have respected the discipline and the dignity of the Muslims' all-black work force.

Many different tales of rhythm & business come to mind that illustrate how this impulse toward self-control manifested itself during the height of the civil-rights movement. Some are in booking, some in retail, onstage, in the producer's booth, and in the presidency of labels.

One story begins in the forties when Ruth Bowen, the child of the marriage of a white jazz musician and a black woman, was touring the country with husband Billy Bowen, a member of the decade's most popular vocal group, the Ink Spots. While traveling through Pittsburgh they spotted a tour bus with the painted sign: "Dinah Washington— Queen of the Blues." Ruth and Billy stopped by to say hello.

Dinah Washington wasn't kidding with her sign, though it should be added that this Chicago-born vocalist claimed to reign over jazz and gospel as well. In any given performance, Washington was capable of projecting gospel fervor and jazzy saxophonelike phrasing into her achingly bittersweet delivery. This combination made Washington, with the possible exceptions of Billie Holiday before her and Aretha Franklin afterward, the most poignant female balladeer in American music. Washington was a queen; she was also a terror, and when caught in a bad mood she could be as mean and foul-mouthed as any man.

Saxophonist Eddie Chamblee, one of her eight husbands (she married one twice), thought Washington's erratic temperament was essential to her artistry. "She had a group of conflicting emotions that had the most to do with how she presented her songs. She sang a ballad better sometimes if she hurt," he told Leslie Gourse. "Not necessarily because of a man but because of her sons or her mother. She would curse you out or she would curse out a club owner, then put a girl in the hospital to have a baby—and pay all the expenses." Washington's explosiveness made her fearless in conflicts with the white men who ran the record business. Raging like blues great Ma Rainey in August Wilson's award-winning play *Ma Rainey's Black Bottom*, Washington would come in hours late for sessions, do songs in two takes, and split as quickly as she arrived. Drummer Panama Francis, who played on her classic "What a Difference a Day Makes," claims that when she came in late for one session and saw that Francis was the only black player on the date, she refused to record until more blacks were called in—suggesting that some of her temperament was fueled by a sense of racial rebellion.

The night she met the Bowens, Washington was in an expansive, friendly mood, joking that Billy had "robbed the cradle" to get Ruth, whom he'd married when she was seventeen. Washington, a dark woman with strong Negroid features, quickly charmed Ruth with her wicked humor, and the two vowed to keep in touch. After Ruth came off the road and settled in a New York brownstone, taking courses in public relations and business to stay busy, Dinah offered her a job as her personal publicist, and Ruth accepted. Working with "the Queen" brought her offers to work for other musicians, such as rhythm & blues band-leader Earl Bostic.

Planting items in the newspapers and setting up interviews are the jobs of a publicist today. But in the 1950s, a time when neither record labels nor booking agencies provided the artist-development services now so common, Ruth quickly found herself involved in all aspects of her clients' careers, taking charge of everything from arranging hotel accommodations to picking up their money from club owners after gigs. The singer, her darker side flaring up, demanded that Ruth give up her other clients and become her personal manager. Ruth didn't give up the others; she just hired some help so she could spend more time with Dinah.

After 1954, that made a lot of sense. With "What a Difference a Day Makes," Washington hit the top of the pop charts, yet she was still unsatisfied with her bookings despite her association with Joe Glaser's powerful Associated Bookings. She felt Glaser wasn't pushing her for the more lucrative gigs that whites and some blacks (Sammy Davis, Jr., Nat King Cole) were getting in Las Vegas and other established show-business venues. Trying to find out why, Ruth began a curious relationship with the old booking agent, asking naïve questions and, much like a mascot, hanging around him as he worked. Glaser liked her spunk.

She would even visit on weekends when he came in to work alone. On one of these visits Ruth heard the show-business vet talk a black star out of an engagement at a white club because, in Glaser's opinion, it wasn't the "right move." So through Glaser, she had a unique opportunity to see how the entertainment establishment pigeonholed and limited the earning potential of blacks. Nobody's fool, Glaser realized her innocent questions masked a growing sophistication. She was picking his brain, but apparently he found it quite amusing. She began to press him about getting better dates for Washington, but Glaser didn't change his mind.

Bowen decided to put her skills to the test. Using contacts she made traveling with her husband, Ruth booked concerts for Washington in Europe and the U.S. To compound Glaser's surprise, Ruth wanted to give him the 10 percent commission, hoping it would encourage him to be more aggressive in booking all his black clients. Dinah, however, took a different view. Never one to be intimidated by white authority figures, she refused to pay him one cent and decided she and Ruth would start their own booking agency. Ruth would do the legwork— she borrowed $500 from Billy to rent office space in the CBS building— but the name came from Dinah: Queen Booking. Dinah would die of a sleeping-pill overdose in 1963, but by then the company was already booking the young Aretha Franklin and the Motown Revue, and would be a significant factor in R&B for years to come.

Today we can see that Washington's spirit of artistic arrogance and willingness to trust a black person in business anticipated some of the coming decade's more progressive currents.

A BLACK FIVE-AND-DIME

Bruce Webb is a stocky Philadelphian with a tough skin and a strong back who entered the recording industry as a "collector" for a record distributor, Progress of Philadelphia, formed in 1961. Distributors were essential to independents, since they were the middlemen between the labels and the small retailers, the "mom-and-pop" stores that were the primary conduit to the public in most neighborhoods. Even some of the biggest labels made use of independent distributors in areas where they weren't strong, and there were hundreds of distributors around the country competing for labels and hit records. Since most of the companies they worked with were small, or based in one region with no national staff, it was the distributors who, if so disposed, promoted records in their areas, encouraging retailers to order, and radio stations to play, certain records. Much of the payola given deejays came from distributors with a financial stake in a record either because they'd ordered many copies of a particular side, had invested money in a label, or were owed money by the record company. One industry truism is that distributors often didn't pay indie labels, or paid them slowly if that company hadn't established a steady flow of releases. But the distributors also had to chase down their own money, which came from records shipped to retailers, people who could be equally slow about accounts payable. That is where Webb came in.

"I didn't mess with white women, drugs, or homosexuals so there was nothing they could bribe me with," Webb recalls. "So Frank Miller, who ran Progress, came to me and said, 'I need someone to collect. Now I have guys who keep the money or want to go to bed with the daughters of these guys.' I'd done some boxing and knew how to handle myself and throw a punch, so I took the job." In Philadelphia, New York, Washington, and down to the Carolinas, Webb and a partner collected or tried to collect for the company. Often Webb found himself forced to "turn guys over or get turned over myself." Nevertheless, Webb, with no regrets, did what he could to keep Progress in business. "They were shipping records out and couldn't collect," he recalls sadly. "Our problem was that we were black. Pop stations wouldn't play our records. White retailers and wholesalers, black and white, didn't want to pay on time."

While Progress continued struggling, Webb used his earnings to open Webb's Department Store in Central Philadelphia in 1962, where he sold hula-hoops, transistor radios, and televisions, but mostly records. For a time, Progress's partners abandoned distributing and joined him in the retail business before exiting the record business altogether within a year. Webb quickly became an important retailer in a city that was then a major center for pop music. With Dick Clark's "American Bandstand" as a hub for white teen idols, a stream of local dance hits (notably Chubby Checker's "twist" songs on the Cameo-Parkway label), and a passionate audience encouraged by a trio of exciting radio stations (WDAS, WFIL, and WIBG), Philadelphia was a town that made hits and started trends. The city was honeycombed with small mom-and-pop retailers just like Webb. He says business was great at his corner storefront. It was the heyday of the small storeowner, whose salesmanship began with sidewalk speakers boasting of the latest hits to attract customers.

Webb remembers fervently, "If you come in to get two records and leave with two records, we didn't sell no record; we just filled an order. The thing is to sell that third or fourth record. If they come in to buy gospel, we'll play all gospel. Somebody wants blues, we play blues. I keep on playing music in his groove." Webb claims he became so adept at this form of salesmanship that he could, in sixty seconds, play the intro and identify hooks of twenty-eight records. "If I see them looking and not listening, I move to the next record. That's selling records."

Cooperation between mom-and-pops and labels was integral to the health of each. The rhythm & blues labels offered the stores "free goods" (promotional copies) or cut-rate prices on 45s in exchange for "yeasting" a record up a couple of spots in reports to the trades or local radio. Personal contact between Webb and label representatives was extensive, either over the phone or in person. Whether black or white, the label reps went directly to retailers to monitor sales and the efforts of their local distributors. So just as with radio, the mom-and-pop stores were financial partners in the R&B world with record companies. This was not the case, however, when it came to majors such as Columbia and RCA, who in the early 1960s had a few R&B artists, though they weren't considered big forces. "The majors wouldn't open accounts with us. I knew only four black retailers who could buy directly from them. If you wanted Johnny Mathis [on Columbia], you had to go to a one-stop wholesaler." It didn't matter to them that Webb sold the pop top thirty in his stores. But, as they had relatively few of the big R&B acts, their hands-off attitude wasn't a serious problem for retailers.

Because of Webb's background and aggressiveness, he did more than simply sell records. For free goods or nice prices on 45s (say, wholesale price of a quarter for a single that would retail for 79 cents), he monitored and stimulated local jukebox play for various record companies, believing the regular patrons were prime record buyers. To Pep's Lounge, the Blue Note, the Northwest, and other bars in Philadelphia's black neighborhood, Webb traveled with records under his arm and a friendly one-hand-washes-the-other proposition. Bar owners, bartenders, and barmaids received free records for themselves and the jukebox, and visits to the bar from entertainers who came to his store. For this Webb gave them anywhere from $1 to $5 in special quarters painted red, green, and blue so they could play the record he was pushing during peak hours. "I'd tell them to play it when the bar's crowded on Friday or Saturday. When it was baseball night or ladies' night or guild night. They felt important because I brought a record to them. Nobody else was doing that. They usually had to wait for the jukebox operator to come by once a month, but I'd go there personally with a record and say, 'You don't have to play it. I'll give you four quarters to play it.' It's that personal touch that helps me stay in business." Without a doubt, Webb's grass-roots entrepreneurship, and that of other mom-and-pop stores, enriched their communities culturally and economically. These stores were the secular temples of rhythm & blues, where the local charts and the lists of new releases were the Bibles of budding converts to vinyl.

TWO SIDES OF THE COIN

During the early days of Webb's Department Store, two of the artists he played most frequently on sidewalk speakers to seduce customers inside were handsome, lean, athletic men with flexible, passionate voices. One was Sam Cooke; the other, Jackie Wilson. These two R&B princes shared much: friendship, tours, charisma, the love of black America, and intense sex appeal. In 1962 and 1963, Cooke and Wilson stood on about equal footing as stars of the rhythm & blues world. But in the long run, Cooke would overshadow Wilson and be generally regarded as having made the more important contribution to black music, not just musically but in terms of the record business as well. Cooke was a marching black, and Wilson was not. Wilson's career in fact illustrated the worst scenario a singular and instinctive black vocalist could face, while Cooke would embody the ambitions of his people and the contradictory ways those ambitions were often satisfied. Wilson was strangled by the status quo; Cooke, a trailblazing businessman and a mass-market commodity, was a vision of the good—and bad—of black music's future.

Jackie Wilson's journey started in Detroit, where, as a teen, he won the Golden Gloves in boxing, took a talent contest sponsored by bandleader Johnny Otis, and replaced Clyde McPhatter as lead vocalist of the Dominoes. With McPhatter, the Dominoes had had a string of seminal R&B hits including "60 Minute Man," but despite Wilson's talents, the quartet was never as popular again. The group's only hit with Wilson was an interpretation of the religious standard "St. Theresa of the Roses," a precursor of the musical atrocities that lay ahead for him. In 1957 Wilson left the Dominoes for Brunswick, a label controlled by his new manager, Al Greene, and after his death, by Nat Tarnopol. Tarnopol managed Wilson and took charge of his recordings. For the rest of his life Wilson was Tarnopol's cash cow. Bound to Tarnopol like Elvis was to Colonel Tom Parker, Wilson received none of the innovative and sensitive guidance his talent deserved.

Though hard to document, it is the unfulfilled immensity of Wilson's gifts that make him one of R&B's greatest tragedies. As a live performer only James Brown, another ex-boxer, could match Wilson for sheer athleticism. But where Brown projected the gritty determination of a heavyweight—left hooks and thrusting thighs—Wilson was a devilishly agile middleweight, pound for pound one of the most graceful entertainers ever. Wilson was able to leap from a platform to the stage, land on his toes and knees and then elevate purposefully to his feet without missing a note. Anyone who ever saw him, either live or on television, will never forget the image of Wilson, snazzy sharkskin pants rubbing against the floor, his shirt open to his waist, his processed hair flying about his head, and the crowds roaring with the frenzy of a ritual sacrifice. There was always an air of danger at a Wilson show, since one never knew what the audience or the singer would do next. At an early sixties show in Boston, Joe McEwen says that Wilson, in an early version of slam dancing, leaped into the audience with mike in hand to distract the crowd from the absence of the announced headliners. If there is another image of Wilson worth recalling, it is of the singer, again semiclothed, but now because frantic female fans had torn his shirt to shreds and were going for his pants.

Wilson's sex appeal, so apparent in concert, was a hit-or-miss affair on records. This wasn't because he didn't project it, for his voice soared, but even in the songs that made his legend—"Reet Petite," "Lonely Teardrops," "That Is Why," and "A Woman, a Lover, a Friend"—the production was laden with white-sounding backing voices, too many strings, and a general ineptness at enhancing Wilson's pleading style. His musical masters may have understood "Night," an overripe, completely schlock ballad that received the kind of lumbering production it deserved. But Tarnopol and company could turn the frisky, light-hearted shuffles he recorded, like "Lonely Teardrops," into a white-bread sandwich. Anyone making a claim for Wilson's greatness must ignore, or at least explain, production that drags down his hits. The fact is Brunswick only sporadically sought out writers and producers who could truly showcase Wilson's talent. Wilson spent the 1960s wading through crap like "Danny Boy," and he only rarely ascended to something as sublime as "Higher and Higher," always without any coherent direction. He disappeared into a circuit of second-rate nightclubs and bars, a musical relic of a once great talent, finally collapsing onstage during an oldie show in New Jersey in 1975. During the 1960s, an era of rising black self-awareness, one would think that Wilson should have demanded more control over his own career. Maybe he did. But he never got it.

In contrast, Sam Cooke always remained his own man. Between the start of his secular career with the release of "You Send Me" in 1957 and his death, just a month shy of thirty, from a gunshot fired by a Hollywood motel manager in December 1964, Cooke was an adventurous, experimental, and contradictory figure, who molded his talent to entice whites, while pioneering new directions for black artists as a producer, songwriter, and businessman. In contemporary terms, Cooke "tried to have it all," and, to a remarkable degree, he succeeded. Born in Chicago, the son of a Baptist minister, Cooke was already performing in gospel groups before he was ten. At Wendell Philips High in Chicago he sang with the Highway Baptist Church, aka the Highway QCs. Then he replaced R. H. Harris as lead vocal of the legendary gospel quartet the Soul Stirrers. While Harris introduced to gospel ad-libs and repetition of key words behind the chorus, Cooke went on to exceed the great singer's popularity by injecting a youthful, sweet sexuality into his performances. Instead of the hoarse shouting so typical of male gospel singing, Cooke used understatement to showcase his satiny midrange and natural vibrato. It wasn't that Cooke never shouted, but at the urging of other vocalists, such as J. W. Alexander of the Pilgrim Travelers, Cooke modulated between the two timbres, giving him greater emotional range. And greater sex appeal. According to every account from the period, his voice, along with his smooth honey-brown skin and innocent yet masculine features, made Cooke gospel's first teen idol.

No analysis, however, can capture the naturalness of Cooke's sound. There was something ingratiating about his voice that entranced listeners and inspired a whole generation of male vocalists to try to approximate his supple sensuality and flowing melisma. (These would include David Ruffin, Johnnie Taylor, Otis Redding, Bobby Womack, Lou Rawls, and Jerry Butler.) But Art Rupe, the owner of Speciality Records who recorded the Soul Stirrers, wasn't convinced of Cooke's appeal until Bumps Blackwell—his artists and repertory head, the mentor of Little Richard, and one of many black tastemakers at white-owned indies—convinced him Cooke had the goods. Cooke was not only an outstanding vocalist but also a prolific writer. Compositions such as his "Touch the Hem of His Garment" are still respected in gospel-music circles. With the increasing use of gospel inflection and song structure in R&B in the late fifties, the charismatic singer was constantly being tempted to sing "the devil's music." Bill Cook (Roy Hamilton's deejay-manager) and Atlantic's Jerry Wexler were among the many who pursued Cooke. Finally, Alexander and Blackwell got a reluctant Rupe to let them cut some secular sides on Cooke.

Instead of tapping into Cooke's passionate side, they stuck to more restrained pop material epitomized by the unexpected number-one R&B and pop success "You Send Me." This record was released on Keen, not Specialty, since Rupe, in an irrational moment, fired both Cooke and Blackwell when he found them recording some Gershwin material and using white background singers at a session. Rupe, unlike Tarnopol, felt that such recordings were unsuitable for the black audiences he catered to. But Cooke's material was usually better chosen and better arranged than Wilson's. Rupe's objections weren't merely artistic, as I've noted. He knew that Cooke's pop experiments would alienate the narrow-minded members of the black religious community and could hurt Specialty's image in the gospel market. Risking that for the hit-or-miss world of secular music didn't make sense to Rupe. Cooke, after all, could have stayed a gospel artist forever. But taking a chance on pop—with the knowledge that if he failed the insulated gospel audience of the fifties might never reaccept him—was a dangerous gamble. Cooke's victory can be attributed in a large part to his own skills as a songwriter. Songs like "Only Sixteen" and "Wonderful World" are remarkable examples of pop craftsmanship. That Cooke could write a powerfully devotional hymn such as "The Hem of His Garment" and teen-pop fluff like "Sixteen" with equal assurance reveals his flexibility.

So it was a natural yet bold move when, in 1958, he and Alexander initiated Kags Music Publishing, one of the first publishing operations owned by a major black artist. As was described earlier, R&B labels traditionally controlled all publishing royalties, leaving the artist-writer only his songwriting royalties. Even then the publisher got half of all songwriting royalties and controlled how the writer's share was distributed. So when white acts covered black hits or when old R&B songs are used in new films, that revenue was funneled to the writer through the publisher. For every J. W. Alexander, who understood the dollars song-publishing generated, there were literally hundreds of black artists who didn't. Of course, few record executives told them. Sometimes when told, they didn't listen. In Peter Guralnick's *Sweet Soul Music,*

In the late 1940s, Louis Jordan and the Tympany Five played the shuffle boogie rhythm to "jump the blues," a precursor to what became known as rhythm & blues. *Courtesy of the Frank Driggs Collection*

Jack Gibson (above), Eddie O'Jay, and Del Shields (seen pre-
senting a NATRA award to Ella Fitzgerald in 1967) were three
of the dark voices in the night that made black radio such a
powerful tool of entertainment and community involvement
in the 1950s and 1960s. *Gibson photo courtesy of Stax Records
(Fantasy, Inc.), Shields photo courtesy of Del Shields*

R&B singers' fate could be servitude or self-
sufficiency, depending on whether they
knew how to take—and keep—control.
Jackie Wilson (left) didn't; Sam Cooke
did. *Courtesy of the Frank Driggs Collection*

The fortunes of Stax Records rose—
and fell—with Otis Redding. *Courtesy
of Stax Records (Fantasy, Inc.)*

Between Billie Holiday and Aretha
Franklin, there was Dinah Washing-
ton. *Courtesy of Ed Giorandino/New York
Daily News*

The hardest-working man in show business—James Brown. *Courtesy of the Frank Driggs Collection*

Aretha Franklin triumphed when white America was willing to accept the sound of raw black emotion. *Courtesy of the Frank Driggs Collection*

Inspired by Eddie O'Jay, deejay Gary Byrd has survived all the changes in black radio in the last twenty-five years, and is still on the air. *Courtesy of Gary Byrd*

James Brown's road manager, Alan Leeds (left), and Hoss Allen, WLAC deejay (middle), at a party at King Records in 1973. *Courtesy of Alan Leeds*

Newly elected Newark mayor Kenneth Gibson meets backstage at a concert with Isaac Hayes, star and a driving force behind the highly politicized Stax.
Courtesy of Stax Records (Fantasy, Inc.)

Alexander describes the disinterest Fats Domino and Little Willie John displayed toward the subject.

Founding Kags was just the first of Cooke's moves with Alexander's shrewd advice. Soon after, they sued Keen for back royalties. Cooke won a settlement so big that the label went belly up. At about this time, Cooke fired his manager, Bumps Blackwell, in part for not making him aware of the many options his songwriting allowed him. Since Blackwell was also Little Richard's mentor, one wonders how that singer's career and life would have been changed if Blackwell had only encouraged him to start his own publishing company back in the early fifties.

In 1960, Cooke joined Elvis Presley on the RCA roster where for the most part he continued in the softer style originated at Keen. Where Presley's escape from the blues at RCA was a manifestation of his essential wimpiness, Cooke controlled his songs and his sound, despite the often obnoxious studio input of white producers Hugo Peretti and Luigi Creatore. As time went on, Cooke developed a catalogue that used his clean-cut, all-American black-boy image to enhance his sturdy gospel roots. What most of his white fans didn't know was that the same man releasing "For Sentimental Reasons" and performing "Bill Bailey" on *Live at the Copa* was also a pioneering soul producer. In fact, a case can be made that SAR Records, owned by Cooke and Alexander, was the first full-fledged soul record company. Johnnie Taylor, the Valentinos featuring Bobby Womack, Lou Rawls—all gospel singers Cooke met with the Soul Stirrers and then "turned out"—recorded rough, gritty love songs that reflected Cooke's deepest musical yearnings and his understanding of black America. Pure pop tunesmith on one hand, soul record pioneer on the other, Cooke tried to embrace mainstream success as defined by Sammy Davis, Jr., and yet retain his roots as well. This balancing act between his instinct for integration and love for undiluted black expression—then very much the music of a segregated people—allowed him to fashion a career that spectacularly navigated the dual tracks of black life after 1960.

Cooke "crossed over" to whites as well as any performer from the barricaded R&B world could dream. However, and this is crucial, he used his money and free time to reach back and give other young blacks an opportunity to share his rewards. Equally important, the catalyst for this action was Alexander, another black entrepreneur. With a spectrum of accomplishments rarely matched before or since, Cooke was, in short, a black American dream come true, one that was still growing when he was shot. Just two months after Cooke's death, Malcolm X was assassinated, robbing black America of two young, dynamic leaders who had closer contact than most people knew at the time. Just as their mutual friend Cassius Clay became, as Muhammad Ali, a symbol of black self-sufficiency and pride, with their vision and intelligence, these two fallen warriors could have significantly redirected events in the decade to come. The examples they set still reverberate.

THE CHICAGO SCENE

While men such as Stokely Carmichael, a civil-rights organizer in the South, would aspire to become heir to Malcolm X's political legacy, there were songwriter-businessmen who would, in a variety of ways, continue Cooke's act of balancing art and business, crossover music and soul. Two of Cooke's most important disciples were Curtis Mayfield, a vocalist, producer, writer, and guitarist, and Carl Davis, a record producer and executive. Together they were the architects of the long underappreciated "Chicago soul" sound of the early sixties. Mayfield was, of course, a singer and writer reared in gospel whose best love songs were as devotional as any hymn and whose dedication to the tenants of brotherhood created a catalogue of stridently pro-civil-rights material. Mayfield's genteel manner mirrored the uplifting imagery favored by civil-rights leaders. Though gospel was at the root of his music, Mayfield, with Davis and arranger Johnny Pate, utilized many musical styles to carry his message. Blaring big-band horns courtesy of Pate, rhythmic and harmonic ideas from Brazilian samba, Spanish flamenco, and the rumba all at times underpinned the Chicago sound.

Not as dynamic as Detroit's Motown or as funky as Memphis's Stax, the Windy City approach had a unique blend of social conscience, emotional restraint, and giddy playfulness. It was the expression of the first postwar generation of black Chicagoans, and as such reflected a more educated, sophisticated attitude than the South Side blues favored by their parents. The Chicago scene never acquired the cultural cachet of the other two great sixties soul centers because no single record label got a lock on the best local talent or developed one identifiable sound. Chicago's soul flowering spilled over several labels: ABC-Paramount, home of Mayfield's Impressions; Columbia's Okeh label, supervised and revived by Carl Davis, and the black-owned Vee-Jay label.

ABC-Paramount and Okeh were major label associations. The big boys were interested in soul but didn't totally understand it and certainly didn't appreciate its commercial potential. Okeh is a good example of black music's up-and-down history in corporate confines. It started with Mamie Smith's "Crazy Blues" in the twenties, was acquired by Columbia in the thirties, kept as a low-priority black label into the fifties, reformed in 1962 under Davis, and was closed for good in 1966. ABC-Paramount, home to Ray Charles's country & western experiments, had an equally spotty record with R&B, as exemplified by the emasculation of Lloyd Price from a ballsy New Orleans shouter in 1952's "Lawdy Miss Clawdy" to the popcorn crooner of ABC's "Personality" in 1959.

While Sam Cooke gracefully walked the line between pop and schlock, many black singers like Price and, for that matter, Jackie Wilson lacked the material and the vision (or at least good advice) to make the shift from R&B to pop with any artistic integrity. As the civil-rights movement was beginning to demonstrate, just because you moved into a white neighborhood didn't mean the neighbors were going to accept you. Chess Records, the powerful indie label of Leonard and Phil Chess, failed to capitalize on the Chicago sound because, like Art Rupe with Sam Cooke, their vision of what blacks were and could be was limited by their proven successes. The Chicago-based Chess brothers had made their money with Muddy Waters on the blues side, and the teeny-bopper blues, i.e., rock & roll, of Bo Diddley and Chuck Berry. As the label's main stars grew older and less popular, Chess made sporadic efforts to retool but never moved into the soul world with any confidence or authority. Originally, Berry Gordy leased his records to them, but by 1963 it was clear that the Detroiter had built Motown, with the use of some Chess-derived capital, into the Midwest's best indie label. Only one exceptional Chicago-sound star emerged from Chess, the rotund, honey-voiced Billy Stewart, whose version of Gershwin's "Summertime" and composition and performance of the wonderful urban love songs "Sitting in the Park" and "I Do Love You" are gently romantic in the Sam Cooke manner.

As a model of local enterprise, Vee-Jay had the most promise—and the most spectacular fall. This black-owned family label, like those of Bobby Robinson and Lillian McMurry, evolved out of a record store. The husband-and-wife team of Vivian and James Bracken, aided by cousin Calvin Carter, entered the recording industry selling 45s in the grim, predominately black industrial town of Gary, Indiana, just outside of Chicago, in 1952. (Vivian also worked in Chicago as a deejay.) As with other popular record stores of the period, young singers hung out there trying to find out how they too could make records. Happy to accommodate a good thing, the Brackens started Vee-Jay and established an office in Chicago. The release of "For Your Precious Love" by the Impressions, with Jerry Butler's strident baritone lead vocal, signaled their understanding of what a rich market there was to tap in Chicago music. Unfortunately, instead of signing the entire group (including Curtis Mayfield), Vee-Jay got only Butler, a miss that prevented them from cornering a big part of the Chicago market. The young Butler wasn't then the consistent seller he'd be later in the decade; his biggest hit on Vee-Jay was a reworking of the Andy Williams standard "Moon River" in 1961. Betty Everett did have some regional hits, but her only significant national sellers were a duet with Butler, "Let It Be Me," and the wonderful girl-group-styled "Shoop Shoop Song (It's in His Kiss)." On the label's subsidiary, Constellation, Gene Chandler did in fact have several major hits, of which the slinky doo-woppish "Duke of Earl" is the best remembered.

Building on a few major commercial hits, Vee-Jay seemed a black company with exceptional promise. However, it turned out that its owners had more ambition than follow-up. They signed artists over the broadest possible range: the Dells, a great doo-wop-cum-gospel group led by the low tenor of Junior Marvin; bluesmen Jimmy Reed and John Lee Hooker; Dee Clark, an R&B wailer with a taste for rock & roll; and the Four Seasons, a white vocal and instrument quartet lead by Frankie Valli's crying falsetto on songs like "Sherry" and "Big Girls Don't Cry"— these were a few of the artists generating profit for Vee-Jay. In what could have been its most prescient move, Vee-Jay had released the Beatles' U.S. debut, "She Loves You," before Capitol Records got smart and picked up the Fab Four from its EMI affiliate in England. In the period before Motown blew its competitors out of the water, Vee-Jay was one of the most ambitious black labels operating; in terms of marketing white pop artists, it was the most effective ever.

Unfortunately, Vee-Jay's owners were not as shrewd at watching the bottom line as they were at spotting talent. Observers remarked that the Brackens never seeemed to take more than a passing interest in the company's day-to-day operations. Vee-Jay is remembered as being extravagant and wasteful even by some black deejays, a group never known to pass up an expensive good time. Still, it was a shock when Vee-Jay filed for bankruptcy in 1965, while it was still turning out hits. With its artists soon dispersed over a number of labels, Vee-Jay's demise left a huge gap not only in the Chicago record scene—one that has never been replaced—but in the history of black music.

Despite the presence of Chess and Vee-Jay, then, it came to pass that ABC and Okeh benefited most profoundly from Chicago because both leaned heavily on Curtis Mayfield, a man whose songwriting bounced easily between frivolity and social commitment. For his comrades around Chicago, Mayfield wrote ephemeral dance music ("The Monkey Time," "Rhythm," and "The Matador" by Major Lance on Okeh) and casually romantic ballads ("Just Be True" and "Bless Our Love" by Gene Chandler on Constellation; "It's All Over Now" by Walter Jackson on Okeh). For the Impressions, Mayfield utilized a more personal voice that made him black music's most unflagging civil rights champion. At first he used his supple guitar strokes and quavering, high tenor, backed by the voices of Sam Gooden and Fred Cash and Johnny Pate's horn, to declare his inspired love for black women ("I'm So Proud" is one of the most idyllic love songs ever written). Starting in 1964, Mayfield composed an ongoing series of "sermon" songs that preached commitment to social change, religion ("People Get Ready" in 1965), black self-love ("We're a Winner" in 1968), and brotherhood ("Choice of Colors" in 1969).

Like a true nonviolent civil-rights activist, Mayfield looked for the best in antagonists as well as friends, gently prodding for change and rarely pointing an accusing finger in anger. There was a dignity in his approach, a feeling that his ideals were for the elevation of his listeners; that this was "love music" in the phrase's spiritual sense. The songs were certainly gospel-derived, at least in part, but the effect was broader. In fact Mayfield prefigured psychedelic bands as a "peace" and "love" advocate in the same way civil-rights movement rhetoric helped inspire the hippies. He was a secular personality who embraced the values of brotherhood in such an openhearted way as to seem at times naïve— which is how some of his sermon songs struck the more militant. Still, Mayfield's songs with the Impressions suggested that R&B-soul was more than entertainment—that it could be as influential a tool for positive propaganda as gospel. Leiber and Stoller knew this. So did the Sam Cooke of "A Change Is Gonna Come." But no other black star or R&B writer of the early sixties put his social philosophy into his music as often or as effectively as Mayfield. Unfortunately, the understated soul of Mayfield and Chicago was overshadowed by magnificent music from two cities blessed with well-organized and integrated record companies.

R&B YIN AND YANG

Motown and Stax were the twin towers of sixties soul, feeding ideas and energy into house parties and love scenes of all colors. Though connected by their simultaneous success, the two companies were total opposites. Motown in Detroit was black-owned, secretive, rigidly hier- archical, totally committed to reaching white audiences, with production styles that ultimately made its producers, writers, and musicians the real stars of the Motown sound. Stax in Memphis was initially white-owned, easily accessible to outsiders, filled with leaders of all kinds. Its records, the offspring of musical miscegenation, appealed primarily to black Americans and were consistently highlighted by some of the most unen- cumbered soul-shouting ever recorded. Because Motown's management and employees were more sensitive to the barriers before them, the label seemed hell-bent on injecting itself into the mainstream. Stax, through chemistry and sensibility (and eventually a strong black distribution base supplied by Atlantic), consistently aimed at R&B fans first, the pop market second.

In the beginning Stax and Motown shared a heavy reliance on the cooperation of black radio to build audiences. John R. Richbourg of Nashville powerhouse WLAC became an important ally of Stax after label president Jim Stewart went out of his way to woo him. Stax, known in 1960 as Satellite, also cajoled local radio legend Rufus Thomas into cutting himself and his seventeen-year-old daughter, Carla, on a tune he'd composed called "Cause I Love You." To generate airplay, Stewart assigned part of the publishing to John R., thus guaranteeing the tune some airplay on WLAC. Rufus Thomas, still on WDIA, got it played there and by a good buddy, Dick (Cane) Cole, at another local R&B outlet, WLDK. Since WDIA was owned by the Sounderling chain of black-oriented stations, Thomas picked up airplay on the record as far west as San Francisco. "Cause I Love You" became a significant Southern hit and won the attention of Atlantic's Jerry Wexler. He leased the recording for $1,000 (the first money Stewart and his sister, Estelle, had made on their label), inaugurating their fruitful relationship with the New York R&B indie, and leading the Stewarts to emphasize black music.

John R. would also be a crucial catalyst in the introduction of Stax's biggest star, Otis Redding. Born in Macon, Georgia, the vocalist began his recording career as an unsuccessful Little Richard sound-alike. He cut a couple of lousy records before landing a job as the driver for a band called Johnny Jenkins and the Pinetoppers. Redding's first Stax recording session came about because of this job. He had driven Jenkins up for a session at Stax's Memphis studio, and when Jenkins finished his performance there were still forty minutes worth of unused studio time remaining. Redding was allowed to cut two songs, one of them the impassioned, self-penned ballad "These Arms of Mine." Stewart wasn't impressed by the twenty-one-year-old singer and apparently allowed the song to be recorded only when offered 50 percent of its publishing profits.

Another part of the publishing royalties on "These Arms of Mine" was again awarded to John R., who, according to Stewart, "must have played that record for six months, literally, every night over and over and finally broke it." Thus, enlightened self-interest gave Otis Redding his first hit and started the career of an amazing vocalist. However, what solidified the union of Stax and R&B radio was the 1965 addition of Al Bell as head of promotion. The tall lanky ex-minister, once active with Dr. King in the civil-rights movement and later a star deejay at Memphis's WLOK and Washington's WUST, brought to Stax's hierarchy an energy and a charismatic black presence as vivid as Redding's voice. Jerry Wexler says he suggested they hire Bell as head of sales—Atlantic initially paid half his salary—surely with the idea that Stax would be a better partner with the addition of an executive beholden to them. But Bell had his own agenda, one that became clear later in the decade. What was apparent immediately was that in 1965 Stax got more records played and sold than ever before. Stax singer William Bell told Peter Guralnick, "Al was the only one who loved to meet people and rub elbows and talk deals, and that was good for the company because we were growing both in terms of the caliber of the artists we were acquiring and the number of records we were selling." Bell's reputation in the R&B world was impeccable. To the deejays, particularly the black ones, Bell was a blood who'd made it, knew what they needed financially, and had no problem providing it.

With Bell in place, Stax finally had a black figure who, especially in inspiring racial loyalty, could compete with Berry Gordy, another exec who used his blackness as a weapon as shrewdly as any civil-rights leader. As all fans of American pop know, Motown promoted Gordy as an affirmative, unthreatening symbol of black capitalism, one as acceptable in the *New York Times* as on the cover of *Ebony*. In his rare public statements and in all Motown promotional materials, Gordy clearly stated that his goal was to buy into mainstream standards. He was amassing wealth and expanding his operations—a sure threat to insecure whites—but his message was, "Don't worry. I just want to be like you." That's what his dreams of acceptance in Hollywood and Las Vegas, and the slogan, "The Sound of Young America" were meant to communicate.

But according to radio personnel from the period, Gordy, an ambitious, hustling dude, knew he didn't have the financial resources to provide black deejays with the same perks Atlantic or Duke-Peacock could. Instead, he used racial solidarity to overcome an early lack of capital. First, he acted as an unglorified gofer for the men he needed. He went to after-hours clubs with deejay Georgie Woods of Philadelphia's WDAS. He hung out after work with LeBaron Taylor of Detroit's WLHB. At black deejay conventions, Gordy bought drinks and sandwiches for all-night card games involving Jack Gibson, top deejay Magnificent Montague, and other jocks.

He also provided the deejays with artists. In some cases, Gordy lent them individual artists for the weekend, free of charge. The jocks booked Motown acts into bars on Friday and Saturday nights—often, before "Where Did Our Love Go," the Supremes—earning travel expenses for the group and pocket money for the announcers. In exchange, Motown received play on the releases of the performing artists. Later, when the Motown Revue hit the road in 1962, Gordy allowed black deejays around the country to get a piece of local dates. One prominent example was Georgie Woods, who made a fortune promoting shows at Philadelphia's chitlin circuit showcase, the Uptown Theater. Woods supported Motown with ample airplay and was rewarded with the exclusive rights to promote the Revue when it reached Philadelphia. This practice of consolidating black radio loyalty by giving deejays acts for shows free of charge was continued even after the hiring of Jack Gibson, in 1962, as the label's de facto head of promotion. Just as Bell had aided Stax, Gibson strengthened Motown's relationship with R&B radio. In fact, it got to the point that Motown began, not totally unreasonably, to take black radio for granted, since these deejays were committed to Motown's success by economics and by race—even cynics in the industry were inspired by the label's exciting music and aura of black upward mobility.

It should be noted that black pride notwithstanding, Gordy knew that it was also important to keep his eye on the future even at the expense of old loyalties. Queen Booking found that out. Ruth Bowen's company was one of the first in the industry to book the acts on the embryonic

Motown-Tamla-Gordy labels around the country, using deejay givea-
way weekends to promote what were then less-than-hot properties.
Even the now-legendary Motown Revue wasn't that big an attraction
in the early sixties, since the featured acts—the Marvellettes or Marvin
Gaye, for example—were not yet consistent national hit-makers. Queen
Booking lost money on many Motown acts but had faith in Gordy. But
as Motown's records began zooming up the R&B and pop charts, Bowen
saw William Morris take over the rights to the Supremes, Temptations,
Stevie Wonder, and others now in big demand. According to Bowen,
Gordy did offer her Motown's lower-echelon acts (the Spinners, Edwin
Starr), but Gordy was so wedded to his integrationist philosophy that
he thought nothing of using agents who would never have booked his
stars prior to their chart success. Nor of refusing to use his sudden
leverage to push Queen Booking into new markets. This was, after all,
big business.

As the decade progressed, Bowen found integration's victories created
new battles for her and other black entrepreneurs bred in the chitlin
circuit. In the fifties the battle had been to get black acts decent money
from black-oriented venues, as well as some consideration from whites.
The fight now was with white mainstream business people for the very
acts they'd once ignored. In the industry there was, in Dave Clark's
words, "white payola" and "black payola," a financial double standard
in which whites were usually given more money for airplay. There was
also, in the minds of blacks raised in the music world and beyond, a
sense of inferiority that gave them little confidence that blacks could
perform traditionally white jobs. Motown's embrace of white booking
agents and implicit rejection of Queen shows the effects that the combination of successful integration and powerful feelings of black inad-
equacy could have. It was a bad omen for the R&B world.

RADIO RAPS AND THE CURRENTS OF HISTORY

Eddie O'Jay saw these omens and occasionally growled about them on
the air. It didn't change anything, but it built him an audience, and up
in Buffalo in the sixties, that was what he wanted most of all. WUFO
opened in 1961 with O'Jay as its star deejay and program director. It
was a rebirth for the deep baritone-voiced jock who'd started his career

in Milwaukee in 1949 and went on to some fame at Cleveland's WMAQ in the fifties before his popularity became a curse. "When you were black and became overly popular, they'd find some way to remove you 'cause people would demand personal appearances," says O'Jay. "They didn't want you bigger than the station." O'Jay's demise at WMAQ wasn't entirely management's doing, though clearly they forced him into an act of insubordination. He recalls that in 1959, "I lost my job at WMAQ as a result of being invited to [a party sponsored by] Stroh's Beer. [I was] selling so much of it, they sent me an invite like the rest of the guys. White guys were going. I wasn't allowed to go. But I went anyhow. As a consequence, I didn't have a job when I went back." With a wife, a kid, and a brand-new tax-free Stingray awarded him for selling many cases of Italian Swiss Colony wine in his broadcast, O'Jay was off the air two years before he landed a job at Buffalo's WUFO, a spanking new station owned by the Sounderling chain. In the first five years of the sixties, R&B stations were just opening up in secondary markets like Buffalo, creating new on-air jobs even if the pay ($150 a week) was still strictly minor league.

After being out of circulation for two years, O'Jay hit Buffalo like a winter storm. "[I] started creating different shows, bringing artists to town that had never been there before, bringing record promotion people into town," he recalls. "There was a market there. WUFO went on the air, people started listening. I'd be out there in the streets meeting people. That's what created the audience. Jocks today just don't do that. They go on the air and they stay three or four hours and they come off and you don't know where they are."

The people in Buffalo knew where O'Jay was, according to WUFO listener and future deejay Gary Byrd. "He was Eddie O'Jay, the Wild Child," says Byrd. "While he was doing his close, he'd be talking and you'd hear an engine revving up. When he'd finish, he'd say, 'Bye, baby' and you'd hear the car drive off into the sunset. Now the thing was that he also drove a sports car, so he'd be coming into the community after the show and you'd hear the car revving off and then you'd look up two or three hours later and here he is *in* the car. It was really powerful stuff, and it made you want to be a deejay." Though not in a major city, WUFO, with O'Jay, George (Hound Dog) Lorenz, and the gospel man Sonny Jim Kelsy, became a significant breakout station—airing promising new records before its big-city brethren—and acting as a training ground for top broadcasting talent. Hank Spann, aka the Dixie

Drifter, Gerry (B.) Bledsoe, Byrd, and Frankie Crocker, a skinny part-time bandleader and college student who called himself Your Record Rocker, would all go on to prominence in R&B circles.

At the same time, a man O'Jay had watched with fascination and a bit of envy was plunging toward an early death. Alan Freed had owned Cleveland and a good part of the rock & roll business he'd created. But in the early sixties, his increasing power, which he flaunted, had made him a target of a reactionary backlash. The rebellious rock attitude, a bastardization of black attitudes toward white authority, were stirring up teens and upsetting white authorities. It was payola, which for Freed was a still growing source of income when he moved to New York's WINS and WABC, that was used to cut him down.

Manhattan district attorney Frank Hogan, acting as a protector of public morality (and as a politician looking to please voting moms and dads), instructed his office to pursue Freed. In 1962, the deejay pleaded guilty to two counts of commercial bribery. Though fined only $300 and given a six-month suspended sentence, Freed was bounced off the air and blackballed from radio, surely the real victory for the prosecution. A prophet without a voice is a man without a reason to live. Freed, always a hard liver off the air, drank like the proverbial fish, and by 1964 he was a broken man living in Palm Springs. The IRS dropped the bomb on Freed that year, claiming he owed $37,920 on unreported income of $56,652 between 1957 and 1959.

In January 1965, suffering from uremia and probably a broken heart, Freed's body died, though his voice, through a hundred other mouth-pieces, could still be heard on most pop radio stations across the land. Freed, like Memphis deejay Dewey Phillips, used black slang and a flamboyant delivery to match the music he broadcast, and now a generation of hip, high-energy white jock voices were flowing out of the radio. They cleaned up the words, perfected the pronunciation, and sold Coke and Clearasil to white teens. Via Freed, white, often ethnic (Italian, Jewish) jocks came to the fore: in Philadelphia there was Jerry Blavat, aka the Geeter with the Heater; from Mexico and, later, Los Angeles, the scruffy Wolfman Jack; in New York, Murray Kaufman, better known as Murray the K. Because of the payola punishment meted out to Freed, that practice was curtailed, and these jocks had less control over the music than their white counterparts in the fifties or black contemporaries like O'Jay. Program and music directors began serving as intermediaries between record labels and deejays, making a playlist of forty or fewer songs for airing and (read this with a knowing wink) putting an end to payola.

The ties between the music known as rock & roll and its original black audience were being severed, and black America didn't seem to care. For one single encapsulating glimpse at what had happened, just zoom back to the summer of 1965, Santa Monica, California, where the Teenage Awards Music International (TAMI) show was taped. Few pop-music films before or since have had as diverse a roster of talent. Gerry and the Pacemakers, the Miracles, James Brown, Lesley Gore, Chuck Berry, the Rolling Stones, the Supremes, Jan and Dean, and Marvin Gaye all shared the bill before an auditorium filled with shrill, screaming teenage fans—predominantly white girls. That constant barrage of noise is particularly significant. It remained loud no matter who was on stage. Some therefore interpreted this vocal benediction of the integrated proceedings as an example of brotherhood: teens of all colors cheering acts of all colors. However, those shouts also suggested that, to the ears of these young record buyers, such foul English products as Gerry and the Pacemakers and Billy Kramer sounded as good as Chuck Berry, who, though fresh from the joint on a Mann Act charge, still outplayed his accented imitators. That they could cheer as Mick Jagger jiggled across the stage doing his lame funky chicken after James Brown's incredible, camel-walking, proto-moon-walking, athletically daring performance— greeting each with equal decibels—revealed a dangerous lack of discrimination. To applaud black excellence and white mediocrity with the same vigor is to view them as equals, in which case the black artist in America always loses.

Sadly, Chuck Berry would suffer even more than others because his pioneering styles would so influence two of the dominating groups of the sixties, the Beatles and the Beach Boys. Adapting his songs and playing style, and, of course, enjoying huge public exposure, they more than filled the gap his absence created. The Beatles, ultimately a more creative group than the Beach Boys, sought the same youthful directness ("I Saw Her Standing There," "A Hard Day's Night") as Berry, but hadn't yet developed enough as storytellers to pull it off completely. Still, they adroitly synthesized his music (with the help of producer George Martin), as they also did Little Richard's leering vocal style. The Beach Boys were more overt (or was it just more determined?) in "borrowing" Berry riffs and melodic ideas. The group's pop genius, Brian

THE NEW NEGRO (1950–65) **93**

Wilson, took Berry's teenage slice-of-life writing, painted it the colors of suntan brown, bikini pink, surfboard orange, and sports-car red, and turned rock & roll music into his personal metaphor for "the Good Life" consumerism. So, the Beach Boys, with their golden all-American image, and the Beatles, with their cheekiness and revolutionary haircuts, unwittingly conspired to make the greasy-haired black man from St. Louis with the red guitar and funny dance obsolete. Berry had taken the rhythm and humor of Louis Jordan and brought it to teenland. But in the mid-sixties, teenland codified heroes who more closely resembled them, or what they wanted to be, as the only fitting rock & rollers. For the baby-boomers, rock became, after 1965, white music made by white people with the occasional black old-timer thrown in.

Jackie Wilson, Sam Cooke, Al Bell, Berry Gordy, Ruth Bowen, and Eddie O'Jay weren't too concerned with the adaptation of black music called rock & roll because, quite truthfully, their audience wasn't. With the coming of the Beatles, blacks, too, in an extension of their fifties attitude, saw rock & roll as white boys' music that didn't reflect their musical taste or cultural experience. That doesn't mean *no* black teens or adults bought Beatles records. Nor does it mean they wouldn't eventually be influenced in some way by them. But by and large, black record buyers and black musicians were moving in another direction, one that would dominate their musical, cultural, and, to some degree, even their political style for the rest of the 1960s. In black America, R&B was about to become "soul," a word which would in its day rival "rock & roll" for social currency and commercial exploitation. Ray Charles may have had the key, but by 1965 the open door was becoming a goddamn expressway. Poor old rock & roll, like blues, swing, and even doo wop and some of the less impassioned elements of R&B, was history to blacks.

Ahmet Ertegun, who spent plenty of time trying to tap the black psyche, recently made a good stab at explaining this cycle of death and rebirth in black music. Ertegun was talking about jazz, but his words are also germane to R&B and its transformation into soul. "Black people tend to think about the future more. Black musicians don't like to play in an old style; they prefer to play in today's or tomorrow's style. If you go down to New Orleans, you'll find some young white kids who play Dixieland; it is part of the heritage of that area. But it's very hard to find black people who play Dixieland today, unless they're very old. Because the young blacks have heard Miles Davis and Charlie Parker. They're thinking of what's next."

FOUR

BLACK

BEAUTY,

BLACK

CONFUSION (1965–70)

Speaking at Howard University's 1965 commencement, Lyndon Baines Johnson pledged his total effort to bring blacks into the mainstream. His rhetoric was met with the cheers of the students and faculty of the prestigious black university in Washington, D.C. For, unlike so many speech-makers of the sixties, Johnson could, as president of the United States, back up what he promised. The legislative landmarks—the 1964 Civil Rights Act prohibiting racial segregation in public accommodations and the 1965 Voting Rights Act barring all forms of racial and religious discrimination in voting procedures—passed because Johnson, a white rural Southerner, believed in them enough to push them through. Johnson moved blacks into the heart of his government, naming five black ambassadors, the first black to a Cabinet-level position (Robert Weaver, director of the Department of Housing and Urban Development), and placed Thurgood Marshall on the Supreme Court.

Marshall's ascension to the nation's highest court was his just reward for successfully pursuing case after case for the NAACP—and black America—over his long career. Throughout the 1960s and into the 1980s Marshall would as a jurist, just as he had as a lawyer, fulfill the integrationist agenda of the "new Negro."

While Judge Marshall prospered and pressed on, two of his most important contemporaries stumbled. In 1965 Adam Clayton Powell, Jr., was one of Congress's most influential legislators. He'd been in the House of Representatives twenty years and, considering how loved he was in Harlem, it appeared he'd be there another twenty. In Chicago on March 28, 1965, he introduced a seventeen-point program, "My Black Position Paper for America's 20 Million Negroes," which was far from the assimilationist rhetoric of his peers. Powell spoke of blacks seeking "audacious power—the kind of power which cradles your head amongst the stars"—and fused the ideas of Washington and Du Bois by demanding that the civil-rights movement "shift its emphasis to the two-pronged thrust of the Black Revolution: economic self-sufficiency and political power." He felt the legislation of Johnson, particularly the 1964 Civil Rights Act, meant nothing in the North without the economic component of "black power" to support it. More than any other leader of his generation, Powell articulated the dissatisfaction of young blacks with the traditional integrationist views of the civil-rights movement and the rising currents of black nationalism it fueled among activists.

Unfortunately, Powell never had a chance to pursue the vision put forward in his position paper. As reckless in his personal life as he was charismatic on the podium, Powell was a poor manager and had messy personal entanglements with women. Both made him vulnerable to attack. A lawsuit by a female constituent charging him with abuse led Powell, in 1967, to be stripped of his committee chairmanship and then his seat. Later that year Harlem would vote him back into Congress, but his colleagues refused to seat him. Finally, in 1969, after a suit to regain his seat was won in the Supreme Court, Powell was returned to Congress, but without his seniority. And by then, he was a broken man. He lost the 1970 congressional election and died two years later.

Martin Luther King, Jr., confronted a different barrier, but one that was almost as damaging to his effectiveness. In the fall of 1965 he announced that his Southern Christian Leadership Conference would begin an offensive in Chicago, hoping to use Southern civil-rights techniques in what King called the most "ghettoized" city of the North. He said, "The nonviolent movement must be as much directed against the violence of segregation. . . . Egypt still exists in Chicago but the Pharaohs are more sophisticated and subtle.''

Alas, King was right. Mayor Richard Daley, last of the big-city Irish power brokers of the North and a man as willful as any Pharaoh, was ready for Dr. King. So were a raft of complications he hadn't confronted during civil-rights triumphs in Birmingham and Selma. In Chicago, many local black leaders had intimate financial ties to Daley's white power structure. As a result, King never enjoyed the undivided support of Chicago's strong black establishment. Also, in contrast to their attitude during the Southern struggle, the national media weren't as supportive of the Chicago campaign and often suggested that the Nobel Peace Prize winner was now misguided. Daley outflanked King by shrewdly offering him a role in an existing antipoverty program. This offer allowed Daley to portray King as a disruptive force in the city. It didn't help that King had come out against the Vietnam War when that was still a radical stance, particularly for a civil-rights leader dependent on the good will of government officials. Many Chicago whites who'd applauded King's victories in the South were uncomfortable when blamed for the economic disparities in their city. While the Southern Jim Crow barriers had presented easily identifiable (and distant) targets for reform, in Chicago it was difficult to convince whites that they had a responsibility to participate in rectifying economic discrimination. For white Chicagoans it was one thing to abolish racist laws. It was quite another to establish government policies ensuring blacks a chance at a life-style equivalent to whites.

Ultimately, after over a year of struggle and the threat of a potentially violent mass demonstration in nearby Cicero—the same city where that black family was almost lynched in the 1950s—King and Daley signed an open-housing agreement. It was a nice piece of writing, full of the right words and positions. But the bottom line was that King's energies had been wasted. Nothing had changed. Chicago was the same divided city the day he left as it had been before he arrived. King's only legacy to Chicago was an organization called Operation Breadbasket he left in the hands of an ambitious young minister named Jesse Jackson.

As King returned to the South, a leader clearly wounded by the lost Chicago struggle, black America bled into the streets. Watts and Chicago experienced black riots in 1965. Within two years, Tampa, Cincinnati, Atlanta, Newark, and Detroit all had similar explosions in the heart of their black communities, and would suffer even more unrest in 1968 when King was assassinated in Memphis. Because of the riots, "Black Main Street, U.S.A." became a series of before-and-after photographs, filled with businesses that in a blaze of anger became burnt-out shells. In place of stores came short-lived antipoverty programs. Once primarily the bane of jazzmen, heroin flooded the streets of black neighborhoods, infecting the children of the 1960s with a horrifying disease which eventually led them to crimes that debased their community and themselves. Civil rights, self-sufficiency, protest, politics . . . all of it faded for those trapped in the shooting galleries of the body and the mind.

The civil-rights struggle was not dead, but its energy was increasingly scattered. The Black Panthers embraced communism. Ron Karenga's U.S. organization advocated an Afrocentric cultural nationalism that saw African tradition as the cure for American ills. Powell's Black Power came to mean whatever its user needed it to. Of course, the assimilationists pressed on, encouraged by government support and antidiscrimination laws, though the leadership vacuum left by King's murder was immense.

But in the R&B world—known by then as "the world of soul"—there was no such leadership gap, no energy scattered, no philosophical conflict. The most powerful individual on the scene had arrogance, black appeal, and a cultural integrity that was the envy of the young-blood political activists of the civil-rights center and the nationalist left. His name was James Brown.

THE GODFATHER

During the 1960s James Brown singlehandedly demonstrated the possibilities for artistic and economic freedom that black music could provide if one constantly struggled against its limitations. Brown was more than R&B's most dynamic performer. "J.B." used his prestige as a weapon to push through innovations in the sound and the marketing of black music. Though Berry Gordy's name tops the list of black music's great entrepreneurs, Brown's efforts—despite being directed in a single-minded celebration of self—are in some ways just as impressive. He was driven by an enormous ambition and unrelenting ego, making him a living symbol of black self-determination. White managers may have made all the business decisions for most black stars, but Brown maneuvered his white manager, Jack Bart, and later his son, Ben, into a comanaging situation, where no crucial decisions (and few minor ones) could be made without the singer's input. In the early sixties, when Brown's contemporaries (and rivals) Jackie Wilson and Sam Cooke traveled with, at best, a guitar and a bass player, Brown built a raucous revue backed by the preeminent big band of its era, one that performed with the flair of Louis Jordan's Tympany Five and the discipline of the Count Basie orchestra. Where booking agents and arena managers often dictated appearances to even the biggest R&B acts, Brown's organization used their clout to demand the best dates and biggest dollars. Eschewing national promoters, Brown handled the chore himself, cutting out the middlemen, which allowed him to offer black retailers and deejays a piece of the action in exchange for special promotional "consideration." Motown may have been the sound of young America, but Brown was clearly the king of black America. How he managed his kingdom illustrates his impact and remains his enduring legacy.

Brown was rightfully dubbed "the hardest-working man in show business" because of a work load of five to six one-nighters a week from the mid-sixties through the early seventies. Until 1973 he worked anywhere from nine to eleven months a year. The only breaks in his nonstop touring came when he played a lengthy stand at the Apollo, Howard, Uptown, or elsewhere. What isn't generally known is that this rigorous schedule was very much of Brown's own making. Every two months or so Brown and his road managers (in the late 1960s it was Bob Patton and Alan Leeds) would pull out the Rand-McNally maps and decide the show's routing. A key city, "a money town" they called it, would be picked for the crucial Friday and Saturday night dates. Brown and company would then study the map and judge the next town they could reach comfortably by the next night. If they played Philadelphia's Uptown on Friday, maybe they'd hit Richmond, Virginia, Saturday, and Fayetteville, Arkansas, on Sunday. An ideal schedule would be laid out and then Brown's employees would call around the country to see if the show could be booked according to their plan. More often than not it was, since Brown was much loved by arena managers. For all the grit and earthiness of his music, Brown put on a clean show—no cursing, no gross sexuality—that brought in the entire family. Since arenas dealt directly with Brown's organization, instead of going through a local promoter, they never worried that Brown wouldn't show up or would be late—all consequences for such unprofessional conduct would fall directly on Brown. Brown's team was very sensitive to not overbooking a lucrative market and squeezing it dry. They tried to space dates in a "money town" between six to nine months apart and played slow markets once every year and a half.

Since Brown controlled his always lucrative shows, he was able to use them to reward and penalize deejays or retailers who had or had not cooperated in promoting his material. In smaller cities, Brown often awarded deejays, notoriously underpaid as we've seen, a piece of the date, ensuring both their loyalty and the play of Brown's current release in the weeks prior to his appearance. In many cases these deejays became known in the market as "Mr. Brown's representatives"—a prestigious title in the black community—and were expected to provide Brown's organization with firsthand feedback on his records and supervise distribution of posters promoting the show.

The local deejays, in conjunction with Brown's national office, co-ordinated radio time buys and the purchase of advertising space in the black press beginning two months before Brown came to town. Usually two weeks before the appearance, Brown's office would monitor ticket sales to see if additional promotional efforts (radio spots, ticket give-aways, etc.) were needed.

Unlike today's tours, where tons of equipment are carried from city to city by a convoy of trucks, the entire James Brown Revue—forty to fifty people and all the gear—traveled in one truck and one bus. In the mid- to late 1960s the show's equipment consisted of two Supertrooper spotlights, one microphone, and an amplifier for the saxophones. The drum and rhythm section (bass, guitars) weren't mixed at all except for their own onstage amplifiers. Road manager Leeds remembers that in 1966, when Brown introduced a flickering strobe light into the act while dancing "the mashed potato, people in the audience were awestruck."

In 1985 it took the recording of "We Are the World" and the Live Aid concert to bring top stars and musicians together. In the R&B world twenty years before, it was customary for any other musicians in town to come around and say hello to the touring star. Backstage at a James Brown concert was a party, networking conference, and rehearsal studio all in one. Part of this was just professional camaraderie, though for many musicians these gatherings allowed them to bid for a spot in Brown's band. In the late 1960s, with Brown's low man making $400 a week and veteran players around $900, he was paying among the most generous rates in R&B.

Moreover, critics, deejays, and even other players generally acknowl-edged the band to be the best of its kind. Some thought Otis Redding's

Bar-Kays were tough. So were the guys Sam and Dave used. Same for Joe Tex's band. But the JBs, as they came to be called, earned their reputation because they were as strong-willed and intense about their music as their boss. Under the guidance of Brown and superb mid-sixties bandleader Alfred (Pee Wee) Ellis, the JBs took the rhythm & blues basics laid down by Louis Jordan and his disciples and created a style, now known as funk, that inspired Sly Stone, George Clinton, and so many others to come.

Funk evolved while the JBs were on the road, on the tour bus, in hotels, backstage, and in hastily called recording sessions. A great many of Brown's pioneering dance jams were cut following concerts, including the early funk experiment from 1967, "Cold Sweat," and the landmark 1970 single "Sex Machine." Often a rare off-day would suddenly become a work day when the musical mood struck Brown. He liked to record his music as soon as he got an idea. The spark often came on the road, as Ellis and the players strove to keep the show fresh. With these rearrangements, new songs emerged from old.

For example, in January 1967, Brown's "Let Yourself Go," a two-and-a-half minute dance track now little recalled, reached number five on *Billboard*'s soul chart. One reason it has faded from memory is that it was eventually overshadowed by a better song created from its chords. On the road that winter, "Let Yourself Go" became a ten-minute jam during which Brown displayed his mastery of several dances, including the camel walk and the mashed potato. While he was performing at the Apollo, someone pointed out that the jam was virtually a new tune. As a result, "There Was a Time," a song marked by one of the JBs' best horn lines, was recorded live and went on to become one of Brown's funkiest hits. As the melodies of Brown's songs became more rudimentary, and the interlocking rhythmic patterns grew more complex, the JBs began to use horns, guitar, and keyboards—usually melodic instruments—as tools of percussion. Short, bitter blasts of brass and reeds now punctuated the grooves and complemented Brown's harsh, declamatory vocals. Listening to recordings of the JBs from 1967 to 1969, the band's most innovative period, it is hard at times to distinguish the guitars from the congas because the band is so focused on rhythmic interplay.

As Robert Palmer wrote in the *Rolling Stone Illustrated History*, "Brown, his musicians, and his arrangers began to treat every instrument and voice in the group as if it were a drum. The horns played single-note bursts that were often sprung against downbeats. The bass lines were broken up into choppy two- and three-note patterns, a procedure common in Latin music since the forties but unusual in R&B." "Sheer energy" is what writer Al Young felt when he first heard Brown's classic "Cold Sweat." "James Brown was pushing and pulling and radiating in ultra-violent concentric circles of thermo-radiant funk," Young said. By the time of Brown's last great recording, "The Big Payback" in 1973, the JBs sounded as tense and sparse as a Hemingway short story, though admittedly a lot easier to dance to.

Brown's relentless flow of singles, many released in two parts, were products of an uncontrollable creative ferment. The grooves simply couldn't be contained by the three-minute 45 RPM format of the day. Unfortunately, the twelve-inch single was not yet in vogue; it would have been the perfect format for Brown's propulsive music. But today Brown's output would be constrained by other marketing strategies and corporate-release patterns—the conventional wisdom that only so much product can be put out in any twelve-month period. At King Records, however, his recording home during his greatest years, Brown had carte blanche. It was a power he had fought for and won.

The sales of his 1962 *Live at the Apollo* were phenomenal. Even without wide white support, the record went gold at a time when most black studio albums sold only 200,000 copies; it stayed on *Billboard*'s album chart for sixty-six weeks, and reached number two. Despite this success, Brown felt his singles weren't being marketed properly. So in an ambitious stab at gaining more control of his career, in 1964 Brown formed Fair Deal Productions, and, instead of delivering his next set of recordings to King, he sent them to Smash, a subsidiary of Chicago's Mercury Records. One of the records was "Out of Sight," a brilliant cut that in its use of breaks—sections where voices, horns, or guitars are heard unaccompanied—anticipated the work of disco deejays of the next decade. With Mercury's greater clout, the song became one of Brown's first records to reach whites.

Syd Nathan, King's feisty president and a charter member of the R&B indie old school, didn't hesitate to sue, and for almost a year, Brown, Nathan, and Mercury battled. The outcome: Brown stayed with King, but Nathan promised more aggressive promotion and gave Brown broader artistic control—similar to what Ray Charles enjoyed at Atlantic and ABC and Sam Cooke had with SAR and later at RCA. It was this control that would allow Brown to make the most controversial and important records of his career.

Dr. Martin Luther King, Jr., was assassinated in Memphis on April 4, 1968. Brown was booked for that night at the Boston Garden. Initially city officials were going to cancel the show, in light of the riots shaking Boston's black neighborhoods. Then the idea of broadcasting the show live on public television stations was suggested as a way to keep angry blacks off the streets. And so it was. Today, tapes of that performance are bootlegged and still treasured by black-music fans. At the time, it served its purpose, keeping the historically tense relations between whites and blacks in that "liberal" city cool, at least for the evening.

For Brown, never one lacking in self-esteem, this confirmed his power in black America, a power that the previous summer had led vice-president and presidential candidate Hubert Humphrey to give him an award for helping quell riots with public statements. A capitalist and a patriot (he played for troops in Vietnam and Korea), Brown was also genuinely moved by the black-pride movement. Seeking to fulfill his role as a leader, he cut "America Is My Home," and was branded an Uncle Tom by radical blacks. (His "Living in America" is the 1986 counterpart.) But he saw no contradiction, and shouldn't have, when he released "Say It Loud, I'm Black and I'm Proud" in the summer of 1968. Supported by the JBs' usual rhythmic intensity, Brown shouted out a testimonial to black pride that, like the phrase "Black Power," was viewed as a call to arms by many whites. For a time Brown's "safe" reputation with whites in the entertainment business suffered. In interviews, Brown has blamed resentful whites for his failure to enjoy another top-ten pop single until the 1980s. (In 1969 "Mother Popcorn" reached number eleven and "Give It Up or Turn It Loose" number fifteen.) Still, it didn't deter Brown from his newfound leadership role, and he went on to cut the message-oriented "I Don't Want Nobody to Give Me Nothing," the motivational "Get Up, Get Into It, Get Involved," the prideful "Soul Power," the cynical "Talking Loud and Saying Nothing," and the nondance rap record "King Heroin," a black jail-house rhyme put to music. The irony of Brown's musical statements and public posturing as "Soul Brother #1" was that he became an embarrassingly vocal supporter of that notoriously antiblack politician, Richard Milhous Nixon.

Much of Nixon's appeal for Brown was the president's advocacy of "black capitalism," a seemingly fine philosophy that saw an increase in black-owned businesses as the key to black advancement. At the time, Brown owned several radio stations, much property, and a growing organization. He identified with black capitalism's self-reliant tone. Nixon, who understood the desire for power, made Brown feel he was a key example of black capitalism at work, which appealed to the singer's gigantic ego. Brown didn't understand the nuances of Nixon's plan—reach out to showcase some black business efforts while dismantling Johnson's Great Society programs, which for all their reputed mismanagement had helped a generation of blacks begin the process of upward mobility.

But naïve though he might have been about Nixon, Brown did choose this juncture in his long career to assume some kind of leadership role in black America. It wasn't enough for him to be an artist anymore; he saw himself as a spokesman with as much right to articulate his world view as H. Rap Brown, Stokely Carmichael, Eldridge Cleaver, or any of the other more obviously political figures who professed authority. The "Godfather of Soul" had decided that he, too, could aggressively project his vision.

Looking back I find it is simply impossible to resolve all the contradictions in James Brown. As a businessman with a long and lucrative career based on astute self-management, he was a sterling example, and advocate, of black self-sufficiency. He was also as happy as he could be within the white-dominated system, buying diamond rings for his fingers with the profits from his white fans. A stone-cold assimilationist in the general political realm, he carried himself with an arrogant, superconfident demeanor that in fact wasn't far removed from the street-corner polemical style of other, far more radical sixties black spokesmen. In a way, it is these very contradictions—and Brown's own unbothered attitude about them—that make him a consummate American.

There is another aspect of Brown, though, that causes some unease if we try to hold him up as a kind of model. Given the unbridled machismo that was part and parcel of the energy driving him (as well as Carmichael, Cleaver, and others), black women were simply attached as a postscript to a male-directed message. As Michelle Wallace, with some overstatement but a lot of truth, observed in *Black Macho and the Myth of the Superwoman*, these men thought of women as mothers, cooks, and servants of the revolution, not as its leaders. It didn't have to be that way. Black women were, of course, as capable of leadership as any male. Fallout from this political patriarchy would be felt in black literature in the future, but in the late 1960s, feminist issues weren't overtly part of the agendas of the nationalist or even civil-rights movements.

THE QUEEN

Yet the one voice that spoke most directly to the aroused black psyche of the 1960s, though apolitical and preoccupied with struggles of the heart, was a woman's. If anyone wondered what "soul" was, all they had to do was play any of Aretha Franklin's Atlantic albums.

From 1967, when she joined Atlantic after six frustrating years at Columbia—when she recorded pop standards and traditional blues that didn't highlight her fiery gospel style—until about 1971, Aretha Franklin was not just indisputably the best singer in the R&B-soul world but the focus for, to use a sixties cliché, the positive spiritual energy of her listeners. As daughter of Detroit's flamboyant and strong-voiced Reverend C. L. Franklin, Aretha was an heir to a legacy of redemption through music. At the same time, her widely publicized marital problems—*Time* made them an essential part of a June 1968 cover story—and her unmistakable voice made her the epitome of soul music, just as Ray Charles had been a decade before. Ah, that voice. One of the more cogent passages from the *Time* piece describes Franklin's approach as a "direct natural style of delivery that ranges over a full four octaves, and the breath control to spin out long phrases that curl sensuously around the beat and dangle tantalizingly from blue notes. But what really accounts for her impact goes beyond technique: it is her fierce, gritty conviction."

Jerry Wexler, in the wisest move of his long career, recorded Franklin at Fame Studio, in Muscle Shoals, Alabama, and at Criteria Studio in Miami, with Southern session men—white and black—who gave her voice the kind of complementary musical backing that had eluded her at Columbia. The songs were written by Aretha, or specifically written for her and chosen by her, with the rhythm arrangements usually built around her gospel-style piano. In a time when popular black, and then white, slang ("Do your thing!" "Sock it to me!") were admonitions to be loose, uninhibited, and natural, few things communicated these values better than Franklin's vocals. Despite singing love songs, many of them quite melancholy, Franklin's voice communicated so wide a range of emotion as to truly defy description.

"Intangible" is a word that music critics overuse daily, but listen to Franklin on "Dr. Feelgood" or "Ain't No Way" or "Say A Little Prayer" or "Think." One discovers not one Aretha Franklin but a cast of hundreds of women: some sweet, some mad, some cool, some sad, some angry, and a great many playful and sexy. Franklin expressed all a black woman could be, while her contemporaries (Diana Ross, Tina Turner, Dionne Warwick, Martha Reeves, even the underrated Gladys Knight) seemed trapped in one persona by the artistic decisions of male producers as well as by their own vocal limitations. Given her talent and the tenor of the times, it wasn't surprising that Franklin became a prime example of "natural crossover." Compared to Motown, Franklin's music made few concessions to "white" sensibilities. She and Atlantic found that white America was, at this point, more willing to accept "real" black music by blacks than at anytime since World War II. Why?

The Western world, politically and culturally, was undergoing a profound upheaval. With the civil-rights movement and the Vietnam War as catalysts, traditional values of every kind—machismo, monogamy, patriotism—were being rejected, or at least questioned. The white teen market Alan Freed once cultivated had matured into a dynamic force for change; its interest in politics, drugs, and free love altered its music. "Rock & roll," that straightforward, unambitious consumer product, was now evolving into something more experimental, less categorizable, roughly dubbed "rock." White musicians were more explicitly articulating their cultural experience in pop music. And in 1967 the broader perspective rock represented was crystallized by the Beatles' *Sgt. Pepper's Lonely Hearts Club Band*. This music had plain old rock & roll drumming, playing, and singing—the adaptation of black R&B—plus instrumentation and melodies from European classical music and English music halls. This was more ambitious than mere rock & roll. It was electronic. It was experimental. It sold albums instead of just 45s (and so got major labels interested). It was art. It was rock. It was white.

It was also liberal—probrotherhood and all that. The civil-rights movement's evolution into various forms of black nationalism and self-assertion had, in music as well as in Democratic politics, caused a breach. Into the late sixties, Motown was still selling itself as "The Sound of Young America," but it wasn't without critics, black and white, who now saw the label's aggressive upward mobility as an unnecessary attempt to escape blackness and sell out to the Establishment. So soul, with the uncompromising Aretha as its star, was enjoyed and purchased by whites and blacks. One of the most intense album-length explorations of soul ever recorded, *Aretha Live At the Fillmore*, with a guest appearance by Ray Charles, was cut at one of white promoter Bill Graham's temples of rock, San Francisco's Fillmore West.

In the 1950s rock & roll overshadowed R&B; in the sixties white musicians had difficulty synthesizing their own version of soul. This was primarily because white singers just couldn't match the intense vocal style of soul, though at the time the gap between white and black music was perceived differently, as less a musical than a political distinction. For example, in his introduction to the 1969 book *The Age of Rock*, Jonathan Eisen explained why only three of thirty-four essays dealt with black music by saying, "I have not placed as much emphasis on the music of the black community as I have on that of the white. The reasons, I trust, are evident. In recent years, young black musicians on the whole have been involved within an entirely different milieu, both social and musical, most of them concentrating on developing greater nationalistic self-consciousness."

In the late 1960s, with soul integral to the lives of black America, the white rock audience revived 1950s electric blues, a music which had been part of the R&B world but which, like rock & roll and straight doo wop, had been forsaken for soul. B. B. King, whose career had been in decline since the early sixties, was suddenly discovered in 1966 by the rock audience through the praise of white guitar heroes like the Electric Flag's Mike Bloomfield and Cream's Eric Clapton, and bookings at Graham's Fillmores East and West.

Muddy Waters, Howlin' Wolf, and Bobby (Blue) Bland were among the grand old electric bluesmen who found themselves getting paid better than at any time in their lengthy careers because they had suddenly started reaching that elusive white audience. Few blacks showed up at rock festivals and concert halls. Older black fans, who'd loved Muddy and company at the neighborhood bar, rarely came to these temples of youth culture partly because they didn't feel comfortable among middle class white teens and college students, and partly because they didn't know about the gigs: advertising, in the underground press and progressive rock radio (the key media of ascendant rock culture), never reached them. To blacks who still valued the blues, it seemed these cultural heroes had been kidnapped by the younger brothers and sisters of the folks who'd led Chuck Berry astray. And to younger blacks—the soul children of the sixties—the blues just wasn't (remember this one?) "relevant" in a world of dashikis, Afro picks, and bell-bottoms. To paraphrase Ahmet Ertegun, black music is in constant flight from the status quo. Young blacks at the time abandoned the blues because it was "depressing," "backward," or "accommodating" to white values.

This argument is crap—"relevancy" irrelevant itself—but then as now a lot of blacks believed it. In fact, blues was only suffering the same fate that, surprisingly, would soon befall soul.

CULTURE SHOCK

The black audience's consumerism and restlessness burns out and abandons musical styles, whereas white Americans, in the European tradition of supporting forms and style for the sake of tradition, seem to hold styles dear long after they have ceased to evolve.

The most fanatical students of blues history have all been white. These well-intentioned scholars pick through old recordings, interview obscure guitarists, and tramp through the Mississippi Delta with the determination of Egyptologists. Yet with the exception of Eric Clapton and maybe Johnny Winter, no white blues guitarist has produced a body of work in any way comparable to that of the black giants. Blacks create and then move on. Whites document and then recycle. In the history of popular music, these truths are self-evident.

But—and here's the paradox—all the great black musicians working in a pop idiom—be it rock & roll, R&B, or funk—become cultural curators or historical critics. By taking established black forms, preserving their essence but filtering these textures through an ambitious creative consciousness, they made astounding music that is in the tradition yet singular from it. For example, Jimi Hendrix used blues and R&B as his building blocks, and Sly Stone worked from gospel and soul. Yet black America's reaction to each was different: Hendrix was rejected, while Sly was viewed, before drug days, as a hero.

The difference was that Hendrix drew from a style blacks had already disposed of; Sly shrewdly stayed just a few steps ahead of the crowd. Both were children of the R&B world. Hendrix had been a sideman for numberous R&B bands after leaving Seattle in his teens, including the Isley Brothers. Sly, baptized as Sylvester Stewart, was reared in a roof-raising, sanctified church and worked as a popular deejay on several Bay Area stations. And both Sly and Jimi rebelled against the narrow-mindedness in which they grew up. It is not coincidental that they blossomed in environments removed from the traditions of black America, Hendrix in London and Sly in "free-love" San Francisco, where they each plunged into the hippie life-styles of those two countercultural centers, emerging with a black-based sound drenched in flower-power rhetoric that had little in common with the soul consciousness of James Brown or Aretha.

Unfortunately, Hendrix fatally damaged his connection with black audiences because of his innovative brilliance on the electric guitar, an instrument that, with the declining black interest in blues, fell into disfavor. At Motown, electric guitars, sometimes as many as four, were locked in intricate patterns. At Stax, Steve Cropper's lead lines were short, concise statements. But in rock, lead guitar extravagance was crucial to the music and the supporting culture. It was the perfect accompaniment to LSD and other chemicals of choice. Hendrix, once frustrated by R&B background work, greedily hogged every available space for his Stratocaster. In essence, Hendrix was the revenge of the R&B sideman, one with the ability to turn the voices inside his head into music—problem was, you just couldn't dance to it. Maybe if you were stoned at a light show the Jimi Hendrix Experience could be boogie fodder. Maybe if the grass was flowing at a local love-in you'd dance. However, to the audiences of Stax and Motown and James Brown, "Purple Haze" and "Hey Joe" just didn't do the do. Jimi's music was, if not from another planet, definitely from another country. In a weird symmetry, Hendrix, with his young white-teen audience, was a sixties equivalent of Chuck Berry. Like Berry, his success with guitar-based music made him an outcast on Black Main Street.

Sly was, alas, just as drug-crazed as Hendrix and just as enamored of "rock culture." He had an integrated band, not just racially but sexually, that looked as if the members had just wandered off the corner of Haight and Ashbury. No slick choreography around the Family Stone. It was organized chaos or, as Dave Marsh wrote, "The women played, the men sang: the blacks freaked out, the whites got funky; everyone did something unexpected." Sly never worked the chitlin circuit. Like Hendrix, he played gigs with rock acts at rock revues almost from the beginning, working through contacts in the West Coast music scene.

But Sly always gave up the funk. His rhythm section, with bassist Larry Graham, drummer Greg Errico, and guitarist Freddie Stone, mirrored James Brown's jagged polyrhythms. On "I Want to Take You Higher," "Thank You (Falettinme Be Mice Elf Agin)," and "Sing A Simple Song," Sly brought Brown's funk to the rock masses almost uncut. Almost, because it would be inaccurate to say that Sly's music just allowed the mass dissemination of Brownish bottom. His memorable melodies and knack for sloganeering ("Hot Fun in the Summertime," "Stand!," "Everyday People," "Everybody Is a Star," "You Can Make

It If You Try") were as infectious as the chant-vocal approach he pioneered. In addition, and this is a crucial point, Sly was the first great R&B innovator raised to stardom on a corporate label.

Two years before the release of Sly's 1968 debut, "Dance to the Music," on Epic Records, its CBS corporate sister of the Columbia label had let Aretha's contract lapse and ended its affiliation with Carl Davis and the "Chicago sound." CBS was virtually out of the black music business. Things turned around at CBS, and the credit goes to its young president, Clive Davis. In 1965, CBS Records (Columbia, Epic, and its subsidiaries) had 11 percent of the overall market. By the end of 1968, CBS commanded 17 percent, and the figure was climbing due to Davis's aggressive signing of rock artists such as "white Negro" Janis Joplin; Chicago; Blood, Sweat and Tears; Simon and Garfunkel; and Sly and the Family Stone. Davis at first wasn't convinced that, in the age of Aquarius, Sly's glittery costumes could reach whites, which at the time was the only market that concerned CBS. In his autobiography, Davis recalls a soul-searching meeting with Sly about his direction. According to Davis, the bandleader contended, "They will know what to make of it soon," he said. "I have a definite idea of what I am trying to do and I want to stay with it. Maybe the kids will be put off at first, but they'll get into it." Davis admitted he underestimated Sly's vision. But Sly's play worked; CBS backed the group all the way. This didn't mean, however, that Columbia had a fully developed strategy for exploiting black music. At the time, while Columbia was becoming a dominant force in rock music, a new entity was emerging as its chief foe in the youth market—the conglomerate Warner Bros., Elektra-Asylum, and (with its stellar black catalogue) Atlantic Records. Eventually, this combination, known today as WEA, would become CBS's chief rival in the industry.

Atlantic's absorption set Ahmet Ertegun and Jerry Wexler financially for life. The influx of dollars also solidified an ongoing sea change in the label's direction. In 1967, Atlantic's ATCO subsidiary signed one of rock's first supergroups, Cream (with guitarist Eric Clapton, bassist Jack Bruce, and drummer Ginger Baker), and the Beatlesque Australian vocal trio, the Bee Gees. In 1969, Led Zeppelin delivered two albums to Atlantic that laid the foundation for a new genre, heavy metal, while Ertegun personally wined and dined the Rolling Stones into a deal. Atlantic was now as closely identified with British rock as it had been with black music. After the late sixties, the balance at Atlantic would be tipped permanently to rock. It began with the death of Otis Redding in a plane crash on December 10, 1967. Then, during a bitter negotiation between Wexler and Stax's Jim Stewart, it was revealed that Atlantic, back in 1962 when the original distribution deal was made, had gained control of all the Stax masters. Taking advantage of a technicality in the contract, Atlantic held on to them. Apparently Wexler first mentioned them merely as a negotiating ploy. Embarrassed and stung, Stewart and Al Bell made a deal with Paramount Pictures Music Division, a subsidiary of Gulf + Western, for almost $3 million plus G + W stock. As part of this transaction, Bell was appointed executive vice-president of Stax and given a piece of the label's growing East Memphis catalogue.

So, unexpectedly, Stax became, just like Atlantic, a part of corporate America—though it was a relatively small acquisition for a huge oil company. Few observers at the time foresaw the negative impact these distribution shifts would have on the music and the institutions that made up the R&B world. It was simply assumed that the sudden influx of corporate dollars would allow everyone to do a better job at making, promoting, and distributing black music than ever before.

NARA

Sly's success at Columbia, and the Atlantic and Stax deals, signaled a significant realignment of power in the R&B world. At the same time, black radio was undergoing an internal political struggle and a stylistic evolution that brought revolutionary changes in how it sounded and was perceived.

The genesis of this change, according to Del Shields, then a jazz deejay at New York's WLIB, was the assassination of King. While James Brown was being broadcast on public TV in Boston, deejays across the country were on all night, sometimes against their owner's wishes, to stifle black backlash against this latest instance of American racism. Shields says, "Black radio came of age the night Dr. King was killed. Up until that time, black radio had never been tested nationally. No one ever knew its power. You knew the popularity of black disc jockeys, the power to sell various products. But on the night Dr. King was killed, all across America every black station was tested and everybody who was on the air at that time, including myself, told people to cool it. We tried to do everything possible to keep the black people from just exploding even more than what they were.

"We were on WLIB, a daytime station that was supposed to go off at sunset. We stayed on till twelve, one o'clock at night. We went beyond the FCC ruling and, of course, had to answer to the FCC later with reports about why we stayed on. The oddity was that we, the black disc jockeys, made the decision to stay on. As a result, the station got the Peabody Award. The owner himself had called and told me I had no right to do that, but I told him I didn't have time to talk to him. When America looked at black radio in that particular period, it suddenly hit them that this was a potent force. If, in every major city, a black disc jockey had said, 'Rise up,' there would have been pandemonium. And that night was also the beginning of the end of black radio. It was never allowed to rise up again.''

In the sixties, Shields was a highly politicized man who, before and after his jazz broadcast from Harlem's Lenox Avenue, hung out with a wide range of people, from Black Power advocate H. Rap Brown to his cousin, Bill Cosby, a rising comedian and costar of TV's first integrated action-adventure show, *I Spy*. Shields saw in the energy of both—a spokesman for radical black America and a mass-market symbol of upward mobility—the kind of mix that would fulfill black radio's potential. But for Shields's vision to become reality, several things had to happen: there had to be more black ownership (in the late sixties, fewer than ten stations had black owners); better trained disc jockeys who could demand higher salaries (Shields, a top deejay in New York, made only $250 a week; white counterparts earned $800); and black deejays needed some form of protection from abuse by station-managers and manipulation by record-label executives. Because of the differences in job description and salary for deejays around the country, unionization was ruled out. An organization of some kind, with the committed leadership and membership of a civil-rights organization, was needed, and the framework for one existed.

The National Association for Radio Announcers (NARA) was an outgrowth of an old-boy network of black deejays that Jack Gibson had helped establish in the fifties. In 1955, Gibson formally dubbed it an organization, though social club might have been a more apt description. NARA's parties were legendary. The deejays, many from small Southern stations, used the organization's annual gatherings to show off as flamboyantly as any recording star or pimp. Gibson recalls one gathering in St. Louis where NARA took over a hotel ''and partied until it was time to go to church,'' which was typical of the organization. Well before the excesses of rock stars became common, NARA had a reputation for leaving an enduring impression on hotel managers. Much of this had to with ego. Gather together four hundred men who make their living with glib tongues and jive, and you've got a hotel full of one-upmanship. Everyone wanted to know, who drank more? Who fucked more and longer? Who played the slyest poker? Who got the most payola? That competitiveness is of some importance to NARA's history since the biggest deejays controlled the organization and set the tone for its hell-raising. NARA and its members weren't oblivious of the civil-rights movement and the changes it brought to the fabric of black life. They gave money; they gave lip service. But their internal will for collective effort was weak. Business as usual was good for many; others feared reprisals from white bosses if they got too political.

In 1965, three years before King's assassination, Shields, then at Philadelphia's WDAS, had a fateful talk with Clarence Avante. Avante, the manager of jazz organist Jimmy Smith and soundtrack composer Lalo Schriffen, was viewed by whites and blacks as one of the most able deal-makers around, and he cultivated close ties with white record and TV executives at ABC, and within the CBS corporate structure. He told Shields it was time to upgrade NARA and asked him to prepare an outline with ideas. Together with Ed Wright, program director of Cleveland's WABQ, and Jimmy Bishop, a deejay at WDAS, Avante and Shields began networking with other jocks around the country to prepare a coup d'etat. At that year's convention in Houston, the group, known affectionately and pejoratively as the "new breed," surprised everyone by winning an election for control of NARA.

Suggestive of this new breed's perspective, they changed the organization's name from NARA to NATRA (National Association of Television and Radio Announcers), feeling that they needed to reach out beyond radio and records to all parts of the communications industry. An awards banquet, the first ever specifically for blacks in the broadcast industry, was held at the Waldorf-Astoria. The choices were intriguing and revealing: Lena Horne, not a popular figure in black America at the time, and Sheldon Leonard, the white producer of *I Spy*, were respectively NATRA's woman and man of the year. Horne was chosen in a generous attempt to refurbish an image unfairly tarnished in black America by what many viewed as her career-long accommodation to whites; and Leonard, to emphasize to NATRA's membership that the world of communications encompassed more than hit records.

More ambitiously, political and social issues were introduced into the organization. Representatives of NATRA visited the Center for Study of Democratic Institutions in Santa Barbara, a liberal think tank, where they discussed strategies to politicize its membership. In 1968 a relationship was nurtured with Vice-President Hubert Humphrey resulting in NATRA's appointment to two presidential commissions on youth. If Humphrey was elected president, Shields thought he would help blacks acquire more broadcast outlets. At the same time, as executive vice-president, Shields began to lobby for increased advertising by Madison Avenue on black radio, meeting with advertising agencies and speaking to trade presses.

Through Shields, H. Rap Brown made an unscheduled speech at a NATRA meeting in Atlanta. The next year, after King's death and the unexpected power it revealed in black radio, meetings were organized by NATRA in New York between the white owners of these stations and their black deejays to discuss their differences for the first time ever. The owners were reluctant participants since they had the same respect for the jocks as the jocks had for them—none. It was testimony to NATRA's growing importance that any showed up at all.

Shields and Avante's boldest move was to propose that NATRA start its own school of broadcast science. In 1968 they found a failing college in Delaware and began negotiations to make it the site. Through Avante's contacts, CBS's and ABC's broadcast divisions promised equipment. Ten record companies at NATRA's 1968 convention said they would donate $25,000 each.

Shields recalls wistfully, "We were going to walk out of the Miami convention with a quarter of a million dollars [in donations] to build the NATRA School of Broadcast Science, and we blew it." He speculates that there were "certain people in the broadcast and TV industry who did not want to see black deejays gain the kind of responsibility and power we were talking about." It sounds like Shields thought some kind of Big Brother was watching—and he may not have been wrong. Someone was certainly on the prowl, jealous of the power NATRA was accumulating and looking for a way to get in on it, and they weren't afraid to use force. A series of violent events over the next few months involving both blacks and whites left the ambitious NATRA plan in shreds.

There was a lot of talk among people in the industry about "pressure" being applied—black activists were strong-arming white record-company owners for "reparations for past exploitation" (which many blacks applauded), but according to Shields, reprisals against black deejays too weren't unknown. For months before the 1968 convention, Shields recalls being the target of a series of threats from individuals who were after a cut of the new breed's action. "I'll never forget," says Shields, "Clarence Avante saying to me, 'Whatever you do, don't sell out.' " Just before the convention, the rumors in Harlem heated up— some dudes were out to hurt Shields—and one night, just after Shields left WLIB's offices on Lenox Avenue near 125th Street, three men beat him to the ground. The perpetrators were never caught.

It was only a prelude. At Miami, between August 14 and 18, white record men and black radio men were threatened, and some were beaten. Marshall Sehorn, Bobby Robinson's old New Orleans contact, was beaten. Phil Walden, Otis Redding's white manager, was threatened. So was Jerry Wexler. Shields spent only one day in Miami. When he arrived at the airport, members of NATRA warned him not to stay: "they" were after him. Meanwhile, members of NATRA's Southern branch complained in sessions that the organization wasn't responsive to the needs of the underpaid Southern jocks because its leadership was too busy politicking.

Once back in New York, Shields was visited by FCC head Nicholas Johnson, and the city's district attorney tapped his phone and put him under twenty-four-hour surveillance for two months—after the events at the Miami convention. After the violence and dissension of that gathering, the commitments to the school evaporated and the enthusiasm for the new breed waned. At the 1969 convention in Washington, D.C., Shields paid $10,000 to hire guards to protect himself and convention attenders. In fact, one of Shields's antagonists chided him for "stooping so low" as to hire his own thugs.

After 1969, the new breed pulled out of NATRA. Shields and Avante moved to Los Angeles in 1971 to fulfill one of their dreams by buying radio station KACE. NATRA's offices moved to Chicago and the organization quickly returned to its historic role as a movable feast for black deejays. Four years of attempted "relevance" proved to be a little too much for the brothers on the microphone. Instead of becoming a unified political force dedicated to raising professional standards, black deejays remained unorganized and unfocused. And even while they tried just to maintain their status quo, the radio industry was evolving in ways that would alter the role of black deejays forever.

GARY BYRD

Gary Byrd, a Buffalo native who grew up listening to Hound Dog Lorenz and Eddie O'Jay on WUFO, can be seen as a transitional figure in black radio. His career began in the era of the personality jock, continued into its period of decline, and then saw the birth of a new style of black radio that emphasized a rigidly defined professionalism.

Byrd's story begins in 1965 when, as a fifteen-year-old actor, he appeared in a "hip" school play called "The In Crowd," based on Dobie Gray's hit record. Hank Cameron, a schoolteacher and part-time WUFO jock, was impressed enough with Byrd's voice to ask the youngster if he had ever considered a career in radio. Byrd, who had aspirations to act and do comedy, thought radio announcing was close enough and said that he had. So Cameron arranged for Byrd to be trained at the station. He was given his own weekend air shift, where he initially concentrated on jazz, but quickly discovered that R&B was the people's choice. Moreover, the audience wanted the music presented with flair. Byrd had a lot to learn, but, as he explains, he developed ways to help himself catch up: "I was writing all this stuff down. I had a little note-book that I kept and I would write things down that seemed to be what you had to do as a personality deejay. Basically, when I came in, I was into jazz. I remember a guy cutting my hair and he said there was a lot of arguing about who could sing higher, Smokey Robinson or Eddie Kendricks. I was like, 'Who's Smokey and Eddie?' I was into John Coltrane. That was what I was into because I had grown up in that side of Buffalo where there was always jazz around me. So when they started talking about these guys Smokey and Eddie, it was a year or so before I realized who they were talking about.

"When those records would come in, I made a little note that said, 'Pick your favorite records and present them big,' and I underlined 'big' to indicate you gotta do something. So I'd take 'Baby Do the Philly Dog' and some of those other records I really liked and I tried to work and build them up in my little primitive way as a teenage jock. And it worked for me, and stuff happened. And it was definitely part of a concept of personality radio which I came in on the last edges of."

By 1966, Byrd's on-air experience had made him a radio junkie, and he vowed one day to visit his favorite station, New York's WWRL. On junior day, a day set aside in Buffalo for juniors to celebrate their ascension to the senior class (students even saved money for it), Byrd informed his grandmother, who raised him, "I didn't really care about junior day. What I wanted to do was go to New York City." His grandmother asked, "New York City for what?" Byrd told her, "I want to hear this radio station, WWRL. I want to try to visit the station." His grandmother said he could stay with an aunt in the city, so Byrd, who'd never flown before, went to New York. "The first thing I did was turn RL on," he recalls. "The second was to call the station and tell them I wanted to visit." It's inconceivable today that at fifteen Byrd could land an on-air job at a station like WUFO, much less gain entry to an important New York radio station on the strength of a phone call. But not long after his call, Byrd was sitting in the WWRL studio with Rocky (G.) Groce. "I went and sat in and he asked me whether I was interested in radio. I said, 'I'm a jock.' Groce said, 'How you going to be a jock at seventeen?' I said, 'I'm a jock. I jock everyday and I do a show on the weekends.' He said, 'Get outta here. You from Frankie Crocker's hometown Buffalo?' I said, 'Yeah.' He said, 'Well, what if I open this microphone and put you on. What will happen?' I said, 'What are you asking me to do?' He said, 'Introduce the record.' So the record was 'Shake, Rattle and Roll' by Arthur Cobbs. He opened the mike, and when he turned on the mike, it tuned off the cuing system, because you can't hear the speakers and I didn't have a headset on. But I hit the cue anyway. I just hit it blind. You hear the first two beats of a record and you kind of get a sense of it. I hit the cue and, of course, when it closed out, he was really surprised. So was Fred Barr, who was the big gospel jock, a white guy, who was there. The general manager came in and offered me a job at seventeen to come on RL. I was real blown out."

Byrd's grandmother, however, was perfectly willing to stand in the way of progress. She called him home to Buffalo where, not prepared to be your average kid, Byrd landed a spot on WYSL, a top-forty station in upstate New York utilizing a format that refined pop radio into a synthetic consistency that station owners loved and old-line deejays hated. Developed by Bill Drake, the format was initiated in 1965 at Los Angeles's KHJ, where Drake turned a money-losing outlet into the number-one station in the second-largest U.S. market. Drake did it by "tightening" the playlist, which meant playing the most popular records with frequency, limiting and shortening station identification, and holding commercials to below fourteen minutes per hour, four minutes under the FCC maximum. Playing two songs back to back, and beginning records under the deejay's introduction or as the news ended were Drake innovations that became American radio staples because they accelerated the pace of the broadcast. It also gave the deejays very little time to talk, for Drake believed that a uniform station sound was more important than cultivating star deejays. From KHJ, Drake went on to consult on the formats of all RKO-owned stations and rose to a vice-presidency at the chain before forming his own very lucrative consulting firm. Byrd describes the Drake format as, "Time, temperature, artist, title of the record. 'It's 4:07 on CKLW. I'm Gary Byrd. Here are the Temptations.' On comes 'Ain't Too Proud to Beg.' "

In Byrd's analysis, the Drake format "started to take over the country because it shut up jocks who basically may have had nothing to say in an entertaining way. And white jocks at the time were more into wacky humor. I'm not saying all the black jocks were doing something great, but it was a different sense of relationship. It wasn't like the craziness kind of stuff. That was the basic thing it did. It equalized the formats. It meant that if a guy didn't have talent, he could still come in and do the format if he had a nice voice and could control himself. He could give the station a uniform sound. If he blows, take him out, put another jock on. It was that simple. Because it was no longer the jock, it was the station."

And this philosophy, to Byrd's chagrin, was being brought into black radio. Looking back, Byrd cites two reasons the R&B world embraced Drake's format. Like Shields, Byrd puts much of the blame for the demise of the black personality deejay on white management's fear of their power. "It was a plantation mentality we're talking about," he says. "What black radio had along this time was powerful personalities who were built through rapping and an ability to relate to the community and then became very popular. Well, again, the station managers were white. They didn't want to see a black jock become bigger than the station."

The other reason was the changing psychology of black America. To a wide cross section of the community—from those who identified with Dr. King's uplifting cadences to those who pursued Ron Karenga's nationalism, from those who embraced the Panther's socialism to the many seeking to prove they were as all-American as any white—the rapid ramblings of the black deejays were embarrassments. At a time when Sidney Poitier was America's number-one box-office star, black folks of every description had no patience with the Eddie (Rochester) Andersons of the airwaves. Drake's format was the leash that reined them in.

As Byrd remembers ruefully, "What I'll say about integration is it was a kind of period where you learn to put on your suit, put on this shirt, and get a job, now. Suddenly management is saying, 'We have white people listening. Let's be careful. Don't talk too ethnically. Talk proper. Pronounce your *-ings*.' It was this sort of thing. What it did was take jocks who were doing that and made them symbolic of all jocks. So even the jock who was doing a very hip personality thing in a hip way got wiped out. He was lumped with the rest."

In the view of Byrd and others, the era of the black personality jock ended in 1967, when the Drake format seeped into black radio. That seems premature. As we know from NATRA, many of the best-known R&B deejays retained their power to move audiences and influence record companies past that point. In addition, there were many stations, including WWRL from 1969 to 1971, that, while adopting a modified top-forty format, didn't sound radically different to the untrained ear from a few years before. Byrd was on the air there in the evening in 1970 when WWRL went to number five in New York City, the highest Arbitron rating in its history.

What finally ended the old era and ushered in a new one was FM radio, a technological development that wouldn't take hold in black America until the 1970s. When it hit, tradition went out the window, taking with it a great many careers.

REDEMPTION

SONGS IN

THE AGE OF

CORPORATIONS (1971–75)

f you go by the numbers, assimilation in the 1960s was a smashing success. From 1965 to 1969, the percentage of blacks making less than $3,000 decreased, while the percentage of blacks earning over $10,000 increased to 28 percent. In 1965, 10 percent of all young blacks were in college; six years later that figure was 18 percent. By 1972, 2,264 blacks served as elected officials, the highest number in American history at that time. The total annual income of black America was $100 billion. At the same time, though, the amount of that income reinvested in black communities was minuscule, and most of that college-trained talent became workers in established white businesses, not independent entrepreneurs. Moreover, many of the economic gains were created by government intervention and monitoring. Blacks were not, then, growing into an independent economic force, but were becoming an increasingly lucrative market for white-provided commodities.

In the early 1970s, an unlikely industry targeted that black market, but only after a maverick black businessman opened its eyes and introduced a relationship between film and rhythm & blues that foreshadowed the synergy of music video, feature films, and pop music of the 1980s.

It all started in reaction to the white-shirted, ultracompetent, nonsexual black film star Sidney Poitier. Poitier was the black American many of his own people, and certainly the ruling white majority, thought of as the perfect role model. As an actor, Poitier was quite effective in his understated, quietly confident way. As a symbol, he was as potent as Dr. King and freedom marches. With *In the Heat of the Night, To Sir, With Love*, and *Guess Who's Coming to Dinner* in the late 1960s, the Caribbean native rivaled Paul Newman, Steve McQueen, and Clint Eastwood as this country's premier film attraction. After decades of jokesters and mammies, Poitier's dignified presence was startling and made him the first—and last—black dramatic film performer to achieve superstar status.

By 1970, however, "Sir Sid" seemed to many a brother from another planet. The era demanded a more virile, assertive black star to match the rampant machismo of black nationalists and the hardening mood of the people. Jim Brown tried nightly to fill that space. Few film actors have had the physical presence of this ex-running back, one of the greatest to play in the National Football League. When Brown was fighting, walking, or just staring stone-eyed at enemies or girlfriends, he was quite convincing. Brown might have evolved into the next big black star by playing action parts that put him in heroic roles, as in his debut, *The Dirty Dozen*.

But the whole game was changed in 1970 by *Sweet Sweetback's Badass Song*. In it, Melvin Van Peebles was the first film director to understand that black audiences (and many whites as well) wanted their black heroes rebellious, to mirror the romantic revolutionaries one saw on the evening news. Van Peebles, who'd made films in France as well as the Hollywood comedy *Watermelon Man*, was shrewd. He made his professional-stud protagonist a de facto revolutionary by having him butcher two brutal cops early in the film and wander through Los Angeles's black community, dependent on its residents for survival. By making his hero a taciturn hustler, Van Peebles didn't have to explain his politics—he didn't even have to have any. The character just had to know how to survive. For the sound track, Van Peebles also showed vision by recruiting a then obscure funk-jazz band called Earth, Wind and Fire.

Sweet Sweetback's Badass Song was scraped together with odds and ends. Some money for the film came from black entertainers. To escape paying dues, he told the film unions *Sweetback* was a porno flick. When completed, he had to "four wall" or rent movie theaters to show the film when no major studio would distribute it and no theater chains would book it. Blacks, and curious whites, packed the theaters where *Sweetback* did play, amazed at seeing such a tough, sexual, damn nearly existential black protagonist on a movie screen. By tapping so squarely into the black mood and doing it outside the structure of mainstream America, *Sweetback* was very much an expression of the unrest and nationalism found in its audience. *Sweetback* was controversial and, as a by-product, so successful that it made the traditional goody-goody roles of Poitier and the more subtle conformity of Brown totally unhip.

From 1970 to 1976, black-themed films were a Hollywood staple. In retrospect, the range and tone of the films were wider than the term "blaxploitation" suggests. Yet there is no question that films bastardizing *Sweetback* into a repeatable formula set the tone. In *Shaft*, the rebel supported by the community in fighting against white authority was an old-fashioned private detective, caught in a struggle between black and Italian mobsters over organized crime in Harlem. The black nationalists were portrayed as well-meaning, earnest ideologues lacking the resources to defeat the establishment.

In *Superfly*, black activists were poorly dressed clowns quickly dispatched by the coke-dealer protagonist when they attempt a shakedown. With a reality that offended the idealistic, *Shaft* and *Superfly* argued that the once-vital black neighborhoods of America were controlled by corrupt or at best indifferent police and cynical criminals of every color with only black supermen (and women such as exploitation queen Pam Grier) able to thrive.

However, in contrast to the way Van Peebles and Earth, Wind and Fire used music in *Sweetback*, these later two films created moments of music-video-like fascination. In *Shaft*, Richard Roundtree's private detective walked the streets of a beautifully photographed Harlem, seeking the whereabouts of the black nationalist group. Underscoring this purposeful tour was "Soulsville," a moody litany of urban ills sung by Isaac Hayes and accompanied by the piercing voices of a female backing trio. For black director Gordon Parks, once an award-winning photographer for *Life*, it was the film's visual high point.

In *Superfly*, director Gordon Parks, Jr., did an even better job, saturating the film in Curtis Mayfield's brilliant soundtrack: the sensual "Give Me

Your Love" made the bathtub love scene an erotic classic; the driving title song hyped action sequences; "Pusher Man" ran under a still picture montage that, a decade before the cocaine epidemic, suggested the wide appeal of this insidiously chic white powder.

Shaft won Isaac Hayes an Oscar plus a slew of music-industry awards. *Superfly* was both the culmination of Mayfield's long career—it summed up his social concerns with the most aggressive music he ever wrote—and the initiation of a new one. After *Superfly*, Mayfield contributed soundtracks to several black films, including *Sparkle, Let's Do It Again, Claudine,* and *Short Eyes*. Blaxploitation soundtracks would inspire in-numerable music-video-like scenes in the films and many hit records, such as Willie Hutch's title song for *The Mack,* Marvin Gaye's title song for *Trouble Man,* the Four Tops' "Keeper of the Castle," from *Shaft in Africa,* and Aretha Franklin's "Something He Can Feel," from *Sparkle*. Few of these films were respected in or out of the entertainment industry, yet by letting some of the more innovative talents in black music work in film, it encouraged all R&B musicians to expand their sound and ambition (for example, Norman Whitfield's "pyschedelic soul" record-ings with the Temptations at Motown, including "Papa Was a Rolling Stone" in 1972; Isaac Hayes's lengthy ballads on *Hot Buttered Soul* in 1969; and Marvin Gaye's *What's Going On* in 1971).

Longer, more orchestrated, more introspective—some black albums had the continuity and cohesion of soundtracks even when they weren't. Latin percussion, in the form of cow bells, congas, and bongos, suddenly became rhythmic requirements, adding a new layer of polyrhythmic fire to the grooves. Minor chords, frowned on during the soul years, began appearing in the work of Marvin Gaye, Stevie Wonder, and the prolif-erating black bands, such as Earth, Wind and Fire, Kool and the Gang, and Mandrill. The gap between jazz-bred players and R&B music was closing quickly, as Miles Davis and his offspring, such as Herbie Hancock, in a most experimental manner, began using electronic keyboards and dance rhythms. Hancock's *Headhunters* (1974) defined the funk end of this jazz-rock fusion and would be much imitated.

It didn't always work, of course. There were equal helpings of am-bitious accomplishment and pretentious crap, but by and large the early seventies sound in R&B reflected the increased sophistication in the mass black audience. Black college enrollment was at an all-time high due to the availability of student loans and subsidies left over from Johnson's Great Society programs. Now a college education was a re-alistic and obtainable goal for young blacks. All those ads proclaiming

"A Mind Is a Terrible Thing to Waste" definitely had an impact. The Buppies (black urban professionals) of the late 1980s were just coming of age at this time. Not surprisingly, then, the prime example of this new R&B sensibility was a black university graduate. Donny Hathaway was raised in St. Louis by his grandmother Martha Pitts, who sang gospel. He attended Howard University during the late sixties, when the campus and the city's black precincts bubbled with political activity. By day, he studied musical theory at the fine but beleaguered music department. For years Howard had refused to teach jazz, feeling for some weird reason that status-conscious blacks who attended the school needed to know only European compositional concepts. As you can imagine, this was a constant source of campus conflict at the time. At night, Hathaway played the piano in jazz trios around town and hung out with a young pianist-vocalist named Roberta Flack.

Curtis Mayfield, seeking talent on the way toward organizing his own Curtom label in Chicago, was introduced to Hathaway. The meeting led to session work in Chicago and New York, with his formal Howard technique and a jazz sense has helped him create ear-catching arrangements for Jerry Butler, the Staple Singers, and Carla Thomas. A meeting with saxophonist and bandleader King Curtis at a music industry convention led to a contract with Atlantic Records. Hathaway's 1969 debut single, "The Ghetto," coproduced by King Curtis and written by another Mayfield protégé, Leroy Hutson (Mayfield's replacement as lead singer of the Impressions), was a perfect example of this ambitious new R&B. It was long, at 6:47; an ominous jazz organ created the mood; congas rather than a trap drum set carried the groove; the vocals were a hypnotic chant of the title. "The Ghetto" had very little to do with the soul music of Aretha Franklin. Hathaway was after a grander vision that embraced soul's religious fervor but used jazzy orchestrations and Third World rhythms.

He also had a different audience from Aretha's in mind, as Arif Mardin found out in 1970 when he went to record a live album in Los Angeles with Hathaway. "When I arrived at the Troubadour where he was rehearsing for the show that night, I found a line of well-dressed, middle-class-looking black people three times around the block with tickets waiting to enter three hours before the show. Donny wasn't famous then, you know. 'The Ghetto' had been memorable, but by no means had he sold a lot of records. I called the office. 'Something's going on here,' I said. 'The electricity was unbelievable.' Then during the live performances at the Troubadour, they knew every song. He opened his mouth and the audience went berserk. It was like *Name That Tune*. On the live recording, we kept the audience exuberance up loud because it was so much a part of the show. He was a star waiting to sell records. Sure enough, it was his first gold record.''

Mardin, who coproduced and did arrangements on Hathaway's *Extensions of a Man* as well as two of his popular duets with Roberta Flack, "You've Got a Friend" and "Where Is the Love," feels that Hathaway—along with his contemporary Stevie Wonder—was a leader in expanding the harmonic language of R&B. "He used a great many jazz chords: major 7ths, minor 9ths, augmented chords. Donny was a pioneer in that direction vocally as well as in his writing." Mardin cites George Benson and Al Jarreau as two singers able to use jazz chords in a pop context by following Hathaway's example. Because of Hathaway's mix of gospel, jazz, and social consciousness, Mardin felt, "He could have been a true hero in our field. Not just a musical hero. He could have been a social force too." Unfortunately, for all his pioneering brilliance, Hathaway was scarred with deep psychological problems that would limit his recordings and lead him to suicide in 1979.

"HOLLYWOOD" AND HOWARD

The imprint of Hathaway and other musicians who shared his direction was wide, and it spilled over into radio. The sounds of Hathaway, Hayes, and Mayfield made the few remaining old-fashioned personality jocks sound anachronistic. Jack Gibson got out of the music business and moved to Orlando, Florida, to do publicity for "The Mousehouse," which is jockey talk for Disneyworld. Eddie O'Jay quit radio to take a job with a black-owned Cadillac dealership in the Bronx. Hoss Allen, feeling uncomfortable with the tighter formating at Nashville's WLAC and disliking the new trends in R&B, started a gospel program, an area where deejays still had freedom to talk and make programming decisions.

It wasn't "off with their head" at every station and in every market, but a definite changing of the guard was under way. One of its most important aspects was the rise to prominence of several black-owned stations in major cities. In Los Angeles, Clarence Avante and Del Shields sold KACE to ex-Green Bay Packer star Willie Davis, who'd made a killing as a Schlitz Beer distributor in Milwaukee. Earl Graves, publisher of *Black Enterprise* magazine, obtained Fort Worth's KNOK, while John

Johnson, founder of *Ebony* and *Jet*, started WPJC in Chicago. Of all these new black-owned broadcast outlets, two, Howard University's WHUR and New York's WLIB, FM and AM, purchased by a group of local black businessmen led by Manhattan borough president Percy Sutton, were crucial to black radio in the early seventies and throughout the next fifteen years.

WLIB-AM had the number-two black station in New York for most of the sixties. Like its rival, WWRL, it was a daytimer located on the far right end of the AM band. It opened every morning with Eddie O'Jay's "Soul at Sunrise" program, which began when the veteran deejay joined the station in 1966.

In 1969, WLIB-FM was inaugurated by white owner Harry Novick, with a jazz format to take advantage of FM's rich stereo sound. From 7 PM to midnight, Del Shields ruled the airwaves. Located near 125th Street on Lenox Avenue, the WLIB operation was a steady, if unspectacular, success. In the early seventies, according to local residents, "activists" pressured Novick to sell. Some say he was intimidated by a group like those who'd blown open the 1968 NATRA convention. Others discount the threat of violence and assert it was pressure from legitimate community groups that forced Novick's hand. What is not disputed is that Harlemites of various backgrounds wanted WLIB to be black-owned. Led by Percy Sutton, the city's most powerful black politician, and veteran black deejay Hal Jackson, a group under the banner Inner City Broadcasting made an offer for Novick's broadcast outlets. The negotiations were rigorous. Novick set different prices for the AM and FM stations, perhaps hoping to drain Inner City's resources on the AM purchase so he could keep the FM for himself and move it downtown. But after considerable gamesmanship on Novick's part, Inner City eventually acquired both stations. Then, in a move with great symbolic meaning, the group shifted them both down from Harlem to an East Side location two blocks from the United Nations.

Next, Inner City brought in a flamboyant deejay, one of the last of the old-styled personality jocks, to program the station. Frankie Crocker, known at points throughout his career as the "Love Man," "Fast Frankie," the "Chief Rocker," and "Hollywood," was cool, slick, and upwardly mobile to a fault. Crocker would do more than program Inner City's FM outlet; he'd present an announcing and programming style to the New York airwaves that would, for good and bad, dominate New York radio and, to some degree, all black radio in the seventies.

While attending the University of Buffalo with an eye toward law school, Crocker met Eddie O'Jay and was impressed by his flair, his money, and the ease with which he seemed to work as a deejay. Crocker was already in a band playing sax and singing, so he thought deejaying would not be a difficult transition. His initial audition at WUFO failed when Crocker foolishly tried to imitate the sound of a top-forty deejay. However, on his second try, Crocker played jazz with enough sensitivity that Joe Ricco, the regular jazz jock, hired this college kid as his weekend relief man.

Between band gigs and his part-time radio job, Crocker made about $500 a week, bought a new Corvette, and grooved on the sudden rush of local celebrity. Upon graduation, instead of entering law school, Crocker took a job at Pittsburgh's WZUM. During his tenure there, Crocker traveled to Chicago for a NATRA convention and noticed that the guys from New York stood out. He thought, "These guys look like they're doing well. They all have beautiful women or wives with them— think maybe I should go and try it in New York."

By the time Crocker arrived at New York's WWRL in 1965, his deep, smooth voice and velvety style earned him the nickname "Love Man"— and a large following among the city's women. When Crocker said, "Music might not heal you, baby, but it'll help your soul. Reach over and touch your radio one time," speakers were fondled all across "Fun City." Over the next three years, including a brief stint with Los Angeles's KGFJ, Crocker came up with an on-air rap that was less frantic than his predecessors', though he would always remain a personality jock. Through appearances at the midtown disco the Cheetah, he developed a hip white listenership. During the late sixties, top-forty stations in New York like WABC and WMCA not only increased the number of black records on their playlists but sought to break out records by black stars who already had a white following.

As Crocker told Ken Smikle, "I could see before I started at WMCA that they were trying to beat us to the Smokey Robinsons, the Aretha Franklins, the Wilson Picketts, and Otis Reddings—they were trying to get them on their station quicker than I could get them where I was. And I could see that to the record companies, it meant more to have records on WMCA or WABC than on WWRL because of the size of the market and sales volume. So I thought to myself at the time, 'If this is going to be the deal, where am I going to be?' "

Crocker decided he was going to be on WMCA, a station legendary for its all-white team of "Good Guys." With this move, Crocker became one of the first black deejays to move from a black station to a pop station. Many in the entertainment industry at the time saw it as a historic move that would open pop stations to blacks. In the highly political atmosphere of the time, some also saw Crocker's move as a sellout. In a *Record World* tribute to Crocker in 1980, Casablanca president Neil Bogart recalled, "[He] went to top 40 when it was not fashionable for a black person to be there, and he got a lot of criticism from the black community. In fact, I can remember a concert that a lot of rhythm and blues stations wouldn't attend because Frankie had broken the barrier." In truth, Crocker's move opened few doors in pop radio. However, for "Fast Frankie" (his less suggestive handle at WMCA), it solidified his position as a black deejay with a substantial white following.

In 1971, Crocker (now "Hollywood") would pull together all the elements of his background—admiration for New York style, roots in old black radio, feel for jazz, college education, and development of a white following—into a programming philosophy at WBLS-FM, the new label for Inner City's station. The building block was Crocker's drive-time program (from 4 to 7 PM) and a programming concept called the "Total Black Experience in Sound." The pop-jazz of Grover Washington, Jr., Miles Davis's fusion, the expansive R&B sound of Stevie Wonder, Donny Hathaway, Marvin Gaye, and Isaac Hayes—all found a home in the WBLS format. All the deejays brought in by Crocker cloned his style: mellow, seductive, no high-energy spiel, and a calculatedly ingratiating hipness. The feeling WBLS sought to convey was, as Crocker often put it, "If we're not on your radio, your radio isn't on."

What wasn't on WBLS were, in Crocker's words, "Ministers that were on the air selling prayer cloths. I wouldn't deal with those Amos-and-Andy type commercials that were selling products for blacks. I think blacks are sophisticated enough to be talked to intelligently, just like any other portion of the market." One of the crucial assumptions, one that new black FM stations all over the country shared, was that an important percentage of WBLS's audience was either college-educated or identified with the values a college education suggested. In New York, the desire to be hip, to be part of the city's trendsetting class, runs deep, and Crocker tapped into this yearning with a psychologist's skill.

From the viewpoint of the station's sales department, this audience of upwardly mobile, integrated listeners was a weapon to be aimed at Madison Avenue to lure more national time buys. Crocker and company didn't just want to get rid of the ads for "five dollars down and ten years to pay"; they wanted them replaced with ads from car companies, expensive colognes, airlines, and other high-prestige products. Part of the WBLS strategy became to increase the percentage of white artists played and, in turn, the number of white listeners, and, ultimately, white advertising dollars. Crocker said, "Stevie Wonder is a black artist, but a lot of his music comes out pop. It's the same way with Diana Ross. I just don't think along those lines. I know I've got to fight the next guy—black, white, or brown—to get a ticket to her show. So there are those artists where the music just transcends the color of the skin. There are clearly those artists that just do black music, just as there are artists, white artists, that just do white pop. But when you have artists that do music that can be successful in three or four different markets—black, Spanish, and so on—it's just a hit."

Crocker was a child of integration and his lack of racial prejudice in music showed it. The Rolling Stones were as much a part of his taste as Sly. Of course, this ecumenicalism is admirable. Yet, implicit in Crocker's attitude, even while the station was billed as the "Total Black Experience in Sound," was an air of expediency. Where Jack Gibson, Eddie O'Jay, and Del Shields made the black community the focus of their energy, whether it was organizing a party, a demonstration, or just a playlist, Crocker saw his community in broader terms. The black community was his base but hardly his primary concern, a philosophy the station's black management endorsed when WBLS suddenly shifted, in the mid-seventies, from the "Total Black Experience in Sound" to "The Total Experience in Sound."

In addition to Crocker's impact on the orientation of big-city black radio, he also helped facilitate the demise of the chitlin circuit's crown jewel, the Apollo Theater. From his days at WWRL up through 1970, Crocker had been involved with the promotion of shows there, though in essence his chief responsibility was to emcee shows and suggest what artists to book. From the 1940s to the 1970s, the personality deejays could bring acts to the Apollo quite cheaply using the awesome power of airplay as leverage. But with the shift to preprogrammed formats, music directors, not jocks, controlled playlists. The power to play or not fell into the hands of program director Crocker and his peers around the country.

And Crocker, as part of his programming strategy, felt the Apollo was not central to his vision. In 1974, Crocker made his move. Using $7,500 of his own money to rent the Felt Forum, a 5,000-seat auditorium that was part of Madison Square Garden's 33rd Street and 7th Avenue com-

plex, he then borrowed $10,000 to promote a show. The artist he se-
lected for his promotional debut, Barry White, shrewdly reflected
Crocker's concept. The rotund producer-vocalist had a deep, deliberate
voice reminiscent of Isaac Hayes and a taste for lush string and horn
chants that fluttered over Latin-inflected rhythms. It was romantic,
danceable, mellow, and Crocker played White and his Love Unlimited
Orchestra like the National Anthem. The audience warmed Crocker's
heart, and his pocketbook. "We could see what kind of audience came
to White's concerts and it wasn't any single group," he told *Record World*.
"We'd see young, old, black, white, Hispanic—it wasn't any ethnic
group. It was basically the audience I reach on my radio program."

The impact of black artists in New York moving downtown to Crocker's promoted gigs didn't affect the Apollo immediately. In fact, Bobby
Shiffman, who took over the theater after his father's death, has said
the 1970–74 period was the most lucrative in the theater's long history.
During those years Gladys Knight, for example, became the first act to
sell out an entire week at the Apollo in advance. Still, it wouldn't be
long before Crocker's WBLS connection and downtown concerts
knocked the Apollo to its knees—just as integration was sending former
Harlemites and their children to the better housing and safer streets of
Queens, Long Island, and New Jersey.

WHUR

At Howard University, a different dynamic was at work. At the school's
new communications department, the kind of exciting learning environment Shields and Avante sought to establish for blacks in the sixties
was finally coming together. Professional journalists such as Wallace
Terry, who'd covered the Vietnam War for *Time* and was then working
on *Bloods*, his landmark book on blacks in that war, were brought in
to give the students "real-world" instruction. An annual black communications conference was instituted to debate issues and encourage
black recruitment by the networks and major publications.

The founding of WHUR was part of Howard's ongoing effort to offer
hands-on instruction for students and to provide information to black
Washington (known to blacks as "Chocolate City" because of its over-
whelmingly black population). The station's public-affairs programming
was exceptional: Sundays were filled with talk of black politics, African
culture, and local news. At six o'clock on week nights, "The Drum"

was aired, an evening news hour with black perspectives on news reports from Africa, South America, and the Caribbean. In an informative and inspiring way, program director and Howard instructor Andre Perry emphasized the links between blacks in D.C. and the rest of the world. This radio-news style elevated the whole community-involvement aspect of black radio and would be imitated around the country.

As far as music went, WHUR was a jazz station that mixed in some mellow R&B. Well remembered from the period is Dyanna Williams, whose mellow style, like Crocker's in New York, reflected the new direction in black announcing, with special implications for female deejays. Women on the air until then had affected a flighty or flamboyant persona, with names like Dizzy Lizzy and Twentieth-Century Fox, often sounding as manic and raunchy as their male colleagues. Dyanna and her contemporaries were allowed to be more self-consciously feminine, urbane, and slightly spiritual: "heavy chicks" for the New Age. Her afternoon broadcast was called, "Ebony Moonbeams," and her voice had an appropriately spacey, sensual quality. Barry Mayo, then a student majoring in communications at Howard and now a vice-president of RKO Radio, remembers Williams as "one of the premiere lady deejays of the time. Men really related to her. She was sexy, but she was no clown. She was classy. She complemented the mood of the music but wasn't superficial. She had substance and many female jocks copied her style." It was rumored on campus that Williams, an acknowledged free spirit, once broadcast in the nude. That wasn't true, but the credence given the story suggests the spell her voice cast. Frankie Crocker was one of those charmed. In the mid-seventies, he stole her for WBLS, knowing quite well her style would work well with his own.

In about 1974, however, the mellow vibrations at WHUR were rippled by protest. Students argued that because it used only professionals on the air, the station was not fulfilling its mission of training Howard students in radio broadcasting. The school administration seemed reluctant to let students broadcast on this increasingly lucrative enterprise. As a result of the protests, though, which included the boycotting of some classes, students got some slots on WHUR and a second station that reached only the campus was created. Its general manager, Barry Mayo, called it WHBC. At WHUR these changes meant an influx on the air of some bright, ambitious communications students—many of whom had led the protest. At the urging of general manager and student adviser Kathy Liggins, student Melvin Lindsay started playing R&B ballads at night. The show was called "Quiet Storm," in tribute to the romantic Smokey Robinson album. It became a D.C. tradition and later had unexpected consequences.

Three other students, Gwen Franklin, Milton Allen, and Sheila Eldridge, worked on a show called "Saturday Night Special." The show itself is not of historical importance, but the trio of Howard students are, since all three, as well as Andre Perry and several others, would become employed in marketing and promotion positions in the record industry in the late seventies. By the late eighties, Howard graduates would form an informal network throughout the recording industry, with alumni holding key positions in various radio and record-promotion offices.

There had always been a few college grads in black radio (e.g., Jack Gibson), but the R&B labels tended to employ streetwise blacks in promotion and sales. It had been, as record retailer Bruce Webb suggested, a business of late payments and strong-arm collections. College grads hadn't been recruited for these jobs, and admittedly, most hadn't been that interested. Up until the seventies, if a black family had a college graduate in the fold, he or she would have been kicked out for wanting to use their degree to sell records. Doctors, lawyers, white-collar jobs—these were what motivated the kids to attend and their parents to dream. Howard University graduates were supposed to be part of Du Bois's talented tenth, not down in the happily corrupt world of R&B. The increasing corporate control of R&B, however, meant that more-educated staffs would be recruited, and from the early seventies on, college-educated blacks started aiming for careers in the music business in a serious way. The best-known example of this shift was the Commodores, five students at Tuskegee Institute who forsook white-collar dreams for the music business.

More representative is the tale of Vernon Slaughter, perhaps the first promotion man who went directly from a college campus into an industry position. Born and raised in Omaha, Nebraska, Slaughter was attending the University of Nebraska in August 1969 when he went to a student convention in El Paso, Texas. Considering what he had learned growing up in the corn belt, Slaughter wasn't surprised to find few blacks in attendance. But he was shocked to see that as part of the convention Stax was holding a showcase with Isaac Hayes, the Bar-Kays, the Staple Singers, and Rufus Thomas, in an attempt to court the white college market.

The day before the Stax showcase, Slaughter met Jim Smith, an executive at the company; the two stayed in touch after the convention.

Smith sent him Stax releases and, since Lincoln had no black station and wasn't a major market, he asked Slaughter to bring the records to the local top-forty and album-oriented rock (AOR) station. Their relationship was more social than professional and really depended on Smith's generosity. But by now Slaughter, always a music lover, was sure he wanted to be in the record business.

In February 1970, CBS Records came looking for a campus rep at the university. "They had just started a college-rep program, and I went to interview along with every other student on campus," Slaughter recalls. But he got the gig. "I think I got the job because I was the only one who thought about going beyond what was expected. I mentioned about checking jukeboxes in the city to see that the records were being added, making that connection as well as retail and radio."

Because of his good work and, maybe, because the company had so few black faces, CBS paid for Slaughter to attend a NATRA convention in Houston. Slaughter will never forget it. "This was my second time on an airplane; my first time in Texas. I was nineteen years old and scared to death." Luckily, in his hotel lobby he ran into CBS's ranking black promotion man, Granville (Granny) White, out of Chicago. The impact of NATRA on Slaughter echoes the words of Frankie Crocker just a few years before. He confesses, "I just made a snap decision that this was where I wanted to be. Here I was in the same room with Nancy Wilson, Isaac Hayes, O. C. Smith, and actually saying things to them. But the one thing that came out of that was my experience with Granny. The awards ceremony was in another hotel. We rode down in a limousine, my first time in a limousine. The limo pulled up to the hotel and Granny said, 'The first thing you have to understand is, when in a limo, you get spoiled. You don't open the doors, you let the driver open the door.' The driver got out and opened up the door and here I am with my Afro. I'm a college student, so I'm looking like a college student. Guys are wearing tuxedos with beautiful women on their arms, the whole thing, and I say, 'Jesus Christ, this is amazing.' To see black people with this type of class, with this type of savoir faire, and with this type of money, flashing their money around."

Slaughter felt that black music, Sly notwithstanding, was still invisible to CBS's corporate hierarchy. Then in 1972, seemingly quite suddenly, CBS established a black-music division headed by a young black executive named Logan Westbrooks. Slaughter was not in their plans. "At first Westbrooks just brushed me off totally," recalls Slaughter. After three attempts and apparently some pressure from white executives to give the kid a shot, Westbrooks hired him for a position in Washington. "I'll never forget, I had a conversation with Richard Mack, director of promotion, about salary. I'm saying $7,000 and he asked me, 'Well, is $12,000 enough?' " Slaughter, openmouthed with amazement, accepted.

His early days in D.C. were rough. "The local radio people and the record community felt the job should have gone to a Washingtonian rather than a twenty-two-year-old kid from Nebraska. When we disagreed or I made a mistake, the thing was to say, 'How could somebody who's been to college say something so stupid.' " Looking back Slaughter sees himself somewhere between the promotion men of the Dave Clark school and the current college-educated generation. "I was part of the protest against Vietnam and civil-rights protest in college. I was a militant. I still am. I had a broader context than most of the guys who just grew up in the street business. That's all they cared about. That was their world. I had broader interests. That created problems for me initially."

At WHUR, with people his own age whose consciousness was shaped by college experience, Slaughter was quite comfortable. As the station's clout grew so did his, in D.C. and at CBS, since Washington is a crucial black-music market. Persistence paid off for Slaughter and put him in the perfect position to capitalize on CBS's phenomenal expansion into black music. Starting in the summer of 1972, a major thrust began at CBS that would subsequently be mimicked to different degrees at other conglomerate-controlled labels, including RCA, Warner Bros., MCA, ABC, and Capitol.

To this day, Clive Davis, who was then president of CBS, claims it was his brainchild to move aggressively into black music. Maybe. But some people feel there is a different story behind the CBS campaign, and they cite a provocative document titled, "A Study of the Soul Music Environment Prepared for Columbia Records Group," and submitted to the label on May 11, 1972.

THE HARVARD REPORT

For six months beginning in the summer of 1971, record retailers, deejays and program directors at R&B stations, and talent managers in the Boston area received phone calls and requests for information from— they could hardly believe it—the Harvard University Business School.

Interviewees were told it had something to do with Columbia Records. To some it was another sign of black progress that the nation's most prestigious business school was interested in them. And it certainly was, though not in the way the interviewees assumed. The resulting fifty-three-page document came to be known in the industry as the "Harvard Report."

The growth of CBS's involvement in black music in the years following the Harvard Report was immense: in 1971, the CBS roster included two cutting-edge black artists, Sly and the Family Stone and Santana. By 1980, it had 125 acts, among them big names like Earth, Wind and Fire, Teddy Pendergrass, the O'Jays, the Isley Brothers, and Weather Report. The report opens with an attempt to define "soul" and "the soul market." There was even a chart labeled "Soul Content of Artist's Repertoire," broken into three categories: Almost All, Mixed, Almost None. James Brown and Joe Tex made column one, Isaac Hayes and Roberta Flack column two, and Gloria Lynn and Columbia's Johnny Mathis column three. By analyzing the total size of the record industry in 1970 ($1.66 billion), the report estimated the soul share at $120 million, or approximately 10 percent. A look at the historical development of black music followed, emphasizing the major labels' lack of interest and the role of indies in distribution.

Of more significance was the next section, "Internal Dynamics," in which the report analyzed how black records moved from black radio to top forty:

> The fact that 30 percent of the top 40 is composed of records which have 'crossed-over' from soul stations underscores the strategic importance of soul stations as one of the most effective vehicles for getting on to the top 40. What this means it that the competition among promoters for soul airplay involves far more than simply the prospect of record sales to black consumers.
>
> In sum, soul radio is of strategic importance to the record companies for two principal reasons: first, it provides access to a large and growing record-buying public, namely, the black consumer. Second, and for some of the record companies more important, it is perhaps the most effective way of getting a record to a Top 40 playlist.

The "competition" was divided into three categories: specialized national companies, principally Motown, Atlantic, and Stax; majors such as RCA, Capitol, and MCA; and smaller indies. The latter two were not viewed as big threats. Against the majors, employment of a "well-planned and well-financed initiative aimed at long-term market penetration" would allow CBS to outposition them, while the small indies were viewed as opportunities for absorption through talent raids and distribution deals.

Not only were Atlantic, Motown, and Stax problems to anyone trying to crack the soul market; further, because of their record sales to blacks, they now had "the base from which to challenge the majors in other segments of the popular music market." Atlantic had already done so with its wooing of English rock bands, while Motown and Stax were, in different ways, trying to do likewise.

The Harvard Report went on to chastise CBS for its historic lack of commitment to black music. R&B deejays, the report said, found CBS promotion personnel "substandard" and full of "arrogance." Harvard's prescription was multifaceted and direct: hire blacks in A&R, production, and promotion; recruit black creative personnel; carefully develop relationships with black radio. The report predicted this commitment would break even in three years and return an operating profit of $1.4 million by the fifth year.

In the "Plan of Action" section, the Harvard Report listed dos and don'ts for CBS, which may prove that Davis didn't read it after all, because he did several of the things it suggested he avoid. First, it warned CBS not to acquire one of the R&B big three (Atlantic, Stax, or Motown) which would risk antitrust complications; second, it advised against seeking established artists at the onset, under the assumption that the cost would be prohibitive and that an artist might not sell as well once picked up by CBS. Harvard thought a more deliberate program guided by a new black-music department would be more effective. Staffing responsibilities, operating budgets, and graphs illustrating the background rounded out the formal presentation.

A handwritten addendum by Marie Tattersall, a Harvard researcher, added some interesting (though also ignored) recommendations. After predicting that by 1978 CBS could control 15 percent of the black market and be as big in the field as Atlantic, Tattersall suggested a special conference with top program directors, one of whom, LeBaron Taylor of Philly's WDAS, would soon be recruited by CBS. She advised CBS to use its influence on the CBS-TV network to get Don Cornelius's black dance program, *Soul Train*, shown on affiliates, helping the program's distribution and proving the company's commitment to black music. In a final and inspired suggestion, Tattersall thought CBS should open retail record stores in black communities and then franchise them to residents, which would help black business and enhance CBS's image.

As you might imagine, CBS didn't follow any of Tattersall's more ambitious recommendations. Cornelius's influential program—a slew of seventies dances were born on *Soul Train*—survived on its own. However, the black retail community could have used the shot in the arm for, like the theaters in black communities, these mom-and-pop stores were suffering from integration, as blacks, now working in white areas, began to shop more where they worked and not where they lived.

The stories of CBS's relationship with two of the most important black-music institutions in history, Stax and Philadelphia International, reveal the change the economics of the music was undergoing, and show how philosophy and politics interplayed with money and melody during this transitional period in the history of the R&B world.

STAX DOWN

From 1968, when Stax signed its deal with Gulf + Western, to 1972, when its star-crossed relationship with CBS began, the Memphis label went through an amazing metamorphosis, though you could argue that Stax was changed forever by Otis Redding's tragic death in a plane crash in late 1967. By 1972, Booker T and the MGs were history, as the band's namesake got married to singer Rita Coolidge, moved to Los Angeles, and signed with A&M Records. The production and writing team of Isaac Hayes and David Porter, creators of the Sam and Dave soul hits, broke up when Hayes, with *Hot Buttered Soul* and *Shaft*, became one of the 1970s' first black superstars. Steve Cooper, the label's dominant producer since its inception, was being displaced by a black Detroiter named Don Davis, who brought a slicker sound to the home of soul with the Dramatics ("In the Rain") and Johnnie Taylor ("Who's Making Love"). Three local songwriters who'd been low on Stax's internal totem pole, Bettye Crutcher, Raymond Jackson, and Homer Banks, wrote "Who's Making Love" and a series of soap-opera soul records with a rich-voiced trio dubbed the Soul Children. Overall, Stax started more subsidiary labels and signed a wider range of artists, including the classic jazz baritone Billy Eckstine and a hilarious foul-mouthed comic named Richard Pryor.

In Stax's executive offices, Jim Stewart sold his control of the company to Al Bell, turning an integrated family company into a black-owned, black-staffed, very political organization. Dave Clark, the original promotion man we met earlier, joined Stax in 1971 to help develop its gospel roster and use his deep roots in the R&B world to strengthen Stax's already solid base.

Pryor's landmark 1973 album, *That Nigger's Crazy*, the work that established him as a certifiable star of the R&B world (even though he was joking, not singing), was aided by Clark's presence and a black grass-roots campaign no large corporate company would have attempted or understood. "We knew we'd get little airplay on the record," Bell says with a laugh about Pryor's scatological monologues on winos, junkies, and raunchy old men. "But we knew there was a market in the black community for Richard. We worked the record in poolhalls, barbershops, beauty parlors, and in the streets across America by getting instant play at small record shops. We went after that record strictly on the grass-roots level using word-of-mouth. Dave's energy, understanding, and relationships in black neighborhoods, not just radio, were quite significant about making it work."

"I was trying to encourage black economic stability," says Bell about his vision for Stax. That is why Bell was so attracted to the Reverend Jesse Jackson. In the early 1970s, Jackson, a former lieutenant of Dr. King's SCLC, was urging people to boycott businesses that profited from black dollars yet gave nothing back. In his essay "The Kingdom Theory," Jackson wrote about the responsibility major companies had to the black community, noting that where necessary blacks should use economic pressure to gain control. He gave a grocery store as an example: "Control of the store means determining who will be clerks and bookkeepers, and who will have such monetarily awarding jobs as butcher and meat manager in the store."

So, according to Bell, Jackson, and former associates of the reverend, Stax got intimately involved with the Chicago-based minister's career. Stax not only contributed large sums to Jackson's Operation PUSH (People United to Save Humanity) but reportedly Stax personnel developed the organization's name and original logo. Jackson also recorded his famous speech, "I Am Somebody," on Stax's Respect logo, all part of Bell's commitment to the reverend's mix of old-fashioned civil-rights protest and black-nationalist-flavored economic policy.

The connection between the two men was illustrated by Stax's greatest effort in making a socioeconomic statement, Wattstax. On August 20,

1972, Bell and Jackson stood side by side in the middle of the cavernous Los Angeles Coliseum, chanted "I am somebody," and then raised their fists in the Black Power salute before a hundred thousand music fans. With that gesture began a long day of live music by every Stax artist to raise money for the Watts Summer Festival. It was a symbol of black self-sufficiency. Wattstax became a film—shot by a predominantly black crew—and a six-sided album. Many in Memphis resented Stax's involvement in a community-improvement project so far from home. In response, Bell says Wattstax was simply a great blend of social responsibility and commerce, noting that after the 1965 riot, the Watts Summer Festival, a community fund-raising activity, had consistently lost money and risked being discontinued. More pragmatically Bell asserts, "Stax had never established a strong identity in Los Angeles. Wattstax did that for us."

Stax underwrote most of the expenses, with Schlitz Beer also picking up part of the bill. No record company before or since has put as much money or time into a charitable activity like that aimed at aiding a black community. (Eventually the donations went to the Sickle Cell Anemia Foundation, the Martin Luther King, Jr., General Hospital in Watts, and, of course, Operation PUSH.) Bell meant it when he told *Soul* magazine, "Wattstax '72 is a prime example of the ways in which Stax thanks the people who support us."

This was the "new" Stax, one that used its resources to aid the black community in adventurous ways. Yet this and other successes didn't still doubts about how well Stax was run. No one questioned Bell's heart, but some wondered how shrewd a money man he was.

To complete the deal with Gulf + Western, Stax agreed to provide the company's Paramount Records arm some twenty-seven albums within a month. In a two-week period Stax recorded that many records, and it was that rush that allowed Hayes to record his idiosyncratic debut, *Hot Buttered Soul*. That Hayes got his chance to go solo during this hectic period was obviously good. But that Stax found itself in such a foolish situation reflects badly on Bell and Stewart. It seemed to observers that in Stax's rush to expand, the company was too often pressed into hasty decisions. This was confirmed when after only two artistically and financially successful years, Stax bought out G+W's shares of the company with money borrowed from Deutsche Grammophon, at a profit to G+W of $2 million. Stax then had to pay the German company its $2 million plus $1 million in interest or Deutsche Grammophon would become a 45 percent shareholder in Stax. Memphis's Union Planters National Bank provided the money that went overseas. All in all, it was a paper-and-money trail that caused awful accounting and billing problems for the independently distributed label. And the situation was further complicated when Stewart requested that Bell buy out his share in Stax with cash.

That's when Clive Davis came along. In his autobiography, Davis says Bell called him (in 1972) to set up a dinner meeting, where he told Davis his network of independent distributors weren't playing him fast enough and not getting him prominent enough retail placement. Davis says Bell offered CBS 50 percent of Stax, but as the Harvard Report suggested, lawyers warned that such a large acquisition by Columbia could violate antitrust laws. Instead a unique distribution deal was negotiated that initially satisfied those skeptical of Bell's business sense. Stax got $6 million up front as a quasi loan/advance and retained creative autonomy. Stax historian Peter Guralnick wrote, "The way the contract was drawn up, Stax was to be paid for every record delivered, irrespective of sales; in other words, the more records Stax churned out, the more money to be made." It was a generous agreement that was built around Davis's "handshake" understanding. The Harvard Report had warned CBS against such a liaison. As it turned out, it was Stax that should have been careful.

In 1973 Davis was unceremoniously dismissed as president of CBS. At the time, the company said Davis was fired for $94,000 worth of expense-account violations during his six years as president. In fact it seems more likely to those in the industry that he was fired because of media speculation about high-level CBS involvement in drug payments to deejays—and because Davis's willful visibility made him vulnerable to suspicious minds. With FCC broadcast outlets to protect, CBS could not risk the hint of scandal at the presidential level of its record arm.

For Stax, the firing was a disaster. "When the deal was made, there was a tremendous amount of interfacing, a lot of meetings between CBS and Stax in Memphis," Jim Smith told Logan Westbrooks. "The daily contact with them was unreal. We spoke to them six to seven times a day, constantly on top of what was going on in the marketplace, anticipating problems, working them out. We saw an attitude of really trying to make it work. When Clive Davis left CBS, the relationship changed instantly."

The new regime immediately began to review Davis's many highly publicized deals and were not pleased with the Stax agreement. Stax was supposed to get $2 a record off the top, without the usual percentage held in reserve for returns or damaged goods. CBS now withheld 40 percent in reserves, giving Stax only $1.20 per record, a situation that made it harder for Stax to repay its loans to the Memphis bank.

Beginning in 1973, Stax and Bell were involved in lawsuits by CBS and the Union Planters National Bank, as well as an IRS investigation and all manner of character assassination. In the aftermath, Bell was cleared of all charges against him, though his reputation was severely damaged. (It wasn't until 1988, when Motown, of all people, hired him as A&R vice-president, that he held another significant industry position.) The loan officer he dealt with at the bank was later found guilty on two counts of embezzlement. It seemed that Bell had been getting bad advice for much of this period.

"It was one battle after another," Bell recalls. "At one point I was in federal court with an antitrust suit against CBS for $67 million. On the other side, I was being investigated by the criminal intelligence division of the IRS for no reason whatsoever." The suit came to nothing. If Bell feels his political stance played any role in his, and Stax's, demise, he never says so directly. Instead, he refers to "fighting the Memphis community." And when it became known that he owned Stax, he says, "I started feeling people wanting to control me—'if you'll be my boy and I pull your chain, then everything will be just fine.' "

In 1976, Stax closed its doors. One of the great record labels of all time fell victim to its own bright ambition and the realities of CBS bookkeeping. At the time Stax was disappearing, Philadelphia International Records, a new power in R&B, was working with CBS with frightening efficiency.

PHILLY UP

While Stax's demise had made some in black music leery of corporate entanglements, PIR's story was a CBS fairy tale come true. Its seeds lay in the fertile Philadelphia music scene of the sixties that spanned the Twist, local retailer Bruce Webb, and the production team of singer-lyricist Kenny Gamble and pianist-arranger Leon Huff. In the mid-sixties Gamble and Huff teamed up to write and produce records, recruiting a young generation of local musicians and arrangers to help them. Bassist Ronnie Baker, drummer Early Young, and guitarist Norman Harris became the core of their band, while arranging assignments were handed to Bobby Martin and a soon-to-be-important pianist-arranger-producer named Thom Bell. Local engineer Joe Tarsia took over a mediocre local studio named Sound Plus, changed the name to Sigma Sound, and was lucky enough to talk Gamble, Huff, and Bell into giving it a shot. By 1968, the pieces of Philly International were in place.

Their first major success came with Jerry Butler. After recording the classic Curtis Mayfield composition "For Your Precious Love" with the Impressions in 1960, Butler's career stagnated as Mercury Records marketed him as a sepia-toned Andy Williams. Surrounding his rich baritone in well-modulated midtempo songs with arrangements rich in contrast—bubbling, dynamic bass lines and Latin percussion combined with strings and a sweet female chorus—the Gamble and Huff team had a string of hits with Butler in 1967–68. The most notable recording was "Only the Strong Survive," which contained all the team's musical trademarks and had, lyrically, a stern parental tone.

Atlantic Records, eager to maintain the career of Wilson Pickett and fearful that his Southern soul sound of "Midnight Hour" and other songs was fading, sought out Gamble and Huff's urbane yet assertive services, and the Philly crew didn't fail them. "Don't Let the Green Grass Fool You" was musically and thematically drawn from "Strong" and solidified the team's reputation as producers adept at eliciting extraordinary performances from male vocalists. Producing and writing assignments came regularly now.

Yet just as their music, in its use of bass, strings, and overall ambiance of upward mobility, echoed Motown, so did their ambitions. Gamble, in particular, was a visionary who saw in his local scene the seeds of a Motown-like operation. He started Gamble Records in 1967 in an effort to institutionalize himself along the lines of Motown and Stax. The Intruders, a quality four-member stand-up vocal group, were the label's mainstays, cutting records as strong as those Gamble and Huff provided for Butler and Pickett, such as "Together" and "Cowboys to Girls." Unfortunately, Gamble Records' distribution and collection lagged behind its music. Moreover, Gamble and Huff were never able to recruit decent management. The balance of creativity and business skill needed to smoothly administer the operations would in fact always elude the pair.

Realizing this weakness, they entered into a distribution agreement with Chess Records in 1968. Ten years earlier, that might have been a good move, but now Chess was on the wane. Black pop music hadn't meant the blues for a long time now, and the Chess brothers had made too much money to really care. Marshall, the son of cofounder Leonard, was logically the heir apparent and the man to overhaul the label. But he had hit the rock big time and was too busy working with the Rolling Stones. Then GRT, a diversified corporation, bought Chess, and chaos ensued. Whatever vestiges of impact the Chess brothers still had with black radio and retail disappeared during the transition, and Gamble and Huff's music lost out in the confusion.

Again frustrated, the two were ripe for the monetary stability Clive Davis could offer. To Gamble and Huff, the founding of Philadelphia International Records was a dream come true: access to a major distribution company, a guarantee of hefty advances, and (relatively) honest accounting. To CBS, it gave exclusive control of a duo already acknowledged to be on the cutting edge of black pop; use of the cream of Philadelphia's singers and musicians; the administration of Mighty Three Music (Gamble, Huff, and Bell's publishing arm) for CBS's April-Blackwood catalogue; and in the long term, just as important, the opportunity to build a black label from the ground up. Once this engine started running, nothing, including Davis's departure, slowed it down.

PIR's achievements set the standard, and over the last two decades most major black-owned record labels have been funded or, at the very least, distributed by a major label. With the majors directing dollars into black music, the desire to start an independently distributed label slackened to the point where only the desperate or bull-headed made a long-term commitment to that form of distribution.

Both PIR and CBS delivered. Financially secure for the first time, Gamble and Huff went on a creative rampage. In the voices of the O'Jays' Eddie Levert, and Teddy Pendergrass of Harold Melvin and the Blue-notes, they found the perfect vehicles for their sophisticated message music. Levert and Pendergrass had a wider technical range than either Butler or Pickett and a gospel singer's earnest commitment to the material that Gamble and Huff's songs demanded.

"Backstabbers" was a dark, ominous meditation on treachery, high-lighted by Bobby Martin's brilliant horn chart and the interplay between Levert's high-intensity vocal and the backing voices. "For the Love of Money" was just as dramatic, propelled by a wondrous ensemble groove by the crew of Philly musicians now known as MFSB (aided on that song by New York bassist Anthony Jackson, who also got writing credit with Gamble and Huff). These were just the opening blows as the "sound of Philadelphia."

Frankie Crocker, WBLS deejay; the Reverend Jesse Jackson; Manhattan Borough President David Dinkins; Inner City Broadcasting general manager Charles Warfield; and David Lampel, program director at WLIB: all gather as Jackson visits black-owned Inner City's offices during his first presidential campaign. *Courtesy of Lem Peterkin*

Dyanna Williams was a pioneering voice in the
sophisticated black radio of the 1970s. *Courtesy of
Dyanna Williams*

Kenny Gamble, the visionary behind the
musical and social messages of Philadelphia
International Records. *Courtesy of Philadelphia
International Records*

Vernon Slaughter, a transitional figure in the evolution of the black record promoter, seen here with eighteen-year-old Michael Jackson in 1977. *Courtesy of Vernon Slaughter*

D. J. Hollywood, pioneering rap deejay.

Backstage at Roseland in 1983. Front row (left to right): rapper Kurtis Blow, producer-writer Larry Smith. Middle (left to right): Darryl McDaniels, Joseph Simmons, and Jason (Jam Master Jay) Mizell of Run-DMC. Back (left to right) Russell Simmons, Run-DMC's manager; Steve Plotnicki, Profile co-owner; Manny Bella, head of promotion at Profile; Cory Robbins, Profile co-owner. *Courtesy of Chuck Pulin*

Clive Davis (president) and Gerry Griffith (vice-president, black music A&R) celebrate Whitney Houston's signing to Arista Records in 1983. *Courtesy of Arista Records*

Anita Baker, retronuevo diva. *Courtesy of Chuck Pulin*

The grandfather of R&B, Dave Clark. *Courtesy of Dave Clark*

Along the way, Gamble and Huff contemplated slavery (the O'Jays' miniepic "Ship A'Hoy), ecology ("The Air I Breathe"), spiritual enlightenment ("Wake Up Everybody"), corruption ("Bad Luck"), and the male-dominated nuclear family ("Family Reunion"). Oh yeah, PIR did record love songs. There are few cheating songs, even in country music, better than Billy Paul's "Me and Mrs. Jones," or songs of longing more bittersweet than the Bluenotes with Sharon Paige doing "Hope That We'll Be Together Soon," or more mesmerizingly danceable instrumentals than MFSB's "Love Is the Message."

Yet during this magic period it was the "message in the music" that gave PIR its defining personality, and that phrase was inscribed on every PIR album, following a little minisermon from Gamble. On the back of the *Family Reunion* album, for example, Gamble wrote: "The generation gap is another evil plan. The result of which divided the family structure, therefore creating a halt to the flow of wisdom from the wise to the young, and stifling the energy of the young which is the equalizer to wisdom and age. . . . Being of truth and understanding of all things, we must recapture the family structure—Mother, Father, Sister, Brother—and give respect to everyone. Remember the family that prays together stays together. Put the 'Unity' back into the family." "Unity" was the name of a song on the album.

By the mid-seventies, Gamble no longer saw PIR as merely a musical enterprise but also a platform from which to proselytize, espousing a world view that obliquely revealed his private belief in the tenets of Islam. Gamble developed a tough, male-dominant, antimaterialist perspective from his earliest hits and was both overtly and subtly disseminating his view to America. Of course, the irony is that his preaching reached its apex while under the protection of CBS records.

CBS didn't care. Not about Gamble's talk at least, because PIR was consolidating the sales of albums in the black market. In the early seventies, black families played albums by the O'Jays and the Bluenotes until the grooves were worn smooth. While the PIR groups had hit singles, CBS intelligently marketed them as album-sellers, just as it would any rock band. The length of the album cuts ("Ship A'Hoy" ran thirteen minutes) made the purchase of PIR albums a necessary pleasure. The length of dance jams like the monumental "I Love Music" and "Bad Luck" once and forever pushed the average length of black singles from approximately three minutes to four and five minutes plus. The Philly sound, inspired by Gamble and Huff's productions on the O'Jays, Harold Melvin and the Bluenotes, MFSB, the Three Degrees (especially

"When Will I See You Again," Gamble and Huff's only massive hit with female lead vocals), came to dominate dance music. The trademarks were percolating rhythm sections with Latin percussion breaks, swirling string and horn arrangements, and a cooing female chorus—minus Gamble's message lyrics. These sounds appeared on records made in Philly by MFSB members Harris, Young, and Baker (producing Double Exposure, First Choice, the Tramps, and Vince Montana with the Salsoul Orchestra), in Los Angeles by Barry White, in Munich with Silver Convention, and in New York by Van McCoy, whose 1975 "The Hustle" inspired a dance craze. PIR's musical influence and crossover sales confirmed the historic truth that good, innovative black music, made by blacks, will naturally sell to whites once they get to hear it.

And so, the age of corporate takeover in black music began with the death of one great record company and the rise of another. Both emerged from fertile local music scenes and were led by strong, politically aware black leaders. But there was a central difference. Stax, an organization with a proud decade of achievement behind it, tried, with its wheeling and dealing, its sponsorship of social action, and its grass-roots activity, to be as politically progressive as it was profitable. Somewhere along the line its deals undermined its smooth operation.

Philly International as an institution was relatively unformed at the start of its liaison with corporate America, but it learned, despite the pronouncements of one of its founders, how to work within a white corporate system. And as the chief commodity of CBS's black music department, PIR benefited handsomely. The message in the music? Assimilation worked, especially for a nationalistic capitalist who could write hit songs.

CROSSOVER:

THE DEATH OF

RHYTHM & BLUES

(1975–79)

ndependent record labels, R&B radio, concert venues, retail stores in black neighborhoods, and the creativity of black Americans had come together in the thirty years after World War II to create rhythm & blues music. The struggle to overcome the overt apartheid of America had given blacks an energy, a motivating dream, that inspired the music's makers. By the mid-seventies, a segment of black America had beaten the odds, leaped over the barricade, and now lived in parts of the country they would have been lynched in a decade before. It struck many of them as time to remove the modifying adjective "black" from their lives. It was in this spirit that the term "crossover" came to dominate all discussion of black music and, eventually, the music itself. In the process, much of what had made the R&B world work was lost, perhaps some of it forever.

There were many forms of crossover, each of which fed on the others to alter the way the business of black music is conducted. A wave of major label signings from the early to mid-seventies decimated the independents, costing them not just top performers and writers but administrative personnel as well. In 1971, James Brown, still one of black America's heroes, signed to Polydor, an American subsidiary of the huge European conglomerate Phillips-Siemens. The exit door at Motown spun overtime: A&R director Mickey Stevenson signed a deal with MGM; Harvey Fuqua, a producer, writer, and artist-development staffer, got a production deal with MCA; the writing and producing couple Nick Ashford and Valerie Simpson wanted to perform and got their wish at Warner Bros.; the team of Brian Holland, Lamont Dozier, and Eddie Holland signed label deals with an indie, Buddah, and a major, Capitol; Gladys Knight and the Pips and the Isley Brothers joined Buddah (subsequently the Isleys would join CBS with their T-Neck label and Knight would shift to Columbia); the Four Tops joined ABC; and the Jackson Five became the Jacksons, on CBS's Epic label. During Stax's collapse, Isaac Hayes signed with ABC; the Staple Singers, with Warner Bros.; and Johnnie Taylor and the Soul Children went to Columbia and Epic, respectively. Curtis Mayfield took his Curtom label to Warner Bros., along with the Impressions and Leroy Hutson.

In fact, by February 1976 Warner Bros. was able to put on a massive four-day series of concerts at New York's Beacon Theater called "California Soul," where thirteen acts performed, including Ashford and Simpson, the Impressions, Leroy Hutson, the Philly female vocal trio First Choice, Graham Central Station (led by Sly's innovative former bassist, Larry Graham), Dionne Warwick, the Staple Singers, and two "jazz" artists, guitarist and would-be vocalist George Benson and singer Al Jarreau. At the show, a souvenir booklet was given away, as well as free sampler 45s featuring album cuts. The concerts were not held at the Apollo but at a West Side theater of similar age. Warner Bros. had also chosen to promote the concerts with top rock promoter Ron Delsner to lend the show added cachet. And in spite of its hip, liberal, adventurous image, Warner Bros. would never allow its black executives too much clout outside record promotion. (It hired its first black A&R vice-president, Benny Medina, in 1987.) White executives in A&R controlled talent acquisition, and those in marketing, merchandising, and promotion (top forty, AOR) had imput as well. The most prominent black executive in the company's history, Tom Draper, joined as vice-president and director of black-music marketing in October 1975. He was the first outside executive hired directly as a vice-president, a movement clearly made to impress the black music community of the label's commitment, and conveniently timed to allow a black face to represent the "California

Soul" promotion four months later. Draper's record-industry career had begun just two years before, when RCA shifted him from home electronics to record promotion after they began to sign more R&B acts. In August 1975, he was made a division vice-president at RCA, while in the same month white Warner Bros. executive Bob Krasnow was signing Benson from the jazz indie CTI, the black rock band Funkadelic from indie Westbound, and traditional jazz acts. Krasnow was a former president of Liberty and Blue Note records, labels with extensive jazz and R&B catalogues (Ike and Tina Turner's "Proud Mary" was on Liberty). Over the next five years, he would be the one to sign Chaka Khan and other top black talent attracted to Warner Bros.' Burbank complex.

Draper made a smart move. Warner Bros., unlike RCA, was well run, aggressive, and truly committed to the music. By October 1976, RCA had disbanded its black-music division; it would be restarted and disbanded again in the eighties. Draper surely got better money at Warner Bros., just as all the black artists signing with the majors did. Money— both big advances against royalties and generous royalty rates once a record began to make a profit—were powerful inducements.

For example, when the Jackson Five signed with Motown they got a royalty rate of 2.7 percent on records sold, had all expenses related to their "grooming" written off against revenues, and though the Jackson family didn't know it, gave Motown rights to the name "Jackson Five." When they defected to Epic—sparking an acrimonious lawsuit and the loss of brother Jermaine back to Motown—the Jacksons found out what corporate dollars could mean: a signing bonus of $350,000 per release and a 28 percent royalty on wholesale album prices in America (and 24 percent internationally), which translated to about 98 cents per album—an increase over their Motown royalty deal by about 500 percent.

CBS retained almost as much control over selection of producers and material as Motown had. The issue of artistic control was as vexed at the majors as it was at indies. However, the vastly differing agendas of the majors and the indies affected questions of artistic control in differing ways. For an indie label, even Motown in the late seventies, every record did not have to be a pop hit to be deemed successful. For example, the Commodores' early records were stone cold R&B party music. At CBS, Warner Bros., RCA, Polydor, MCA, Capitol, and ABC, there was more pressure, caused in a large part by the big contracts, for black artists to reach quite intentionally for white sales.

The Harvard Report's observation about black records moving readily from black to pop radio wasn't lost on CBS. In 1976, LeBaron Taylor, head of CBS's black music division, gave an unintentionally chilling interview to Geoffrey Stokes for the *Village Voice*. Taylor outlined CBS's strategy for institutionalizing "crossover"—the sale of black hits to whites. CBS emphasized releasing a first single from an upcoming album with white as well as black appeal. The ideal—implicit in the Harvard Report—was to break it on black radio, build sales into the half million (gold) range, and then aim this "hit" at "mainstream" audiences.

In 1975, Johnnie Taylor's "Disco Lady," a record aimed expressly at capitalizing on the disco vogue, sold 2.5 million singles. The Manhattans' 1976 ballad, "Kiss and Say Good-Bye," sold over a million copies. Following Taylor's outline CBS withheld these albums until almost two months after the singles. "I don't want an album out—especially to radio programmers, who love to play some other cut and tell you that you picked the wrong single—until the single is established," Taylor said. "That way the consumers and the programmers don't have a chance to second-guess you." But, as the *Voice* pointed out, "that policy—especially since the single is chosen primarily for its crossover potential—means that black radio listeners are reduced to auditioning records geared to white audiences." For many of the soul singers who signed with CBS in hopes of attracting crossover audiences—R&B veterans Gladys Knight and the Pips, Bobby Womack, Tyrone Davis, Z. Z. Hill, and Johnnie Taylor—this strategy proved a disaster. Black radio emphatically rejected many of their "pop" efforts or, in some cases, simply didn't like the first single. With no album cuts to play in its place, these acts were left with no airplay for long periods of time, and since CBS had an overabundance of acts to promote, including the consistent hitmakers of Philly International, all the veterans just mentioned suffered at CBS. Eventually, all except Knight would be dropped. Womack, a protégé of crossover pioneer Sam Cooke, a prolific songwriter, and a top session guitarist, had been a significant progressive soul artist on indie United Artists in the early to mid-seventies, writing the classic "I Can Understand It" and the score for the superb blaxploitation film *Across 110th Street*, among many other credits.

With his gutsy voice vividly echoing Cooke's gospel recordings, Womack should have remained a vital force in R&B through the decade. Instead, his career was lost in the flood of black CBS releases. The omens were bad from the start. Just after signing with Columbia in 1977, Womack traveled to a top black station with a CBS promotion man. He wryly recalls, "After he got through giving them the new Isley Brothers, the new Earth, Wind and Fire, the new Teddy Pendergrass, the new Jacksons, he asked if there was any room on that playlist for good old Bobby Womack." There wasn't. By 1978 Womack was gone from CBS and, after a failing album at Arista, ended the seventies a nonentity in R&B.

Some say that Womack's failures were purely musical, that his Columbia albums were simply inferior to his work on United Artists. That was part of it. But there is no question that CBS's crossover consciousness and growing roster buried a great many veterans. Tyrone Davis, though not as gifted as Womack, was another solid R&B citizen whose career died on the vine in the rich fields of CBS. He was a tall, elegantly streetwise Chicago singer with a light baritone. He was coming off a number-one black single, "Turning Point," and a string of other top-ten R&B singles on Brunswick—the indie label Jackie Wilson's records built—when he signed with Columbia in 1977 in search of more dollars and a white audience. At CBS Davis would be a victim of sociology as well as economics.

The white executives who signed Davis were impressed by his sales figures but didn't fully understand what made him popular. They had no idea that his black audience tended to be older and less upscale than new-breed artists such as the O'Jays and Earth, Wind and Fire. In contrast, many members of the black-music department were less than enthused with Davis. Yes, he sold records, but his music was "old." Why work with him when there were so many new acts with fresh sounds around? However, at the time he signed, the consistency of his sales dampened their criticism.

His first single, "Give It Up, Turn It Loose," was a substantial black hit. The lead single from his second album, "Get on Up, Disco," a bow to the disco craze, was Davis's anxious attempt to match Johnnie Taylor's massive "Disco Lady." The record was marginally successful, but no "Disco Lady." This frustrated Davis, and he spent too much time on his next two albums seeking "that crossover hit." Davis had a bad case of disco fever, seeing in its rigid rhythms and hi-hat cymbal pattern the big casino success that would change his life.

Then in 1979, Davis cut a song called "In the Mood," a very old-fashioned string-laden ballad that brought out the richness of his voice. It was syrupy but it worked, though Davis feared that releasing the song as a single would kill his career. But Paris Eley, a young promotion man then recently elevated to the post of Epic's black promotion head and one of the few young blacks sympathetic to Davis's music, decided "In the Mood" was a hit and made it a priority record. At about the same time, Polydor, defying disco's dominance, had followed up Peaches and Herb's (disco) smash "Shake Your Groove Thang" with the beautiful ballad by Freddie Perren and Dino Fakaris, "Reunited." Together these "outcast" songs moved up the black singles chart. "In the Mood" would eventually sell 700,000, and "Reunited" went on to sell nearly 2 million copies, becoming a pop standard.

Both were excellent cuts, but "In the Mood" sold far fewer because, Eley's efforts notwithstanding, Columbia's internal agenda worked against it. Polydor acted on white radio's good initial response to "Reunited" and crossed it over. Columbia got "Mood" on a few pop stations but basically accepted the record's surprising sales without pushing any further.

Johnnie Taylor never had another "Disco Lady," and Tyrone Davis never matched "Mood" at CBS. "No one at the company thought of them as career artists," recalls one Columbia staffer about the attitude toward the soul veterans. "They were artists we tried to get a hit on, and when that hit was over, it was over. The kind of artist development commitment made to a Deniece Williams or Teddy Pendergrass during the same period wasn't considered for them." This attitude wasn't limited to CBS. Candi Staton, a sultry-voiced vocalist who'd built a Southern following with gutsy tales of unfaithful lovers, had a couple of major soul-disco hits on Warner Bros. ("Young Hearts Run Free," "Victim") but was never an album-seller, at least in part because Warner Bros. didn't work as conscientiously at developing her as it did more urbane acts such as Ashford and Simpson and George Benson.

In the case of Taylor, Davis, Staton, and most of the traditional R&B acts in the era of crossover, once one major label dropped them, no other major would sign them. The white execs had no interest in the effect this would have on the traditions of black music. If youthful black record buyers didn't identify with these artists, neither would they. The black executives surely knew that a substantial audience still existed for these records, albeit older and less impulsive in its purchases; they could have fought what amounted to a forced changing of the guard in black music. Many of them, however, felt the difficulty of pushing older acts wasn't worth the effort. Moreover, in their closed-door meetings, some ridiculed these soul survivors, laughing at their processed hair, white suits, and "chitlin circuit ideas" at a time Earth, Wind and Fire headlined Madison Square Garden with state-of-the-art pyrotechnics. The audience these executives—black and white—wanted either went or aspired to college and the middle-class values it represented. It was an audience too young to be attracted by the mature tales of the R&B veterans. Black music had been a family affair in the sixties, with the Temptations, Aretha Franklin, and Curtis Mayfield appealing to a wide spectrum of blacks. A partial result of black music's incorporation was a fragmenting of the market by class and, for the first time since the swing-bebop break, by age.

DISCO FEVER

The crossover mentality and the overstuffed rosters of major labels were internal industry problems that weakened the R&B world. An outside force that helped destroy R&B, pulling the music from its roots and eroding the connections made with white America in the 1960s, was disco. The irony is that disco began as an extension of black dance music. First in Europe and then in the U.S., discotheques became popular as places you danced to recorded music, just like at a house party. And most of the music initially played at discos was supplied by black artists.

From 1971 to 1975, self-contained post-Sly funk bands like Kool and the Gang ("Funky Stuff," "Hollywood Swinging") and Ohio Players ("Skin Tight," "Fire"), and vocal records with extended instrumental vamps, personified by ex-Temptation Eddie Kendricks's "Boogie Down" and "Keep on Truckin'," were early harbingers of the disco sound. TK Records of Florida, owned by Henry Stone, an old "white Negro" of the fifties and sixties, had the first hits that moved from discos to black radio and ultimately crossover sales: George McCrae's "Rock Your Baby" and Gwen McCrae's "Rockin' Chair." The rhythm section of these hits then began cutting behind the poorly shouted vocals of a white keyboardist named Harry Casey. Under the name KC and the Sunshine Band, they cut simple-minded but irresistible dance tracks ("Get Down Tonight," "Shake Your Booty," "Boogie Shoes") that, like the McCraes' records, were based on R&B-funk riffs and arrangements. Two bands from Brooklyn's East New York section, B.T. Express ("Express," "Do It 'Til You're Satisfied") and Brass Construction ("Changin' ") added strings and horns to these extended-play dance records but again, the basic grooves were in the R&B tradition.

But between 1976 and 1980, two musical forces combined to de-funk disco and turn it into a sound of mindless repetition and lyrical idiocy that, with exceptions, overwhelmed R&B. Ironically, one factor was the musical formula of the Philly sound. Separated from the message songs and love stories of the PIR hits, the overripe strings, flowing French horns, and Latin percussion became the soundtrack to a season of drek. MFSB's drummer, Early Young, whose innovative use of hi-hat and kick-drum patterns had fueled PIR's music, found himself spending much of the late seventies repeating those ideas ad infinitum. The same players who performed with such fire on "Bad Luck" and the anthemic "I Love Music" made, recording as the Ritchie Family and Salsoul Orchestra, a series of incredibly insipid records, eventually helping drown the Philly sound in clichés.

At least the Philly disco records sounded like they were made by humans. Soon, Eurodisco invaded America, initially from Munich, and later from Italy and France. It was music with a metronomelike beat—perfect for folks with no sense of rhythm—almost inflectionless vocals, and metallic sexuality that matched the high-tech, high-sex, and low passion atmosphere of the glamorous discos that appeared in every major American city. Silver Convention's "Fly Robin Fly" was the first Eurodisco crossover hit direct from Munich. The biggest star to emerge from the scene was Donna Summer, along with her producer, Giorgio Moroder. Her 1976 album, *Four Seasons of Love*, would define the worst tendencies of Eurodisco while at the same time making Summer—with the extravagant backing of Casablanca Records president Neil Bogart—the period's biggest black female star. That KC and the Sunshine Band, Salsoul Orchestra, and Summer all made their impact on indie labels showed that despite the increasing incorporation of black music, smaller companies were still on the cutting edge, as dull as that edge may have become. But it was the glossier Philly style and the rigid Eurodisco that came to dominate the music's sensibility—a reflection of the attitude of the core disco audience as well as the influence of black music's incorporation.

Disco's movers and shakers were not record executives but club deejays. Most were gay men with a singular attitude toward American culture, black as well as white. They elevated female vocalists like Summer, Gloria Gaynor, Diana Ross, Loleatta Hollaway, Melba Moore, and Grace Jones to diva status, while black male singers were essentially shunned. Funk, which in the late seventies was enjoying great popularity in the South and Midwest, was rarely on their playlists. It was too raw and unsophisticated, and one thing dear to the hearts of disco fans, gay and straight, was a feeling of pseudosophistication. Barry White, who dubbed the collected session musicians on his records an "orchestra" and had arranger Gene Page conduct White's simple string arrangements with a baton, was an early disco hero because he realized that a large part of the American public sought nostalgic elegance in reaction to the dirty jeans and back-to-the-earthiness of the sixties and early seventies.

The sales of White, Summer, Eurodiscos, and the fake Philly sound of Salsoul Records—with a stamp of approval by prominent deejays—made the majors believe that these musical techniques would accelerate the black crossover process. So the new dance music inspired by the inventions of Gamble and Huff, came to celebrate a hedonism and androgyny that contradicted their patriarchal philosophy. At the same time, a glossy, upwardly mobile corporate black music, based on some Philly sound hits (e.g., Billy Paul's "Me and Mrs. Jones," the Stylistics' "You Make Me Feel Brand New," the Spinners' "Could It Be I'm Falling In Love," the last two produced by the soft-soul guru Thom Bell). Some, such as George Benson's "This Masquerade" on Warner Bros., "Jack and Jill" by Raydio, with Ray Parker, Jr., and Deniece Williams's "Free," weren't danceable but launched careers as upscale, polished, and mellow as giving Harvey's Bristol Cream for Christmas. The danceable tracks tended to be sweet, highly melodic, and unthreatening. Gamble and Huff themselves cut some of these with Lou Rawls ("Groovy People," "You'll Never Find," "See You When I Get There"). Producer Quincy Jones, making the transition from big bands and movie scores to pop, contributed two of the more interesting examples with the Brothers Johnson ("I'll Be Good to You," and "Strawberry Letter 23") on A&M, a Los Angeles indie with the mentality of a major. Other prime examples of this new corporate black pop were Marilyn McCoo and Billy Davis's "You Don't Have to Be a Star (To Be in My Show)," produced by ex-Stax staffer and "Disco Lady" writer Don Davis; Barry White's "Your Sweetness Is My Weakness"; and Stephanie Mills's "What You Gonna Do with My Loving."

That is not to say that soul or funk disappeared. Maurice White's Earth, Wind and Fire and the Commodores of Lionel Richie's tenure mixed rough-and-tumble funk with exciting arrangements, midtempo songs, and ballads as pure pop as anything being recorded. But it should be noted that the more successful these bands became, the more mellow and less intense their music got.

Only an aggregation of bands (Parliament, Funkadelic, Bootsy's Rubber Band, the Horny Horns, Brides of Funkenstein, Parlet, among many) under the chaotically creative leadership of George (Dr. Funkenstein) Clinton stuck to their grooves, weaving humor, parody, tons of slang, and the skills of some extraordinary funk musicians, including key-boardists Junie Morrison and Bernie Worrell, guitarists Gary Shider and Mike Hampton, vocalist Gary (Mudbone) Cooper, bassist Bootsy Collins, arranger-saxophonist Maceo Parker, and arranger-trombonist Fred Wesley. George's troops made antidisco dance music of the highest quality: "Tear the Roof Off the Sucker," "Flash Light," "One Nation Under a Groove," "Bootzilla." The whole P-Funk concept was a mus-ically amusing way of thumbing one's nose at what Clinton dubbed "The Placebo Syndrome," aka funkless black music. Disco, combined with the crossover consciousness of the majors, created music for those who sought mainstream acceptance and didn't want to fight about it.

YOU COULD LOOK IT UP

Economic integration (read: if you made enough money you lived any-where you wished) was made possible for more blacks than ever before through civil-service jobs, low- and middle-level management positions, and programs that encouraged college attendance. These factors affected the pocketbooks and tastes of black America. Equally symbolic of this attitude was the rise of pop-jazz, while bebop and the more radical "free jazz" of Ornette Coleman was almost invisible. Pop-jazz—melodic, easy listening, unimprovisational—in albums by saxophonists (Grover Wash-ington, Jr., Ronnie Laws), keyboardists (Bob James, Joe Sample), gui-tarists (Earl Klugh, George Benson), and bands (the Crusaders, Spyro Gyra), was the perfect accompaniment to that quintessentially seventies endeavor, brunch.

It was all a long way from soul but just as reassuring as reading an article in *Black Enterprise* about Caribbean vacations. Such articles told the magazine's middle-class readership that they had the disposable income for such a venture, the foresight to investigate their leisure-time options, and the black consciousness to patronize black-run countries.

Sadly, in this new environment, R&B, as a metaphor and a music, looked like a terminal case; the world that had supported it no longer existed. The connections between blacks of all classes were loosening, as various forms of material success (or the illusion of such success) seduced many into the crossover mentality.

Of course, the loser in all this was the music. If you study the charts, it's clear that crossover was far from a dream come true. The tendency is to acclaim crossover a triumph after looking at the 2.5 million copies of Taylor's "Disco Lady," the 5 million copies of Chic's "Good Times" in 1979 (then the biggest selling 45 in Atlantic's history), or the 9 million copies of Michael Jackson's *Off the Wall*, also in 1979 (produced by Quincy Jones, it was then the biggest-selling album by a black performer in history). But what developed was a deadly feast-or-famine syndrome. If you won, you won big. And if you failed, no one noticed and you could easily disappear.

The test of crossover is how effectively popular black recordings can be sold to whites. Using the placement of number-one black hits on the *Billboard* pop chart as a barometer, one finds the best year for crossover was 1970, when fifteen of the top black songs in America reached the top fifteen on the pop chart, and seven went to number one (though the fact that four were by the Jackson Five at the height of their early appeal somewhat skews the count). Still, the most successful years were between 1967 and 1973, when independent labels still controlled the music: the period of soul's most majestic performances, of funk's popularization by James Brown and Sly, of ambitious new arrangements by Norman Whitfield, Marvin Gaye, Stevie Wonder, Isaac Hayes, and Curtis Mayfield, a time when blackness still fascinated whites and inspired Afro-Americans of every stratum—that's when crossover really worked.

In those years, according to Paul Grein, an expert on the *Billboard* chart, "The average pop peak of each year's #1 soul hits was at least #9. In other words, a typical #1 hit on the soul chart could be expected to, at least, reach the top 10 on the pop chart."

According to Grein, "The road for black crossover started to get rougher in the disco era. From 1974 to 1976, the average #1 black hit peaked right around #15 on the pop chart. In 1978, when disco fever was at its peak, the average #1 black hit reached #22 on the pop chart." Studying the chart another way confirms the results. In 1973, thirty-six records moved from the black chart to the top-100 on the year-end pop chart. In 1974, twenty-seven did. In 1975, twenty-eight took the journey, and in 1976, the number rose to thirty. But 1977 was a disaster, as only twenty-three records moved from black stations to *Billboard*'s year-end top 100 (and that number includes such disco drek as Meco's "Theme from *Star Wars*").

One unexpected result of the disco-crossover nexus was that black radio, the backbone of the R&B world, would no longer be a safe haven for black artists exclusively. In fact, it became a vehicle for developing "white Negro" artists.

THE NEW WHITE NEGROES

The Bee Gees, a family vocal group born in England and raised in Australia, debuted in 1967 with a series of Beatlesque albums based on the ornately psychedelic style of *Sgt. Pepper's Lonely Hearts Club Band*. The brothers Gibb—Robin, Maurice, and Barry—seemed washed up seven years later when their "Mr. Natural" died at 178 on the *Billboard* chart. Robert Stigwood, who managed the group and owned RSO, the label they recorded for, was a flamboyant Australian wheeler-dealer. Quite aware of the black dance-disco scene growing in Europe and New York, Stigwood hired Atlantic staff producer Arif Mardin to bring his black-music experience to bare on these unfunky clients. In 1975 they recorded in Miami, tapping into the city's pool of session players. The result was a profound redirection of their sound: Robin Gibb, a falsetto, became an echo of Eddie Kendricks and Smokey Robinson; Barry started emanating in the low-tenor range reminiscent of David Ruffin; and Mardin's intimate knowledge of R&B recast the Gibbs as the best blue-eyed soul men since the Righteous Brothers. With the uptempo "Jive Talkin'" and the soaring dance ballad "Nights on Broadway," *Main Course* went platinum and generated amazing amounts of black radio play. Stigwood realized he was on to something. He pulled RSO out of its distribution agreement with Atlantic and hired two young musicians, Karl Richardson and Albhy Galuten, to coproduce with Barry Gibb. *Children of the World* repeated the *Main Course* formula with a very fast dance record, "You Should Be Dancing," that reached number one, and another R&B ballad, "Love So Right."

While *Children of the World* was firmly positioning the Bee Gees as a force on black and white radio, Stigwood backed the production of a disco exploitation movie called *Saturday Night Fever*, starring TV actor John Travolta and featuring a soundtrack dotted with disco standards (Trammps' "Disco Inferno," Tavares' "Heaven Must Be Missing an Angel") as well as Bee Gee originals "Stayin' Alive" and "How Deep Is Your Love." *SNF* is important on many levels: it confirmed the arrival of disco as a cultural force in mass America; made Travolta's honky, dancing-fool Brooklynite a seventies icon; showed that the blaxploitation films' catalytic effect on record sales was no fluke; and again showed the power of a black-based music to capture the national imagination.

For black radio, it began a period of reverse crossover, where on playlists nationwide white dance records in the disco style replaced songs by black artists.

It should be no surprise that Frankie Crocker proudly led the way. At the time, Crocker said, "*SNF* was what WBLS is to me, what we try to do on the air." When you consider the history of black radio, that is an amazing statement. The black program director of a black-owned station in the nation's biggest market was defining his station's sound with a recording spearheaded by three Australians imitating blacks. What a departure from the way black deejays, from the beginning of black radio, had seen the role of their stations. And Crocker was far from through. He'd play the rockabilly-style "Crazy Little Thing Called Love," by British rockers Queen, before introducing the group's mean, lean "Another One Bites the Dust," a clever rip-off of Chic's "Good Times." As Brits jumped quite cynically on the disco band wagon (Rod Stewart's "Do You Think I'm Sexy," Rolling Stones' "Miss You") and Eurodisco flowed through import shops (Cerrone's "Love In C Minor" and "Supernature," Gino Soccio's "Dancer"), Crocker played it all. After all, "the Total Black Experience in Sound" was history. So what did WBLS stand for? In the late seventies, just a few blocks from the Apollo Theater on 125th Street, the station ran ads on the side of bus-stop shelters. In one, a blonde sat cross-legged in front of the WBLS logo. Under her, a slogan said, "The World's Best Looking Sound." It is one thing to be hip; it is another to completely abandon your station's original identity as a voice of the black community. But for Crocker, it was the era of disco glamour, when entry to Studio 54 was considered the apex of New York clout, and WBLS's program director walked in any time he wished. Black radio—not everywhere, but in too many cities—became disco radio, just as not all but too many black artists made beige music.

LIVING FOR THE URBAN

By the end of the decade, disco radio would give way to "urban" radio, a format that like rock & roll was at first more a marketing term than a musical concept. Coming out of the black FM radio and disco, urban was supposedly a multicolored programming style tuned to the rhythms of America's crossfertilized big cities. And at its best, it fulfilled that goal. But more often, urban was black radio in disguise. On urban you still heard Earth, Wind, and Fire and George Benson and Ashford and Simp-

son, and, down south, Cameo and the Bar-Kays. But the Bee Gees and
Hall and Oates and even Kenny Rogers, with the ballad "Lady," written
and produced by Lionel Richie, was there, too. Moreover, identifying
with the black community of a given city was deemed unnecessary and,
in fact, counterproductive. Urban was aimed as much at Madison Avenue as at black listeners.

The mentality behind urban was well defined by Sonny Joe White of
Boston's KISS-FM in the early eighties. White, a black programmer with
top-forty experience, had much of the same influence in his city as
Crocker had in New York. "KISS 108 has evolved from its initial image
as a disco station that today plays up to 70 percent soul/r&b/disco and
the rest rock, pop and whatever is selling in Boston," he told *Billboard*.
"Seventy percent of our announcing staff is white, the rest is black.
While I am black and want to do whatever I can to help young black
announcers moving up, I do not like quota systems of any kind."

When asked why KISS, which plays 70 percent black music, doesn't
see itself as a black station, White replied quite straightforwardly, "It's
a marketing problem, unfortunately. Many advertising agencies still
seem to believe there is no black middle class and they know very little
about the buying habits of today's black consumer. So stations call
themselves urban to make themselves more attractive to those agencies
which would never buy a black station. Such stereotypic thinking forces
even black stations to downplay their blackness in order to compete for
the advertising dollars. Right or wrong, urban is a more acceptable term
to many agency people. . . . certain black stations that are, in fact, doing
well and could demand top dollar for spots are reticent to do so because
there is still a poor image of black radio."

So, because white account executives didn't (couldn't) appreciate
black radio's power to motivate blacks (and many whites), many in
radio abandoned their ethnic identity, hoping to do with semantics what
the civil-rights movement couldn't do marching in the street: make
white businessmen respect black institutions.

In the long run, it was a march of folly. In the short run, it made
many black artists unacceptable on urban stations. Just a decade after
James Brown cut "Say It Loud, I'm Black, and I'm Proud," urban
program directors began telling promoters that many black artists were
"too black" for their format. Millie Jackson and Cameo: too black. The
phrase echoed with the sound of self-hate. Too black. A retreat from
the beauty of blackness. Too black. The sound of the death of R&B.
Jack Gibson could feel the pulse weakening. In 1976, he started a black

radio tip sheet called *Jack the Rapper* which, aside from hyping potential hit records, served as one of the few public forums for attacking the too-black syndrome that grew out of crossover. "I feel that black stations should not play any white records," Gibson said more than once. "Every time they do, they take airplay away from a black artist who couldn't get it anywhere else but in black radio. I can accept Teena Marie, who is white, because she works for a black-owned and -operated company, Motown. But other than that, black radio should be for black music. I've been accused by some of being a reverse racist, but the truth is I'm not anti-white, I'm just pro-black." That last sentiment surely marked Gibson in the late seventies as either a radical or a fool. He wasn't completely alone, but the voices that supported him were frequently those as far from the new black mainstream as Gibson. The black mom-and-pop stores on Black Main Street were dying in the period of cross-over, and not too many people seemed to care.

MOM-AND-POP RETAIL REVISITED

For CBS, Polydor, Warner Bros., RCA, MCA, and other major labels, the main concern was increasing the presence of black records in the primary retail chains, such as Sears. In many cases, it was a battle that black and white executives at the majors fought with real gusto. What good was crossover airplay if the white audience couldn't find the album in the record stores of the great American mall? Because black mom-and-pop stores ordered and sold relatively little inventory at a given time, they were low priority. It had always been true that few black retailers had ever had any intimate contact with the majors, but R&B's incorporation put them at a still more troubling disadvantage. Black stores usually purchased major-label products from one-stops or whole-salers, who gave them decent prices. But those prices were still not as good as the high-volume chain stores received directly from the labels.

In 1956, Joe Long started working at Birdel's record store in the heart of Brooklyn's Bedford-Stuyvesant neighborhood. Twelve years later, when Long bought the store from its white owner, there were twenty or so black-oriented record stores throughout Brooklyn, serving an area with more blacks than most major cities. By the late seventies Long estimated there were, maybe, five left. "Several of those specialize in just Caribbean music for the West Indian population," he said. Many so-called record stores in the New York area are "actually selling herb out of the back." The problem was "that we haven't gotten the credit and deals we need to remain competitive. We'll get a deal every six months, but not on a regular basis. There have been a lot of meetings with us mom-and-pop stores. But we've received nothing that can keep us moving. We can't capitalize on hit material with profit margins so small. Discomat [a New York retail chain] is charging $5.99 for hit black albums, while we pay $5.39 just to get them."

Ted Hudson opened his first retail store in St. Louis in 1958 and later opened up several other stores and a one-stop operation, too. "There is a dual system of credit, one for blacks and one for whites," Hudson charged. "No matter how long you're in business you have to battle the companies just like the black star who has to prove himself to the pop market with each record. Yet, we sell what we buy because we know what our market will take. Still, whites have unlimited amounts of credit and we, stable businesses that help make hits, are being squeezed tighter and tighter. They have black executives with lots of titles making several hundred thousand dollars a year. Yet, almost none of the major companies have these blacks in positions to give you what you need when you need it."

In the late seventies, Philadelphian Bruce Webb, owner of Webb's Department Store since 1962, used his money to advertise his few price breaks in the local black press, hoping to counteract chain ads highlighting low prices on black records. "You can't depend on the major labels to help you with advertising, not if you're black and want to stay in business," he observed bitterly. "It has been a problem, despite all the lip service given it over the years. A couple of black stores get made into Uncle Toms and are given a little bit so the companies can say, 'Hey, look what we did for this guy.' But until we get some black executives who can do something and get ourselves together as a group, we're not going to get the advertising and credit we deserve."

Joining the chorus of dissatisfaction were black concert promoters who found that crossover didn't include them. The Apollo, the Howard, the Uptown, the Regal, all were dead or dying. The Apollo had a curious period when, through a front, it was bought by Harlem drug king Nicky Barnes. Despite his millions, Barnes sank no money into refurbishing the building and it, like the other chitlin parlors, continued to deteriorate. Noteworthy during this period were week-long engagements by James Brown, P-Funk, and reggae's Bob Marley as signs of solidarity with the Apollo's audience. More important in the long run would be the music and rhymes provided between songs at some shows by a local teen named D. J. Hollywood. The kid was on to something.

Integration had opened downtown to black acts and, once the reluctant owners of those facilities saw the dollars that could be generated, black artists were greeted with open wallets. Bobby Shiffman of the Apollo broke it down to writer Ted Fox in dollars and cents: "Toward the end of the '70s an act who was in demand—and you need acts who are in demand—could make more money in one night in a bigger and better location than they could make in the Apollo in a whole week. The Apollo . . . had the additional chore of trying to keep prices at a level that the people could afford to pay. If you had an act in the Apollo for $6, that act could sell tickets for $16 downtown or $20 or $50." While the Apollo had 1,683 seats, Madison Square Garden had 20,000, the Nassau Coliseum 19,000, Carnegie Hall 2,800 and Avery Fisher Hall at Lincoln Center 4,500. The economics were clear. But to black concert promoters, men and women who had worked with Queen Booking and Buffalo Booking Agency for years, the death of the Apollo was also tied to racism and neglect.

FINGERS IN THE DIKE

Veteran black artists were leaving the old-line black booking agencies, and new acts were signing directly with William Morris and International Creative Management for career guidance—guidance in the name of crossover that didn't involve black promoters except for acts low on the totem pole. In 1977, Teddy Powell, who had been in the music industry thirty-two years, was the first black promoter to handle tours not just regionally but on a national basis. He was an old-line denizen of the R&B world, and he was pained to see it breaking down. "We [blacks] still believe that in order to be a success you have to act white," he said. "You may start black. Your first records will be R&B. You'll play the chitlin circuit. But as soon as you get in a position to help the black promoters who built you up, they want somebody who doesn't need help. That's why white promoters will always be on top. They reap the cream we are making. They have their audience and our audience." Another black promoter put it more bluntly: "Your white boys look out for your white boys. Since most of the booking agencies are white they go to the white promoters first."

Times changed to such a degree that when major black stars of the crossover era would send out bids for tours, no black promoters would be told. One alternative strategy was exercised by Dick Griffey, in Los Angeles. Though he handled the biggest concerts of any black promoter in that city, Griffey made a deal to copromote gigs by black stars with a large white promotion company. It was a shrewd move for him, but one that didn't appease or help the many smaller black promoters who were being run out of the business by the new status quo.

Black promoters appealed to the racial consciousness of black artists and cited the role black promoters could play in building their acts to superstar status. Unfortunately, a lot of black artists didn't view them with great affection. In 1982, singer Richard (Dimples) Fields, hot with "She's Got Papers on Me" and "If It Ain't One Thing It's Another," quite eloquently presented his position: "It's not about black. It's not about white. It's about people treating you with respect and working like a professional. There are a lot of black promoters out there doing a fine job. I worked with many of them when I toured this year. But I also ran into some practices—primarily among blacks, but whites as well—that disturbed me. All across the country I found promoters who were not willing to meet their contractual obligations. By that I mean they would ask you to take a cut in your pay, usually as much as half, because advance ticket sales were slow. Depending on the circumstances, I was willing to go along. However, I often found that they would be premature in asking for this, since black audiences tend to buy their tickets the day of the show. Often it isn't until half an hour before the concert that you can really tell what kind of attendance you'll have."

In many cities black promoters—often local businessmen or local club owners but sometimes hustlers wanting to try their hand at show business—were inexperienced. Fields found that "too many promoters were not laying the groundwork in the market to make a successful concert. A couple of times I dealt with promoters who didn't know as much as I did." Belinda Wilson, his black manager, agreed, adding, "If you can get a good black promoter, that's fine. But once you get to a certain point in time, it doesn't matter who it is as long as they're professional."

Whether it was racism or a lack of professionalism, in the late seventies black promoters were feeling as vulnerable as black retailers and they fought back often fitfully. Boycotts of black stars were suggested, though rarely carried through. Black-promoter organizations were founded but quickly died since their members, by nature a competitive bunch, were always worried about the other guy gaining an edge. It was a road to destruction, and the black promoters ran toward it.

With black music turning beige, white artists tapping into black rhythms via disco, corporations using black radio as a launching pad, and retailers and promoters based in black America fading away, the Black Music Association was born September 10–13, 1978, in La Costa, California, to "preserve, protect, and perpetuate" black music. Or, as Stevie Wonder said, "Bring Minds Alive." The roots of that historic meeting were in a Newark grand-jury investigation into payola in black radio. No one went to jail. But in 1976 Kenny Gamble was fined $2,500. Jackie Wilson's boss Nat Tarnopol of Brunswick Records was fined too. Frankie Crocker, a target of the investigation, wasn't convicted of anything, but he left WBLS, later came back, and exited again to a gig at the cable video channel VH-1. Since 1980 Crocker has been up for numerous radio slots, but in at least one instance, his "reputation" kept him out of work.

Most blacks in the industry believed the investigation was racially motivated. What Dave Clark called "white payola" went on unabated, with much higher stakes involved. Moreover, investigation or no investigation, payola continued in black radio. Program directors were not usually courted, though some music directors and influential deejays still were. Pay in black radio remained notoriously low outside major markets, and even at the larger black-oriented stations, black- or white-owned, salaries often lagged behind industry standards. In 1974, there were over 8,000 commercial stations in America. Maybe 300 played R&B or its derivations. Only 127—barely one percent—were black-owned.

The threat to black music and radio suggested by the grand jury led to a series of meetings with member of black radio, organized by Gamble and ex-NATRA head Ed Wright. Could NATRA be revitalized? Close inspection showed the organization's well-earned party image and shaky finances rendered it a poor tool for agitation. A new, more broad-based organization was needed, one that could bring all elements of black music together.

At La Costa it happened. Berry Gordy, who never went anywhere, came and was the life of the party, telling jokes and speaking stridently about the power of black music. Maurice White and Earth, Wind and Fire; Stevie Wonder; *Soul Train* host and producer Don Cornelius; and Smokey Robinson were other celebrities in attendance. Every significant black executive and entrepreneur was there, and many of the most liberal (or politically astute) whites were, too. The air was ripe with rhetoric, much of it aimed toward the record industry and threatening to whites. Gamble presented a report to the membership titled "The Final Call," after an image from Black Muslim ideology. In it he wrote, "We the BMA have a responsibility to our community. The communities that you and I were born in, the communities that have been the birthplace for black music, the communities that are dying while the record industry flourishes. We no longer have time for mistrust or deceit. We have no time for jealousies or lies. We only have time for the business of survival, because otherwise, we will only have ourselves to blame."

From the beginning, in La Costa, and at the inaugural conference in Philadelphia in 1979, the BMA was burdened with three contradictory dynamics. First, most of the financial support came from record companies, entities any true black-music organization would undoubtedly confront on many issues. Second, though born out of a radio controversy, the BMA's hierarchy was quickly dominated by black record-industry executives (Gamble, ex-Motown president Ewart Abner, CBS's Jim Tyrell), with radio personnel like Wright pushed to the background. Finally, the very existence of the BMA, and its apparent willingness to tackle all black music's ills, raised expectations incredibly high.

To the general public, the BMA began auspiciously on June 7, 1979, hosting a party at the White House for President Jimmy Carter featuring Chuck Berry, Billy Eckstine, Andrae Crouch, and Evelyn King; there was also an impromptu jam with Bob Marley and Stevie Wonder at the Philadelphia conference later in the month. But underneath the cooperative surface, a battle was under way over the association's direction. Would it be a political organization with some of the ambitions of NATRA under Shields and Avante? Or would it be more of an industry-oriented trade organization in the style of the Country Music Association? A tumultuous session on concert promotion—where black promoters openly attacked black artists and white promoters for driving them out of the business—may have settled that question. No one who attended will forget the raw emotion of the meeting, as Smokey Robinson, Stevie Wonder, white promoter Dick Klotzman, and a host of black promoters argued over the needs of the artists, the black promoters, and money.

Few BMA sessions would be as spirited or pointed in distilling the tensions between crossover and the R&B world that were running through the black music community. Cooler heads, such as Abner and LeBaron Taylor, took control, toning down the organization's rhetoric, while Wright and Gamble receded from leadership positions. The next conference in D.C. was quiet and, for most attendees, unsatisfying. The energy of Philly gave way to disappointment.

Black radio, feeling the BMA was not responsive to its needs, threw its support behind J. D. Black's southern-based Young Black Programmers Coalition, a forum for discussing programming. And for social functions like those associated with NATRA, many radio types attended conferences sponsored by Gibson's *Jack the Rapper* and the magazine *Black Radio Exclusive*. "There is a rule of thumb in this business; where the deejays go, everybody must go," one-time BMA executive director George Ware wrote in 1986. "Thus in losing the jocks, BMA began losing the support of everyone, including the record companies." Ware also observed that "the black retail community had always felt left out and its support was moderate to nonexistent. The artists' community has never given organizational support to BMA even though it has supported tributes and concerts." The BMA wasn't dead, but it has remained so preoccupied with internal problems, especially financing and leadership, that it has yet to develop long-term strategies.

Looking back at the 1975–80 period, it is clear that the interconnections between black musicians, independent black (and white) business people, and the black community were being torn by an economic integration built on conglomerate control of black music. For the veterans of R&B, especially those not employed by major labels, it was a sad time, and not just because they had nostalgic feeling for the old days. In 1979, the crash came. The bottom seemed to fall out of the record industry as sales slumped, returns ran rampant, and budget cuts came down with unexpected swiftness.

As CBS executive Vernon Slaughter explains, "This industry had always been known as a growth industry of unlimited potential. It was always a case of, 'This year we'll do better than last year.' In '74, the recession had some effect on the record industry. That's when they first really started saying, 'Well, maybe we're not recession-proof.' But things got better, and it took '78 and bits of '79 before they finally realized that the record industry was subject to shifts in the ages of population and other economic factors just like everybody else. Before that they thought they were immune to it."

LeBaron Taylor's division at CBS was hit hard. Slaughter remembers, "When the first layoffs came in 1979, LeBaron's staff got decimated.

That was really the beginning of the end, because it became a rationalization process. 'Records aren't selling so we don't need the people.' Certain people in the company felt that LeBaron's department was too big. It got to the point that our market share got to be over 25 percent, one in every four records sold at CBS was black music. That's when the real problem started in terms of who was going to control.

"LeBaron Taylor became the target; he was pulling too big a portion of the dollars for people to sit and be content with. That's when the initial chipping away of his authority and of the department started happening, and it's been downhill ever since." Taylor, apparently aware that despite his success he'd go no further in the CBS record division, created a job as a kind of lobbyist and public-affairs executive, coordinating activities reaching out to blacks such as the yearly talent-showcase dinner with the Congressional Black Caucus. With no bitterness but obvious chagrin, Slaughter says, "LeBaron decided to change directions and go into what he's doing now, and it simply left us in the hands of people who really didn't care about the overall direction."

It seems curious that all this happened while CBS Records was in the midst of selling what was then the most popular black album of all time. Michael Jackson met Quincy Jones on the set of the film version of *The Wiz*, and out of that collaboration came *Off the Wall*, a densely arranged celebration of the body's will to move and of Jackson's captivating voice. Jackson proved once and for all he was no longer the kid star of the Jackson Five days. He was a real creative talent who could write, produce, and arrange as well as sing, as in "Don't Stop 'Til You Get Enough." On *Off the Wall* Jones utilized an all-star lineup of musicians and writers who could work in a variety of styles. Both Jackson and Jones were respected before this album, but its fusion of sweet funk grooves with pop melodies and its interpretation of a remarkably wide range of pop styles—from Rod Temperton's midtempo pop, "Rock with Me," to Stevie Wonder's silky ballad, "I Can't Help It," to Jackson's own rhythmically complex "Don't Stop," to Paul McCartney's winsome "Girlfriend"—pegged the duo as pop Renaissance men as comfortable with New York disco as California mellow.

CBS saw the mass appeal of *Off the Wall* and, as they say in the industry, pushed a button on the record. In all, the company released four singles and marketed Jackson to whites with an enthusiasm usually reserved for the likes of Journey, Billy Joel, and Pink Floyd. So a product of R&B and Motown, of Los Angeles glitter and his own childlike innocence, sold 9 million records. *Off the Wall* was a masterpiece, and it was a natural crossover. Yet with a subtlety few noticed at the time, top-forty radio, CBS, and Michael Jackson himself began describing the singer as a "universal" artist, a "pop" performer. That ethnic stuff wasn't necessary and, in the eyes of production directors, promotion executives, and the artist, it was self-defeating. Jackson's sales were so remarkable that he'd never have to cross over again. To those that mattered, Jackson had rediscovered his "honorary pop pass"—originally given to the Jackson Five—and could now go through the checkpoints with ease. It was economic integration. It was the black American dream.

And if the major black stars and their white managers, promoters, and labels truly controlled the music as completely as it seemed, only Jackson-like ambitions should have defined black music for blacks as they entered the 1980s.

Then the strangest thing happened. Out of a black-owned New Jersey label, by way of the South Bronx, Brooklyn, Harlem, and Queens, a record called "Rapper's Delight" by the Sugar Hill Gang came out and climbed up the pop chart in 1979. In Canada, it went top five. In most of Europe it reached the top ten, at least. It sold so many twelve-inchers in the U.S. that in 1980 the National Association of Retail Merchandisers (NARM) named it black single of the year. Over the groove from Chic's "Good Times," three black teens from New Jersey talked rhythmically about "def" cars, "fly guys and fly girls," hanging out at "hotels, motels, and Holiday Inns." What the hell was it? Just some New York crap. A jive-ass novelty record. At least, that was the opinion of the black industry pros on Sunset Boulevard and Sixth Avenue. It just goes to show you that by 1980, being black didn't necessarily mean you knew a damn thing about what was happening in black neighborhoods.

SEVEN

ASSIMILATION

TRIUMPHS,

RETRONUEVO RISES

(1980—87)

ooking at the eighties from a black perspective, two obvious focal points stand out: one, America's total aban-
donment of the civil-rights struggle under President
Ronald Reagan and, two, Jesse Jackson's run for the presidency in 1984.
Reaganomics—more guns, less butter, and the failure to enforce civil-
rights legislation—just stone cold stopped black progress in this country.
For the first time since the New Deal, the government, including Congress and the Supreme Court, didn't support the civil-rights agenda and,
in fact, did much to dismantle the laws on the books and encourage a
resurgence of racism. Jackson's Rainbow Coalition campaign counter-
attacked this reactionary spirit by attempting to increase the number of
black voters and call attention to issues previously ignored in presidential
campaigns, such as U.S. contributions to South African apartheid. Al-
though Jackson failed to build the Rainbow Coalition into a much-
needed third party, abandoning the idea before the 1984 Democratic

convention, this didn't negate the clear accomplishments of his campaign.

Yet it strikes me that the real story of blacks in the eighties is not about a quest for political access. Instead, the community has had to confront deep internal tensions over income disparity and the accountability of leaders to the grass roots. The real issue, in short, has been racial solidarity. The conflict could be seen both on city streets and, most unexpectedly, on the faces of black entertainers. A good example is Washington, a city whose local infrastructure is controlled by blacks. As a result of the fight for integration and the failure of blacks to develop a strategy of self-sufficiency, two distinct communities emerged. In the 1960s, Marion Barry was considered the city's most dangerous activist, as he often stormed city-council meetings in a dashiki and shades. In the 1980s, he became mayor, and his biggest challenge was not battling whites for political power—he was firmly entrenched—but developing programs to use his power most effectively. A mid-decade survey showed more blacks in D.C. were in high-income groups and fewer in poverty than in a half-dozen cities of comparable size. Howard University, always a force in the city's life, would by 1985 spend $300 million a year in the city and employ eight thousand. In 1986, its radio station, WHUR, made history by being the first broadcast outlet owned by a black university to be number one in its market.

All of which was fine, except for the nasty flip side to D.C. In 1985, one of every two black households was headed by a female, most of them teenagers; twenty-five years earlier the ratio was only one in every five. And, according to government statistics, one third of all black children in D.C. lived in poverty. The commercial strips on H and U streets, not far from the site of the abandoned Howard Theater, had been decimated by riots in 1968 and remained barren. On a boulevard that once supported innumerable black mom-and-pop stores, young blacks sold crack and angel dust, profiting by the sickness they inflicted on their "brothers and sisters."

"Black Washington has fractured into haves and the have-nots; or perhaps a split more ominous," wrote black Washingtonian Eugene Robinson. "The already-haves and the never-will-haves." Even WHUR's victory was short-lived. NBC-owned WKYS hired away "Quiet Storm" deejay Melvin Lindsay and, under the direction of black programmer Donnie Simpson, put together a massive promotional campaign. Within months of WHUR's triumph, WKYS was on top and looked like a sure bet to stay for a while. Just as telling, even while

WHUR was on top, it still billed five to six times less in advertising dollars than its NBC rival. So even when WHUR had the ratings, it lost out in the war to woo Madison Avenue.

A similar picture could be painted of all the nation's major cities: while differences between middle-class and poor blacks grew, white entertainment outlets consistently defeated black institutions for the loyalty of black audiences.

Another sign of the times was that many children of the middle class, raised in suburbia or neighborhoods removed from poor and working-class blacks, had little sense of their racial identity or why the struggles of less fortunate blacks should command their attention. Harvard University admissions officer David Evans told *Essence* magazine that he found black students "lacking an emphatic insight into what's happening to 70 to 80 percent of black people in this country. . . . In order to feel any kind of urgency one must be reasonably close to the problem. But if one has grown up in suburbia and vacationed in Europe, the infant mortality, illiteracy, teen pregnancy, or the grossly disproportionate imprisonment of black males doesn't disturb that kid." When Du Bois talked of a "talented tenth," these were the young people he meant, yet there is no doubt in my mind that advocacy of race consciousness would have seemed irrelevant, passé, or plain boring to a great many of these black best-and-brightest. In their eyes, darkness was apparently not a virtue. Bryant Gumbel, the popular black host of *The Today Show*, knew what time it was. He told a reporter from *New York* in 1986: "I have become colorless. I have clear speech and non-ethnic characteristics."

Sometimes it seems really funny, but it's also quite sad that in surveying black America through its music in the eighties, much of the discussion revolves not around music but skin color, cosmetic surgery, and the rejection of Negroid features. Case in point: Compare current photographs of George Benson with pictures from early in his career. You will be confronted with facial alterations that have nothing to do with age. Surgery has reshaped him into a commercial product for mass consumption. It's as simple and, I think, as frightening as that. Change your face to sell a hundred thousand more units, to do the movies, to make more money. Stop looking like your mother and father, in the name of commerce. Maybe, like Whoopi Goldberg, Oprah Winfrey, and the otherwise sweet Janet Jackson, wear blue or green contact lenses. After all, it might help you achieve that most tempting symbol of eighties assimilation: an MTV video.

The two greatest black stars of the decade, Michael Jackson and Prince, ran fast and far both from blackness and conventional images of male sexuality (and their videos got on MTV). Michael Jackson's nose job, often ill-conceived makeup, and artificially curled hair is, in the eyes of many blacks, a denial of his color that constitutes an act of racial treason. Add to that a disquieting androgyny and you have an alarmingly unblack, unmasculine figure as the most popular black man in America.

Prince is similarly troublesome. Where Jackson's androgyny was like that of an innocently unaware baby, Prince preached sex as salvation in explicit and often clumsy terms. "Head" (oral sex), "When You Were Mine" (sexual ambiguity), and "1999" (sex as resignation in the face of nuclear war) were just a few of the songs in which Prince expressed his funky yet fanciful fascination with physical engagement. Onstage, he went from wearing black bikini, g-strings, and leg warmers to taking seductive pseudobaths and dry-humping his piano, all with a wink and shimmy that suggested his lover could be of any sexual persuasion. No black performer since Little Richard had toyed with the heterosexual sensibilities of black America so brazenly.

Prince's more irksome trait was that, like Jackson, he aided those who saw blackness as a hindrance in the commercial marketplace by running from it. Unlike the many black stars who altered their face to please "the mass market," Prince didn't have to; his features suggested he was a product of the interracial marriages so popular in Minneapolis. But he really wasn't. Both his parents were black. Yet in the quasi-autobiographical film *Purple Rain*, Prince presented his mother as white, a "crossover" marketing strategy as unnecessary as Jackson's tiresome claims to "universality." In fact, it can be argued that Prince's consistent use of mulatto and white leading ladies convinced many black male (and some female) artists to use romantic interests of similar shading in their videos, hoping to emulate Prince's success. The resulting videos seem to reinforce the stereotypic idea that dark-skinned black women are not as attractive as their lighter sisters. As icons of style, Jackson and Prince were assimilation symbols as powerful as Bill Cosby. But, thankfully, there was more to them than image. There was music, but we'll deal with that a bit later. . . .

On November 18, 1982, I wrote a story for the front page of *Billboard*, "Times Tough for Black Retailers," that revealed the social schism found between the assimilated and unassimilated in the R&B world and in the larger black society. "Black-oriented mom-and-pop retailers are going out of business in increasing numbers, and are not being replaced by new enterprises. At the same time, black music is holding its own in the depressed sales environment and is generating a slew of popular new performers. This dichotomy emerges from a *Billboard* survey of black retailers, label executives, and other industryites. As reasons for the problems of the small operator, they cite unemployment, poor management, locations in declining inner-city neighborhoods, and competition from stores in active city centers. General market retail chains are said to be increasing their awareness and sales of black music.

"Says Skippy White, owner of two Boston outlets specializing in black music, 'Around 1978 and 1979, I had a one-stop operation with about 60 solid clients. Now I don't do one-stopping anymore, and if I did, we'd be lucky to have twelve accounts. And some of the remaining twelve would be shaky.' Comments Ted Hudson, owner of Ted's One Stop in St. Louis. 'Here I'd say that 70 percent of the mom-and-pop stores have closed. There are only five guys making good money, and a couple of those have added video games to keep it going.' Similar tales of woe can be heard in Philadelphia, Detroit, New York, and the nation's other largest markets.

" 'Even in the days of the industry's greatest growth, black retailers had a hard time staying afloat,' says Hank Cauldwell, a marketing vice president at WEA. 'So in a day that everyone is struggling, it is no surprise that so many are failing.' While there are no hard figures available on the number of recently shuttered black-oriented retailers, conversations with surviving mom-and-pop operators suggest that those that fail are not being replaced. 'It used to be that for every eight stores that went out of business, maybe five might come in,' declares Bruce Webb, owner of Webb's Department Store in Philadelphia. 'People these days don't want to take that chance anymore.' "

COUNTING THE LOSSES

Despite these deaths in the rhythm & blues family, the music continued on as a number of artists, including Luther Vandross, the Time, Vanity, Jeffrey Osborne, and Lionel Richie, developed acts and put out albums without the aid of black retailers. Many undoubtedly assumed that the death of these stores would have minimal impact on how the industry did business. Cauldwell, a supporter of mom-and-pop stores, couldn't help but reflect this view as a label executive. He told *Billboard*, "I've found awareness among chain stores that black music is growing. They are more willing to get involved in promotions with black acts, to do in-store, have acts visit, etc." And for the majors, it was the big chains that really counted.

Elliot Lee, associate editor of *Black Enterprise*, was less than encouraging when asked by *Billboard* about the state of black mom-and-pop stores nationally. Lee said, "The black consumer market is being exploited more successfully by white businesses than ever before, and unless black businessmen are prepared to compete, they'll lose out. With government so deeply in debt, they are competing with other small businesses in the credit market, a market that had never been receptive to helping black businesses in the first place. Many of the loans that black businesses received in the past were due to government guarantees, and now Reagan is planning to cut back those programs. Another problem is the cost of doing business in the inner city. Insurance, security, and the cost of crime all raise prices, putting black businesses in a less competitive position vis-à-vis whites."

Lee held out a little hope. "More and more black businesses are in 'crossover' areas where they can attract both white and black customers." More black retailers, in his view, needed to shift to these potentially lucrative areas. A select few black retailers were following the editor's advice, but the same lack of capital that stifled them in their own neighborhoods made such a radical and risky gambit impractical. By the middle of the decade, the black mom-and-pop store, inspiration for record labels, entry point for talent, and center for musical education, seemed destined—like neighborhood movie theaters, the soda fountain, and a slew of other wonderful institutions—to be buried alive by a business that found them expendable.

Though not as burdened with the structural liabilities of black retailers, blacks in management, booking, and concert promotion were also just hanging on. Ruth Bowen's Queen Booking was a memory. She still was working with a few of her long-term clients, including Aretha Franklin, but in the battle for new talent, Bowen was now not a factor. After Don Robey's death, Evelyn Johnson had pretty much confined her activities to Houston, making Buffalo Booking a piece of history. Norby Walters, who for most of his career booking entertainers in cocktail lounges used disco to cross over to black music, stepped in to take the place of these black-owned institutions. In the seventies, Walters saw most of the lounges converting to discos and realized that most disco acts existed in name only. Using his contacts, Walters created "instant" acts to perform these dance-floor hits live. By the mid-eighties, he was booking

Rick James, Cameo, the Bar-Kays, Stephanie Mills, Skyy, and almost every other significant middle-level black act. In the vacuum left during the transition in black music from R&B to disco to crossover, Walters had seen an opportunity and taken advantage of it.

Walters, however, did not have most of the biggest crossover stars. This was not because he ran a bad company but because his intimate association with what passed for the eighties chitlin circuit made him something of a white Negro—a role Walters relished except when it barred him from business, which it definitely did. In late 1987 Walters changed the name of his company and added new staff members as he attempted to entice more "pop" clients.

The many black attorneys, MBAs, and industryites to flow from American colleges in the seventies and eighties could sympathize with Walters. Even being black was no help in getting a crack at winning crossover stars as clients. A typically upbeat *Ebony* story in 1984, titled, "Black Stars with Black Managers," inadvertently undercut its premise—black star entertainers and athletes were "keeping it all in the family." Aside from Sammy Davis, Jr., Nancy Wilson, and Stephanie Mills, *Ebony* could cite no other black household names with black management. Stevie Wonder basically managed himself. But Michael Jackson, Lionel Richie, Prince, Luther Vandross, the Pointer Sisters, Earth, Wind and Fire, Ray Parker, Jr., and Donna Summer all relied on white figures for guidance. I don't cite this to imply that these performers were obligated to have black management, accountants, or attorneys. But it does illustrate how little interaction there is between the crossover stars and the black business class, groups that are both products of integration.

The Commodores' black manager, Benny Ashburn—"the sixth Commodore"—who died of a heart attack in 1982, was one of the few black managers to build and hold on to a mainstream rhythm & blues group capable of million-selling albums. It was not unexpected that after Ashburn's death, Richie split from the Commodores and signed with Kenny Rogers's manager, Ken Kragen. But it was surely disheartening to those who hoped he'd give a brother or sister a shot at managing one of the industry's most promising careers.

Richie went for a manager who had turned a country singer, for a time, into America's most popular male vocalist. Richie wanted the same thing, and Kragen, if not for the incredible ascendence of Michael Jackson into pop heaven, would have accomplished it. However, Richie's acceptance by Middle America didn't mean he had escaped the turmoil of the rhythm & blues world. Richie, like Jackson, Prince, and other crossover stars, was a target of verbal abuse and boycott threats from black concert promoters, as the bitterness revealed at the 1979 BMA conference continued into the next decade.

In the early eighties, Anheuser Busch began a black concert series, the Budweiser Superfest, that packed concert halls and football stadiums. The beer company footed all the bills for these multiact affairs and guaranteed the performers' pay, so they got top dollar for relatively little work. They made gravy. A very competent white promoter named Michael Rosenberg had helped develop the Superfest concept and was its inaugural promoter. He did a good job, too.

But a group of black promoters, united under the banner of the National Association of Black Promoters, felt their track records had earned them the right to control the Superfest. At first, Rosenberg seemed to have it locked up indefinitely. In 1982, the group was offered what it characterized as "a sharecropping arrangement which would result in our surrendering all major decisions and development of the contracts to a primarily white promotions agency [Rosenberg], while blacks took on the essentially subordinate tasks, did the leg work, and received an inconsequential amount of money."

Enter Jesse Jackson. As part of his Economic Justice Movement, Jackson, by now the most visible if not the most effective black leader in America, had asked black Americans to boycott Anheuser Busch products in protest against their hiring practices. The promoters issued a statement: "Since our rejection and humiliation, Operation PUSH and the Economic Justice Movement have made us aware of other inequitable practices that A-B has unfairly forced on the black community."

The NABP then went on to state the specifics of their case: "For example, black promoters provide work for black caterers, limousine services, sound and electrical contractors, carpenters, plumbers, and many other service companies. White promoters tend to give these jobs to other whites. When A-B denies us the opportunity to promote its concerts, it further pauperizes a community that represents a very substantial proportion of the audiences and nearly 90 percent of the artists who make its Bud Fests successful."

Two years after that statement, or just about the time Jackson was scaring America with his first run for the Democratic presidential nomination, the black promoters won. Al Haymon, the most polished of the black promoters, was running the Budweiser Superfest and parceling out pieces of the pie to his peers. While this victory wasn't enough to ensure the economic well-being of black promoters, it did set a lucrative precedent.

The black promoters were a maverick bunch who, in demanding that black performers remember (and reimburse) those who have helped them up the ladder, were tapping into black consciences with the anachronistic "buy black" slogan. Their attack on Anheuser Busch was nothing but "mau-mauing the flak catchers," as Tom Wolfe once described it. How long these strategies of finger-pointing would work in the face of economic integration is hard to say, but one couldn't chide the black promoters for having no sense of history.

MOTOWN GIVES IN

In the eighties it took a sense of history to remember the days when rhythm & blues, jazz, and gospel were all primarily disseminated through independently owned and distributed labels, because that wasn't the case anymore. It was made clear in 1982 when Motown signed with MCA for national distribution, ending an era in black music and in the industry. Berry Gordy's privately held company had prided itself on its production-line hits and its status as the last major independent label. From the sixties through the seventies, as corporate America realized the pop impact of black music—a lesson the "Sound of Young America" taught—Motown was a jewel they all sought for their crowns. When Gordy declined bids for the Jobete catalogue, they seduced his writers and producers. Even after the escape of Diana Ross to RCA and Marvin Gaye to CBS in the early eighties, Gordy held his ground. What may have finally pushed him over the edge was the growing instability of independent distributors. Between the ongoing loss of major accounts to the corporate labels and the recession of the early eighties, many distributors had filed for bankruptcy or shifted operations to other areas.

So Motown got in bed with MCA, a company going through a period of intense expansion, and for the first time corporate America was getting a slice of Motown's profits. That was the way of the world. No significant black-owned record company or white label with significant black acts had risen and stayed important without corporate assistance since Philadelphia International established the pattern in 1971. Solar Records, headed by manager-promoter Dick Griffey with the inspiration of producer Leon Sylvers, had hits with the Whispers, Shalamar, Dynasty, as well as Lakeside through a distribution deal with RCA. Later Griffey, who called black music as important to blacks as "oil is to Arabs," split his roster in half, signing the bigger acts to Elektra and developing performers to MCA. In 1987 he got into a nasty dispute with Elektra over loans used to build Solar offices in Hollywood. Via a deal with Capitol, Griffey remained a black music force, though he spent much of his time working with Jesse Jackson and on other political projects. Lonnie Simmons, an aggressive Los Angeles businessman who moved from small operations (a clothing store and nightclub) to owning a recording studio and finally a record company—all named Total Experience—coproduced albums by the Gap Band and Yarborough & Peoples for Polygram and later RCA. This was the age of "ring around the record company," as declared by that sage, George Clinton.

Alas, Philadelphia International Records, which had legitimized the game, suffered in this environment. At CBS, they were no longer the top priority. With Earth, Wind and Fire, the Isley Brothers, Michael Jackson, and others signed directly to CBS's Columbia and Epic labels and depositing all their income directly into corporate coffers, they became the top priorities. The same blues that Bobby Womack cried in the seventies, PIR sang in the eighties. But there were other roadblocks to PIR's continued vitality. One was the tension between Gamble and Huff. Despite their long relationship, the pair had never been close, and success, instead of bringing them together, exacerbated their differences. They stopped working together and for a time, according to PIR staffers, even stopped talking to each other. It wasn't an atmosphere conducive to creativity. MFSB's original members split from PIR over money. So did most of the company's staff producers and many of its acts. Thom Bell, for a time, had moved to Seattle for health reasons. Symbolic of the changing atmosphere in Philadelphia, and the use of black talent to satisfy corporate needs, was that the best Philly sound album released between 1980 and 1985 was *My Melody*, produced by Bell with the angel-voiced Columbia Records signee Deniece Williams. In 1988 Gamble and Huff decided to go back to independent distribution under the banner "Gamble and Huff Records." Their first twelve-inch single was, appropriately, "Run Jesse Run," a tribute to Reverend Jackson sung by Lou Rawls, Phyllis Hyman, and Reverend James Cleveland.

Another aspect of PIR's decline was its inability or unwillingness to adjust to a profound change in black popular music. For all Gamble and Huff's influence on dance music, the pair always considered themselves songwriters first and foremost. But in the eighties, songwriting went right down the toilet as the balance between riff and melody went awry. Fewer and fewer songs seemed written from an adult point of view. You might call it "Chuck Berry's revenge" as black music became as juvenile in attitude as much of rock & roll. One didn't hear a story in sync with a groove but marvelously well-produced records with some words thrown on top. As that esteemed music critic Prince told *Rolling Stone*, "Today people don't write songs, they're a lot of sounds, a lot of repetition. That happened when producers took over." Synthesizers of every description, drum machines, and plain old electric keyboards began making MFSB and other human rhythm sections nonessential to the recording process. For producers, a control-oriented bunch, this was heaven. No more rehearsals. Low session fees. An artist who envisioned himself as a future Stevie Wonder—the first great one-man synthesizer band—could express his creativity in the basement or the bathroom.

But this influx of technology didn't make the music any better. No indeed. For every song that merged keyboard-laden production with words of lyrical and melodic interest, such as "Love Come Down," sung by Evelyn King and produced by Kashif, Paul Laurence Jones, and Morrie Brown, or "You're the One for Me," sung by James (D. Train) Williams and produced by Williams and Hubert Eaves, there were so many others with all the personality and warmth of a microwave. The songwriter-producers who appeared during this time inherited the crown of Jesse Stone, Smokey Robinson, Isaac Hayes, and David Porter. Did they embellish it? No, they dropped it, and danced around the broken pieces.

This situation played a role in the growing difficulty black artists found reaching the pop charts. Musically the songs weren't as good as in the sixties or early seventies. As dance records, the grooves were still inventive, but they were hampered by a disco backlash at pop radio. As a cultural force, the term "disco" went out as quickly as it had come in. Unfortunately, all black dance music was for a time labeled "disco." It was stupid. It was racist. It revealed again how powerful a force semantics can be in the reception of pop music. Just as rock & roll came to mean white music, disco came to represent some ugly amalgam of black and gay music. The Bee Gees went straight down the tubes because of such labeling. They were, after all, disco's biggest white group.

As for the decline in black crossover, you can look it up. Of the fourteen records to reach number one on the black chart in 1983, only one reached the pop top-ten, "She Works Hard for the Money" by Donna Summer, the only disco-bred artist to escape the genre's career-deflating stigma. In contrast, some of that year's great number one black singles—Mtume's sensual "Juicy Fruit," the hard-core funk of Rick James's "Cold-Blooded" and George Clinton's "Atomic Dog," the melodic and danceable "Candy Girl" by New Edition, the soulful boogie songs "Get It Right" by Aretha Franklin and "Save the Overtime for Me" by Gladys Knight and the Pips—only went to number forty or lower on the pop chart. That of course was the same year that Michael Jackson's *Thriller* sold 20 million copies in the U.S. and Lionel Richie's singles "All Night Long" and "Can't Slow Down" sold over 10 million, only confirming the feast-or-famine cycle in popular music. A black who crossed over could sell a humongous number of records. And the fact that so few succeeded didn't stifle the dream.

For many black entertainers, chasing that dream was a fixation, and one that could destroy a career. Peabo Bryson, a smooth, soulful vocalist and distinctive, if limited, songwriter, began his career in the early seventies as a songwriter-vocalist with a number of bands on independent labels. In 1977, he signed with Capitol and immediately became one of the best-loved singers in black America. Deep in the heart of disco he recorded ballads like "Reaching for the Sky," "I'm So Into You," and one of the rare soul classics to be written and recorded in the 1975–85 period, "Feel the Fire." With its devotional lyrics, dramatic piano chords, and wonderful arrangement by coproducer Johnny Pate, a former Curtis Mayfield collaborator, "Feel the Fire" was one of the most respected and covered R&B compositions of the period.

From 1977 to 1983, every new album released by Bryson sold at least half a million copies, and he became a major concert attraction. However, in the age of crossover, Bryson wanted what Lionel Richie and Michael Jackson had, a white audience, and he attempted to get it. A duet with Roberta Flack on the Barry Manilow-like ballad "Tonight I Celebrate My Love" in 1984 gave him his first taste of pop success. In 1985, he jumped to Elektra and had another top-ten hit with "Whenever You're in My Arms Again," another mushy mainstream ballad. Bryson did not see the drop-off in his album sales during this transition as a bad omen. Sure that a pop audience awaited him, Bryson changed his image: gone were the white suits and modest Afro of his Capitol years. He draped himself in ultratrendy English threads and had his low Afro styled into a "fade" cut, high on top, low on the sides. His Elektra debut was synthesized, uptempo, and contemporary, and it was received with all the enthusiasm of a broken computer chip. His old audience hated it, and without a breakthrough single, whites paid no attention. It was clear that the whites who had bought his hit singles had liked the record but didn't know who Bryson, the artist, was. As a result, this album sold a meager 200,000 copies and his concert bookings dwindled. Peabo Bryson, once a staple of what was left of the old R&B world, had tried to leap the barrier and stumbled. It remains to be seen whether he can pick himself back up.

RADIO DAZE

Clearly, one of the consequences of crossover was that if you altered your style but failed to broaden your audience—and most did—you ran the risk of alienating your core audience and never getting it back. On black radio, crossover, even when "successful," often backfired. Urban radio (classic crossover) had been a qualified success. Though its programmers complained that the radio ratings services didn't effectively monitor black listening habits, urban stations throughout the eighties ranked at or near the top in most major markets. The ideas Frankie Crocker popularized at WBLS worked. But now black-owned and black-oriented stations were no longer the only ones who knew it. In New York in 1977, out of nowhere, "Disco 92" WKTU, owned by a company in San Juan, Puerto Rico, exploded onto the airwaves. At its peak, WKTU registered an amazing 14 percent share in New York. Within five months, Crocker and WBLS had overtaken them. But WBLS's monopoly position in the city was history. In August 1981, a more substantial challenge was mounted by RKO's WRKS, aka KISS. Programmed by Barry Mayo, a graduate of Howard University's School of Communications, and backed by a substantial promotional budget, KISS would become the dominant station in New York's five boroughs. By 1985, its position was so solid that Mayo, a New York native, was made the first black general manager in the history of the RKO radio chain. In Cleveland, Philadelphia, Chicago, San Francisco, and Boston, as we saw earlier, the battle between the traditional black-urban stations of the seventies and the new urbans with the KISS name was won in advertising—no matter what the ratings—by the corporate-owned interlopers.

In addition, CHR (contemporary hit radio) (in reality old top-forty in disguise) rose up by aggressively playing black hits mixed with white mainstream artists. These stations, again white-owned with high-powered promotional budgets, gave black stations fits. For example, the competition was intense between Dallas's KVIL, a white adult contemporary station, and the urban contemporary K104. In 1985 they were considered two of the top stations in the country. In the summer 1985 Arbitron book, K104, after years of chasing, pushed KVIL out of the top spot in the Dallas-Ft. Worth listening area. Yet, Dan Flamberg of the Radio Advertising Bureau estimated that in 1986 KVIL's billings were $22 million, while K104's were only $8.5 million. As Flamberg told the *Dallas Times Herald*, "You get the picture. Major national advertisers—and some large regional advertisers—still have a problem believing [urban contemporary] listeners are worth reaching: that everyone tuning in is not an unemployed youth with a boom-box down on the corner rolling dice."

Losing their audience and discriminated against by advertisers, many in black radio called for a reevaluation of the urban philosophy. Just holding on to black listeners was now a struggle. In the February 5, 1986, edition of *Jack the Rapper*, Jack Gibson, in a voice as colorful and old-fashioned as the rhythm & blues world that spawned him, published this open letter:

Come back HOME where you BELONG and quit tryin' to BE somethang that you'll NEVER be, leave that urban contemporary or what-ever you wanna call it ALONE. THE RAPPER is comin' at you ONE on ONE, behind this LAST book (that so many of you LIVE and DIE by) showed BLACK RADIO took an ass kickin' and when you boil it down, the REASON is so MANY of you are TRYIN' to go ofay or pop on us. Figurin' the MORE pop or ofay records you PLAY daily will 'cause YOUR ofay or pop LISTENERS to INCREASE. This is FURTHEREST from the TRUTH as could be. BLACK RADIO, who has SOLD you THAT bill of goods? "If you PLAY pop music, white folks will flock to YOUR station," TORO POO POO, the logic ISN'T even there. WHY would ofay listeners come OVER to BLACK RADIO to HEAR a FEW pop records you PLAY when they GOT their own pop stations that CAN and DO play MORE of their kinda MUSIC then you'll EVER be able to, if you STAYED on the AIR 28 hours a day! You CAN'T be white, so COME on home, BACK where you BELONG and START playin' what you KNOW best—GOOD BLACK MUSIC. Nobody can BEAT you at this, but ONCE you step out your CLASS and TRY bein' SOMEBODY else, THEY got'cha. Don't you see you are PLAYIN' right into THEIR hands and IF you think THE RAPPER is jivin' just CHECK your bible of ratings "THE BOOK" this past FALL that's

just out and you'll SEE you are SLIPPIN', SLIPPIN' Oh! a few
BLACK stations are HOLDIN' their own, but that's to BE expected,
but on the WHOLE, a lotta of you are BITIN' the bullet. You all
are LOSIN' out to ofay stations in YOUR markets, just cause you
AIN'T playin' what you SHOULD be PLAYIN' and that's GOOD
BLACK MUSIC, it's as SIMPLE as that! Funny thang, ofay radio is
playin' MORE and MORE BLACK records, while you all are TRYIN'
to find MORE and MORE ofay records to shove down the EARS
of loyal BLACK listeners. Dig this and this is the truth, RUTH . . .
A BROTHER PD asked his BROTHER MD "to GO and FIND some
MORE ofay records for THEIR station to PLAY cause they DIDN'T
have ENUFF on their play list." Now ain't that a bitch. "Knee-
grows" TRYIN' to BE ofay and ofays TRYIN' to be (but ONLY to a
CERTAIN point!) "knee-grows." THE RAPPER IS STILL laffin'
'cause we KNOW the way they SWING thangs, they'll wind-up
BEIN' better BLACKS than MOST of us! Even if there is a good
BLACK record that is a bit POLITICAL, you'll AVOID that, too!
What are you TRYIN' to prove? From where we sit, NOTHIN'! Keep
on TORO POO POOIN' and you WON'T have any BLACK RADIO
to PLAY any BLACK MUSIC. So THE RAPPER sezs to you our
BLACK RADIO stations, COME ON BACK HOME WHERE YOU
BELONG and STOP all this nonsense TRYIN' be to somethang that
you'll NEVER be. COME ON BACK HOME and PLAY GOOD
BLACK MUSIC AGAIN, and watch those RATINGS go back UP.
Isn't THAT what'cha want? Don't desert your BLACK listener and
your BLACK communities, 'member they NEED YOU and YOU
NEED them. Take this OPEN LETTER in the GOOD intentions it is
written. THE RAPPER ain't got NO *hang-ups* 'bout this EXCEPT we
want you all BACK HOME doin' what you all DO so well—PLAY
GOOD BLACK MUSIC. It's as SIMPLE as that! You won't GO wrong
IF you DO, in fact THE RAPPER will expect a THANK YOU for
pullin' your coat—BLACK MUSIC is WHERE it's at—so what'cha
you all WAITIN' for? It's UP to you WHITHER you SINK or SWIM!!!

With his "black is beautiful" stance and uncompromising language,
Jack Gibson, some forty years after his radio debut, had become a genuine radical. That is quite a long trip, considering his adversary relationship with the "new breed" that took over NATRA in the sixties. Yet
in the eighties Gibson's stance irritated many in what he called "the
leisure-time world" (while winning a lot of support too) as he opposed

the imposition of the crossover philosophy on all elements of the R&B community. His broadsides against black programmers, the "We Are the World" record ("Why no charity record for America?" he argued), and the artists who played South Africa's Sun City resort were always hard and unremitting, while his pleas for young blacks to respect the blues, pure R&B, and the deejays of his generation were quite touching.

RETRONUEVO

It was in listening to Gibson and studying the history of rhythm & blues that I came to admire those in the eighties who have been able to break away from, ignore, or battle the crossover consciousness and remain true to the strength of R&B, while not conceding that that approach left them unacceptable to white America. Inspired by that attitude and the music it produced, I created in 1986 the term "retronuevo," which can be defined as an embrace of the past to create passionate, fresh expressions and institutions. It doesn't refer just to music. The willingness of broadcaster Percy Sutton to revive the Apollo Theater in New York and of black haircare kingpin Robert Gardner to do the same in Chicago for the Regal Theater showed that some black businesspeople possessed the heart and moxie to understand how much symbolic importance and economic potential these once grand R&B showcases hold for now downtrodden inner city neighborhoods. With *She's Gotta Have It* and *Hollywood Shuffle*, Spike Lee and Robert Townsend used hustle and comedy to create non-Hollywood, profoundly black films that partially realized the ambitious dreams of Booker T. Washington in the 1920s and Melvin Van Peebles in the 1970s.

But mostly retronuevo means black music that appreciates its heritage. Until the eighties, R&B never emphasized looking back—one reason for its ongoing creativity, as I've said in earlier chapters. But as too much of the music became as enticing as a ripped diaphragm and not nearly as dangerous, artists emerged to bring back some of the soul and subtlety its audience deserves.

Maze, featuring Frankie Beverly, had been retronuevo from record one. From 1977 to 1985, this Bay Area band released five albums on Capitol, each selling half a million but never breaking the million mark. Many a black artist would have been frustrated by this inability to crack the magical million mark, and Beverly often complained about Capitol's inability to cross him over. But, crucially, Beverly wasn't willing to sell his soul to crossover. He just continued with an idiosyncratic sound that balanced the street feel of his native Philadelphia with the relaxed mood of his Bay Area home. He'd been signed by Larkin Arnold after touring as an opening act for Marvin Gaye. Arnold was a black attorney who'd been brought in to mastermind the expansion of Capitol's black music. Coming on the heels of the jazzy Earth, Wind and Fire and the raunchy Parliament-Funkadelic, Beverly's Maze established itself as a less frantic, less abrasive alternative. Moreover, Maze had the kind of cross-generational appeal that eluded most other young black acts of the time. The 1981 *Live in New Orleans* double album was classic Beverly, with all but one of the twelve songs featuring slow to medium tempos with arrangements rich in glowing electric pianos, humming organs, and tasteful synthesizer figures. The rhythm section—drummer Billy Johnson, bassist Robin Duhe, and percussionists McKinnley William and Roame Lowery—interlocked as smoothly as the keyboards, never pushing the beat, a discipline vital to the aura of Beverly's soothing compositions.

With these sultry grooves as the frame, Beverly paints his wholesome pictures on top with voice and pen. In his phrasing, I hear echoes of his benefactor, Marvin Gaye, and his idol, Sam Cooke. But Beverly's voice has an understated, more working-class quality that differentiates him from those love men. Instead, he sounds like a dedicated husband still madly in love with his wife after all these years. His love songs exist in a world where one-night stands are spurned and real affection is sought, appreciated, returned.

Beverly also has a real gift for nonspecific protest songs in the tradition of the Isley Brothers' "Fight the Power"—songs that refer to the troubles of black America without the nuts-and-bolts rhetoric of an overtly political songwriter like Gil Scott-Heron. In addition to "We Need to Live," a tribute to Atlanta's murdered children, *Live* includes two inspirational numbers with the upbeat sixties flavor of Mayfield's "People Get Ready" and Cooke's eloquent "A Change Is Gonna Come." "Changing Times" assures us, "We'll get through these changing times," while "Running Away" preaches, like Booker T. Washington, that "the things you want are the things you have to earn."

Just as Beverly grew stronger by swimming against the tide, so did the radio format originated by WHUR in 1976 called "the Quiet Storm." Ten years later, stations in every major market and in many of the secondary markets made three- to five-hour blocks of mellow music a crucial part of their programming day. Some stations, like Los Angeles' KUTE, went totally Quiet Storm, while others utilized the format, if not the title, from late evening into the morning. The program gave new life to the title of one of Smokey Robinson's last great compositions and proved a comfortable home, not just for Beverly, but for singers more interested in ballads than boogie. My favorite example is the woman who originally inspired the retronuevo idea: Anita Baker.

Baker's brilliant *Rapture* album, one of the surprise hits of 1986, was an album of contemporary intelligence and old-fashioned pipes. The intelligence was primarily Baker's. As executive producer, Baker made an eight-cut album with no uptempo songs, a complete reversal of the norm for black female vocalists in the post-disco era. In making that decision she displayed an understanding of her voice as instrument and demonstrated why more women should demand control of their recordings. The pipes were Baker's, too. Wrapping her voice in supportive arrangements and using real live bass players and drummers, Baker shone with the maturity of a Dinah Washington. It is unashamedly adult music that, as did her 1982 Beverly Glen hit "Angel," sounds progressive despite its old-fashioned values.

Baker's impact was profound because it exposed how superficially so many vocal divas had pursued their crossover dreams, diluting the power of their voices in the process, and because in *Rapture*'s wake the industry allowed some of its most gifted young voices (Miki Howard, Regina Belle) to record with a minimum of production overkill.

Yes, Baker made music for assimilated black Americans, though unlike that of crossover artists, her work tapped into the traditions of jazz and blues with a feeling that suggested being middle class didn't make your taste the musical equivalent of a Big Mac. Where Baker, a homegirl from Detroit's rich musical tradition, represents one aspect of retronuevo, from New York came a frenzied, always funky updating of Louis Jordan, Sly Stone, and James Brown that will be remembered as the dominant R&B music of the eighties.

RHYTHM METHODS

In retrospect, rap or something like it should have been predicted. Each decade since World War II has seen the emergence of some new approach to black dance music. The 1940s brought forth rhythm & blues, the 1950s rock & roll, the 1960s soul, the 1970s funk and disco. Something was due in the 1980s, though the contemporary taste-makers of

R&B conspired to hold off the inevitable. The black A&R men of the major-label era sought new music from an established pool of writers and managers. The bulk of new signees came through these channels, and this incestuous cross-pollination stifled innovation. The New York–based talent scouts were so office-bound, taking meetings with managers and listening to tapes from song publishers, that they failed to venture up the road to Harlem and the South Bronx where, in the middle of the nation's most depressing urban rot, something wonderful was happening. Because the big boys were asleep at the wheel, rap would spend most of its young life promoted and recorded by independent labels run by hustling entrepreneurs. As music and as business, the rap/hip-hop scene was retronuevo because it was a small mirror image of the pre-crossover R&B world.

Rap started in discos, not the midtown glitter palaces like Studio 54 or New York, New York, but at Mel Quinns's on 42nd Street and Club 371 in the Bronx, where a young Harlemite who called himself D. J. Hollywood spun on the weekends. It wasn't unusual for black club jocks to talk to their audiences in the jive style of the old personality deejays. Two of the top black club spinners of the day, Pete (D. J.) Jones and Maboya, did so. Hollywood, just an adolescent when he started, created a more complicated, faster style, with more rhymes than his older mentors and call-and-response passages to encourage reaction from the dancers. At local bars, discos, and many illegal after-hours spots frequented by street people Hollywood developed a huge word-of-mouth reputation. Tapes of his parties began appearing around the city on the then new and incredibly loud Japanese portable cassette players flooding into America. In Harlem, Kurtis Blow, Eddie Cheeba, and D. J. Lovebug Star-ski; in the Bronx, Junebug Star-ski, Grandmaster Flash, and Melle Mel; in Brooklyn, three kids from the projects called Whodini, and in Queens, Russell and Joey, the two youngest sons from the middle-class Simmons household—all shared a fascination with Hollywood's use of the rhythmic breaks in his club mixes and his verbal dexterity. These kids would all grow up to play a role in the local clubs and, later, a few would appear on the national scene to spread Hollywood's style. Back in the 1970s, while disco reigned in the media, the Black Main Streets of New York were listening to D. J. Hollywood, and learning.

If innovation equaled success, Hollywood would have gone on to some kind of stardom, but usually life is a series of unnecessary hassles. So Hollywood, ignored by more established music-industry figures, black and white, got hooked up with a series of ineffective managers and saw his career recede into legend while those inspired by him, in uptown parlance, "got paid."

Initially, it was older black music vets, still in touch with the streets, who put rap on record. The always musically aware Bobby Robinson, on Enjoy, and fellow doo-wop-era survivor Paul Winley, with Winley and Sound of New York, were the first to record such uptown favorites as Grandmaster Flash and the Furious Five and Spoonie Gee, respectively. Robinson would also introduce the Treacherous Three and producer Pumpkin to the recording process; both acts were seminal early underground rap stars. Winley cut *Superbreaks*, now a collector's item as the first rap album, which contained a series of raps that sounded like they'd been recorded in Winley's bathroom. Coinciding with rap's arrival on vinyl was the appearance of its first radio program. A Harlem party-giver who called himself Mr. Magic bought radio time on WHBI, a barter station filled with ethnic broadcasting near WBLS on the dial. He aired a rap show after 2 AM on Friday and Saturday nights. Magic's broadcast were a throwback to the days of the personality jocks, with the program's brash host hyping shows he was emceeing, taking requests, and flooding the airwaves with stock phrases his listeners loved ("Money Making Manhattan" was a favorite). Mr. Magic's program was, like the rap clubs and low budget twelve-inchers of Robinson and Winley, a reflection of the growing underground sense of community the music and its listeners shared. The show was streetwise, young, definitely rhythmic—to the point of being antimelodic—and a totally black-sounding board for people who not only identified with the rappers but very often were also rappers and spinners, just a twelve-inch deal away from being played on Mr. Magic's show themselves.

Before Mr. Magic was wooed to WBLS in a desperate attempt to combat KISS's strength with young blacks—an admission that much of the core black audience didn't buy that "urban" stuff—his program was sponsored by Sugar Hill, the label that would push rap out of New York and in front of the national audience that the majors didn't believe existed for it.

In the summer of 1979, Sylvia and Joe Robinson, a husband-and-wife team who owned the eight-year-old All Platinum label, were in the midst of a series of lawsuits. Sylvia, who as Sylvia Vanderpol sang on the 1957 hit "Love Is Strange" and recorded the soft-core porn single "Pillow Talk" in 1973, was at a niece's birthday party at the Harlem International Disco when, "All of a sudden I heard these three guys rapping over the microphone. Something hit me—I thought they were fantastic. An inner voice said to me, 'That's a concept.' "

Sylvia and Joe recruited the three youngsters to cut a record that was virtually a rap's greatest hit. Over the rhythm track of Chic's "Good Times," which along with MFSB's "Love Is the Message" was the groove of choice, Sylvia's rappers, dubbed the Sugar Hill Gang, culled rhymes from every rap of note on the uptown scene. The result was a record that went top ten in several countries, sold over 2 million in the United States, and grossed $3.5 million for the suddenly solvent Robinsons. Out of the ashes of All Platinum rose Sugar Hill Records. Using the Sugar Hill Gang and Grandmaster Flash and the Furious Five as their sales core, and then signing almost every other solid rap act, the Robinsons mined a virgin field. In fact it was suspected that Sugar Hill just wanted to corner the market, signing acts just so they wouldn't compete with the label's Hill stars.

The only major label involved in the early stages of the rap game was Mercury, through original Harlem rapper Kurtis Blow, whose novelty record, "Christmas Rappin'," would eventually sell 500,000. Then based in Chicago, Mercury Records enjoyed a 500,000-plus selling twelve-inch single with Blow's "The Breaks" in 1980 (only the second twelve-inch to reach that sales level), but the company always seemed wary that any minute rap was going to disappear, and Blow's audience with it. It was an attitude shared by most people in the industry, which treated rap and its decidedly nonupwardly mobile fans like a social disease.

Rap and the electronic-drum-machine-driven music that it evolved into scared the hell out of major label executives. And it was black executives who were most repulsed by it. Image conscious and bound at the navel to crossover styles, they were generally unwilling to give rap a break. Sugar Hill's dominance of the rap market might have continued if the Robinsons' reputation for unfair contracts and their tendency to take all the credit for creating rap hadn't begun alienating the staff as well as upcoming rappers. When Grandmaster Flash and most of the Furious Five signed with Elektra in 1984, Sugar Hill's rap hegemony ended.

Filling the gap came several independent labels, Tommy Boy, Profile, Def Jam, and Sleeping Bag the most prominent. All four employed a mix of young blacks, whites, and Latinos, some refugees from disco, some hard-core hip-hop fans who brought back a sense of daring and hustle to the record industry. From 1982 until now, these labels have marketed rap with a youthful enthusiasm and sensitivity that shocked old hands. They made videos. They developed fan clubs and newsletters. They put the kind of artist-development efforts into their rappers and other young hip-hop-inspired singers usually reserved for established stars.

In conjunction with these marketing efforts the music itself became simultaneously more complex and more simple. Where Sugar Hill's and Blow's records had backing tracks that one could have sung to as well as rapped over, Russell Simmons and the coproducers of Run-DMC, first Larry Smith and later Rick Rubin, used drum machines, synthesizers, and guitars in a way that was specifically tailored to rap. It was this kind of sonic experimentation that made the scratching sound of club jocks like Grandmaster Flash a standard part of pop music's aural landscape.

The connecting thread between rap's marketing and music was the young black manager-producer Russell Simmons, through his management company, Rush Productions, and the rap label he co-owned, Def Jam. Simmons started his career promoting rap shows in Queens and Manhattan featuring his friend and City College schoolmate Kurtis Blow. Blow's appearance as the only rapper on a major label and his strong visual image drew other rappers to Rush (though Simmons's most important signee was his own brother Joey, aka Run of Run-DMC), and the company became a veritable Motown of rap. On Def Jam, Russell introduced the aggressively articulate rapper L.L. Cool J, the neo-Nationalist rap group Public Enemy, and the old-fashioned retronuevo love man Oran (Juice) Jones, enhancing a reputation as a molder of solidly masculine black male acts started by his work with Blow, Run-DMC, and Whodini.

Partly at his instigation, a revue, under the name New York Fresh Fest, was organized in 1984 to tour the country in the manner of the early barnstorming rock & roll shows. Almost all the tour's drawing cards, including Run-DMC, Blow, and Whodini, were managed by Simmons; only the Fat Boys weren't, but their humorous raps were produced by Blow.

To the utter surprise of the record industry, the twenty-seven-city tour grossed $3.5 million, sold out 15,000-seat arenas, and moved lots of records. So many, in fact, that a month after the tour, the Fat Boys' debut album on Sutra, Whodini's *Escape* on Jive distributed by Arista, and Run-DMC's debut on Profile all went gold, while Blow's *Ego Trip* sold 300,000. Sales of this magnitude could not be ignored. And it wasn't just the record industry that started to pay attention.

The hip-hop style, in clothes, language, and dances, spread through these records and through commercials into every corner of the country and right into the voraciously consuming homes of the suburbs. Sneakers untied in Delaware. Caps worn backward in Oklahoma. And breakdancers like spinning locusts overran more music videos than MTV veejays could mispronounce the titles of.

While skepticism about rap's long-term viability remained, its ability to speak to urban youths went unchallenged. And the reaction of older blacks to it unfortunately mirrored all too accurately the gap between middle-class and poor blacks. Rap was the music of "b-boys"—a term applied to urban males who in style, dress, speech, and attitude exemplified hip-hop culture. It reflected a world far from the proudly middle-class home of Bill Cosby's enormously well-received sit-com. Cosby was a doctor, his lawyer-wife delightfully "bougie," and his kids bright and well behaved. The temptations of drugs and adolescent sex, the trials of ingrained youth unemployment, and the swirl of violence inflicted by blacks on each other and by the police happened far from the Huxtables' front door.

Rap records said quite explicitly that life for so many young black Americans had nothing to do with Harvard T-shirts and sorority pins. The gap between street-corner culture and middle-class comfort had never seemed so large in postwar America because, unlike young blacks twenty years before, b-boys rarely connected to concepts like "hope" and "I have a Dream." The optimistic agitation of the 1960s was not even a memory to the kids purchasing rap records. The most pungent rap records dealt openly with teenage sex (Whodini's "Freaks Come Out at Night") in an era of rampant teen and subteen pregnancy, or a brutalizing urban life-style (Dr. Jekyll and Mr. Hyde's "Fast Life," Run-DMC's "It's Like That," and Grandmaster Flash and the Furious Five's masterful "The Message").

The best rap artists, Melle Mel, Run-DMC, and Doug E. Fresh, all shared an intimacy with their listeners, an outsiders' view of mainstream America, and the ability to reach beyond the so-called limitation of the genre to recast pop culture into a vehicle for their expression. So, in his lyrics Melle Mel could praise Jesse Jackson's run for the presidency ("Jesse") while mainstream black acts avoided singing about this historic event, make allusions to Hitler in discussing America's attitude toward the poor ("Beat Street Breakdown"), and anticipate by several years the antidrug movement of the mid-eighties ("White Lines"). So Run-DMC can recapture a piece of the rock audience ("Walk This Way") without dissolving themselves like Jimi Hendrix into white rock culture, yet they can still be the first black act in years to (*sic*) the praises of their racial identity ("Proud to Be Black")—with both cuts on the same album, *Raising Hell*. So Doug E. Fresh, aka the "Original Human Beatbox," can, as miraculously as late jazzman Eddie Jefferson and singer Bobby McFerrin, have an orchestra in his mouth and use it to allude to the Beatles ("The Show") and New Orleans second-line rhythms ("All The Way to Heaven"), while maintaining his mischievous sense of humor.

This is the eighties, and some of the best rap companies have made deals and peace with corporate America (Def Jam with Columbia, First Priority with Atlantic, Tommy Boy and Cold Chillin' with Warner Bros.), though rap still shows no signs of the dreaded crossover fixation. Yes, the rap/hip-hop world has maintained its rebel status and integrity, and probably will until a Hall and Oates of rap appears—which, by the way, the Beastie Boys are not. The white rappers from New York are charged with exploiting rap and making it safe for white suburbia. As I see it, the Beastie Boys are a historic inevitability and at the same time a profound historic departure. There was no question that there would eventually be a white rap star. Marketingwise it made sense. But no one would have predicted the act would be managed by a black man, Russell Simmons, and have some of its material written by Run-DMC. In fact, Beastie Boy profits underwrote Public Enemy, Oran Jones, and other black singers signed to Def Jam. What did the Beastie Boys think? "Rock and roll was started by Chuck Berry," Beastie Boy MCA told *Rolling Stone*, "but it's Elvis who is called the King. So it's not so surprising that it took the Beastie Boys to popularize rap. That's typical of America."

Considering my earlier comments, the following conclusion may be a surprise, but the two most important retronuevo artists have been Michael Jackson and Prince. Despite the unfortunate impact of their imagery, this dynamic duo proved to be the decade's finest music historians, consistently using techniques that echoed the past as the base for their superstardom.

During his epochal 1983 performance on *Motown 25*, Jackson suggested Jack Wilson's athleticism, James Brown's camel walk, the intensity of the Apollo amateur night, and the glitter of Diana Ross. In *Purple Rain*, Prince, with the sensitivity of a poet, made historical allusions to Hendrix, Little Richard, Patti LaBelle, and Brown, while his employee, the Time's Morris Day, was molded into a modern-day Louis Jordan. Both Jackson (on "Beat It") and Prince (on "Let's Go Crazy" and "Purple Rain") made rock & roll for black folks while injecting their own idiosyncratic perspective into black dance music. Jackson's "Billie Jean" and "Wanna Be Startin' Something" raise superstar paranoia to a high art over grooves just as technologically assured as they were funky. "Don't Stop Til You Get Enough" is an incredible dance record, an anthem of spiritual and physical liberation in a wonderful synthesis of disco, the Philly sound, and Quincy Jones's own understanding of the drama in musical arrangement.

Prince, the auteur of the Minneapolis sound and himself a major talent scout, created the only competition to hip hop in the eighties, injecting fresh musical ideals into black music. Vanity, Morris Day, Jesse Johnson, the production team of Jimmy Jam Harris and Terry Lewis, Alexander O'Neal, Monte Moir, Andre Cymone, Sheila E., and quite a few others were ripples that came to our attention when Prince hit the shore. Not all these folks have great affection for Prince, but either their image or their music owes a debt to his fertile, cunning mind. Prince says that when he was a kid he didn't hear much black radio or music, but if his Brownesque 1986 *Parade* tour and the dancing in the film, *Sign "O" the Times*, is any indication, this retronuevo innovator has done a lot of catching up.

More, if we look at Jackson and Prince from the perspective of economic self-sufficiency, there is no question that this duo exercise a control over their careers and business that neither James Brown nor Sam Cooke, as ambitious as they were, could have envisioned. All major decisions, and even a great many minor ones, involving their money and artistic direction are determined personally by these performers. In Jackson's case this has meant, most significantly, the multimillion-dollar acquisition of the song catalogues of Sly Stone and the Beatles, two of his major influences, and the willingness to pay major directors like John Landis and Martin Scorsese big-budget money to expand the scope of music videos.

Where most of Jackson's business activities have been designed to promote and perpetuate his larger-than-life persona (much as with James Brown), Prince has used his energy to build and direct a multimedia empire that has spawned a slew of artists, launched a record label (Paisley Park), and led to the production of three feature films (*Purple Rain, Under the Cherry Moon,* and *Sign "O" the Times*), two of which he's directed himself.

Also as with James Brown, of course, there are disagreeable elements in the way that they each manifest their power and in the images of themselves they choose to project to both black and white audiences. However, to ignore their power, artistically and within their own organizations, solely because of their cosmetics would be ignorant. By using star clout to further their own interests (and, yes, whims) in unprecedented directions, Michael Jackson and Prince have set new standards of autonomy for black musicians—and for black-music businesspeople, too.

Down in Jackson, Mississippi, in the offices of Malaco Records, Dave Clark doesn't wonder about Prince, Michael Jackson, or rap. No, after almost fifty years in the music business, he is still working away, trying to get airplay for records. Jimmy Lunceford and almost every artist he worked with in the 1930s and 1940s are dead. So are Don Robey and Duke-Peacock, Stax, and TK, too. An entire insular, segregated community of entertainers and business people has passed into history. Even Z. Z. Hill, who with Clark's help had the biggest-selling blues album of the early eighties—*Down Home,* a gold record that spent 100 weeks on *Billboard*'s black chart—died in an auto accident after finally finding success in a journeyman career.

Now some seventy-seven or so years old, Clark's victory is that he is still active, working as head of record promotion for the black traditionalist label Malaco (they only sell soul, blues, and gospel), a living legend that connects the past to the present. He doesn't dwell on himself unless you ask. And even if you didn't know it, Clark would never mention that he discovered LaVern Baker, Big Maybelle, Carl Carlton, and Rance Allen; that he cowrote B. B. King's signature song "Why I Sing the Blues;" and that he helped Quincy Jones and Steven Spielberg research locations in the Mississippi Delta for *The Color Purple.* Yeah, he's got a million of them. Now gray-haired, razor thin, and still wearing $500 suits, Clark refuses to retire, continuing to preach the value of "real" black music. When he's asked whether promoting gospel, blues, and soul in the 1980s isn't a frustration gig, Clark doesn't get reflective, defensive, or melancholy. With the same confidence that led him to con a Jimmy Lunceford record onto Martin Block's playlist back in 1938 when rhythm & blues was new wave, he replies, "I'm not gonna let them stop me. Those doors I opened that were closed, locked, and bolted, I'm going to get a saw and saw them open. If I live twenty more years— I probably won't cause I'm a pretty old cat now—I'll still be trying to get a record played."

EPILOGUE

Self-sufficiency alone has never been the answer to the problems of black America. The interaction between blacks and the mainstream culture are too intimate for a total separatist philosophy to work in the United States. But certainly the philosophy of integration, for all its incremental improvements, has not altered the basic condition of most blacks in America. Poor education, racism, and constant struggle have defined black life here since our arrival. What I've attempted to argue in this book is that a more committed effort at self-sufficiency, in politics and economics, would have given (and still might give) blacks a better base from which to work for integration and practical power. As the Jewish scholar Nathan Glaser wrote in 1964, at the height of the civil-rights movement, "The Negro now demands entry into a world, a society, that does not exist, except in ideology. In that world there is only one American community, and in that world, heritage, ethnicity, religion, race are only incidental and accidental characteristics." Twenty-five years later Glaser is still right, and many blacks are still searching for an America that doesn't exist.

Moreover, as a cultural weapon, progressive black control (or, at least, assertive black involvement with sensitive whites) is one way to keep some of the spirit in black music. For all its vitality, black music has shown itself quite vulnerable to dilution. In *Blues People*, his magnificent history of black music, Leroi Jones wrote: "Negro music is always radical in the context of formal American culture. What has happened is that there are many more Negroes, jazz musicians and otherwise, who have moved successfully into the featureless syndrome of that culture, who can no longer realize the basic social and emotional philosophy that has traditionally informed Afro-American music. In one sense, they have traveled a complete circle, stepping right back into the heart of a paternal and parochial society—from slave to citizen—and have run through blues and discarded it on the way. But they had to. It was one of those ugly reminders that they had once been outside the walls of the city. And there are not too many people in this country, black or white, who'd be willing to admit that." Jones also observed that near the end of the swing era the black elements were so watered down that, without liner notes and pictures, you couldn't tell black bands from white. "So," he wrote sardonically, "many of the citizens had got their wish. At that particular point in the development of big-band jazz, the Afro-American musical tradition seemed indistinguishable from the commercial shallowness of American music."

In 1986, those assimilationist music buffs would be listening to the hits of Peter Gabriel ("Sledgehammer"), Robbie Nevil ("C'est la Vie"), Stevie Winwood ("Higher Love")—all white Negroes, all songs with retronuevo elements—and would find them equal to and often superior to most of the music on *Billboard*'s black chart. Factor in Phil Collins, Paul Young, and George Michael, and you realize that whites no longer have to imitate R&B but have, to a degree unprecedented in the postwar era, matched their black contemporaries. How? Through a deeper understanding and (dare I say?) love for the currents in black-music history.

As the 1980s roll into the 1990s, it is clear that black America's assimilationist obsession is heading it straight toward cultural suicide. The challenge facing black artists, producers, radio programmers, and entrepreneurs of every description is to free themselves from the comforts of crossover, to recapture their racial identity, and to fight for the right to exist on their own terms. Such a philosophy would have a positive impact on all the institutions that support the music and, because of music's special role in the black American psyche, a strong impact on its audience's thinking. For this to occur, black America has to acknowledge that racial pride is as worthy a goal as equality under the law, and, moreover, that the two agendas still go hand in hand.

NOTES

The following is a chapter-by-chapter breakdown of some of the books, articles, and interviews that went into the writing of *The Death of Rhythm & Blues*. It is not a comprehensive list, since a lot of the ideas contained in the book were inspired by long bull sessions on airplanes, in bars, and restaurants, at sundry music-biz conventions, and on the many long-distance calls that haunt my telephone bill. At *Billboard, Record World*, and the *Amsterdam News* over the past ten years, I've listened to many theories about the ins and outs of music and the business, and, in retrospect, I see that these many voices profoundly influenced my thinking. These pages trace just a few main currents and not the whole river.

CHAPTER ONE: Philosophy, Money, and Music (1900–30)

All you bookworms out there should give a look at: Albert Murray's *Stomping the Blues* (McGraw-Hill, 1976), Thomas Cripps' *Slow Fade to Black* (Oxford, 1977), Robert Palmer's *Deep Blues* (Viking, 1981), Art Rust's *Illustrated History of the Black Athlete* (Doubleday, 1985), Leroi Jones's *Blues People* (Morrow, 1963),

Harold Cruse's *The Crisis of the Negro Intellectual* (Morrow, 1967), Lerone Bennett, Jr.'s *Before the Mayflower* (Penguin, 1985), the Recording Industry Association of America's *Inside the Recording Industry: An Introduction to America's Music Business* (1985), and Louis Harlan's *Booker T. Washington: The Making of a Negro Leader (1856–1901)* (Oxford, 1972).

CHAPTER TWO: Dark Voices in the Night (1930–50)

Interviews with Gary Byrd, Jack Gibson, Quincy Jones, Eddie O'Jay, Bill (Hoss) Allen, Al Bell, and Mr. Dave Clark were essential. So were back issues of New Orleans's *Wavelength* magazine, Canada's *Soul Survivor*, Los Angeles's *Players*, and England's *Juke Blues*. The chapter in Peter Guralnick's *Lost Highway* on Bobby (Blue) Bland, and his liner notes on an Epic Records' Chuck Willis compilation again show why he's America's premier folk-music historian.

CHAPTER THREE: The New Negro (1950–65)

Albert Goldman's much maligned *Elvis* biography (McGraw-Hill, 1981) provided a rich picture of Memphis in the 1950s, while Robert Palmer's excellent profile of Leiber and Stoller in *Baby, That's Rock 'n' Roll* (Harvest, 1980) is the best study to date of those marvelous tunesmiths. Thank you, Karen Glover, for giving me access to your talks with Ruth Bowen. Session drummer Panama Francis backed up the observations of Dinah Washington in James Haskins's *Queen of the Blues* (Morrow, 1987) and Leslie Grouse's *Louis' Children* (Quill, 1984). Ray Charles's *Brother Ray* (Dial, 1978) is still the most clear-eyed and honest celebrity autobiography I've read. Finally, I actually got more out of Philadelphia deejay Georgie (the Man with the Goods) Woods during an interview over WDAS-AM than he did out of me when I was promoting my 1985 Motown book.

CHAPTER FOUR: Black Beauty, Black Confusion (1965–70)

Between talking at length with Alan Leeds, now a member of Prince's organization, and reading James Brown's autobiography, *The Godfather of Soul* (Macmillan, 1986), I found out more about the hardest-working man in show business than I wanted to know. Clive Davis's *Clive* (Morrow, 1974), Jonathan Eisen's *The Age of Rock* (Vintage, 1969), and Guralnick's *Sweet Soul Music* (Harper & Row, 1986) talk not just about the mechanics of selling music but about the attitudes toward that side of the business. *Time* magazine's 1968 cover story on Aretha Franklin is a collector's item. Gary Byrd, when not broadcasting or songwriting, gives great interviews. Del Shields, now a reverend, though still a radio broadcaster, gave me access not just to his memories but many of his papers and articles outlining the changes NARA-NATRA underwent. Stephen

Oates's biography of Dr. King, *Let the Trumpet Sound* (Harper & Row, 1982), Landess and Quinn's antagonistic look at the head of the Rainbow, *Jesse Jackson and the Politics of Race* (Jamerson Books, 1985), and E. Curtis Alexander's self-published Adam Clayton Powell celebration (1983) helped with the politics.

CHAPTER FIVE: Redemption Songs in the Age of Corporations (1971–75)

Arif Mardin injected some musicality into my profile of Danny Hathaway. The big shifts in black radio were outlined in interviews with Dyanna Williams, Barry Mayo, Melvin Lindsay, Hoss Allen, Shelia Eldridge, and Vernon Slaughter. A special 1980 *Record World* supplement on Frankie Crocker, built around a lengthy talk with Ken Smikle, provided a crucial view of how Crocker saw the role of urban radio. Stax newsletters, loaned to me by Fantasy's Terri Hinte, along with interviews with Al Bell and Dave Clark, helped me understand the politics of that label. And essential, not just to this chapter but the entire book, was the copy of the Harvard Report passed to me by Slaughter.

CHAPTER SIX: Crossover: The Death of Rhythm & Blues (1975–79)

From this point on a lot of the interviews and material cited came from work I did, either at *Record World*, *Billboard*, *Black Enterprise*, the *Village Voice*, or in researching my Motown history, *Where Did Our Love Go?* (St. Martin's, 1985). Ted Fox's *Showtime at the Apollo* (Holt, Rinehart & Winston, 1983) was again helpful. George Ware's letter to *Billboard*, published in a condensed form as a commentary, was a detailed guide to the failures of the Black Music Association. Attending its conventions also helped. Of all the interviews I conducted at *Billboard* that ended up in this chapter, those with ex-critic and current Columbia A&R man Joe McEwen and the great singer-songwriter Bobby Womack made the most sense.

CHAPTER SEVEN: Assimilation Triumphs, Retronuevo Rises (1980–87)

Eugene Robinson's 1986 look at the two black cities within Washington, D.C., in the *Washington Post Magazine*, Erroll Louis's look at black college kids of the late 1980s in *Essence* (1986), and my *Billboard* piece on the dichotomy between black-music growth and black-retail depression, all crystallized my feelings about how deep the split in black America has become. The Sugar Hill Records special I organized at *Record World* (August, 1981), interviews with D. J. Hollywood, Sylvia Robinson, my friendship with Russell Simmons, and life as a "B-Boy Intellectual" influenced my observations about rap's role and future.

EPILOGUE

Leroi Jones's *Blues People* and Harold Cruse's *The Crisis of the Negro Intellectual* are two of the best books about the black condition in these United States this side of *The Invisible Man*.

The following books round out the list of the books I found most useful while thinking about and writing *The Death of Rhythm & Blues*:

Adler, B. *Run-D.M.C.* New York: New American Library, 1987.

Berry, Chuck. *Chuck Berry*. New York: Crown, 1987.

George, Nelson. *Fresh, Hip Hop Don't Stop*. New York: Random House, 1985.

———. *Top of the Charts*. New Brunswick, N.J.: New Century, 1983.

———. *The Michael Jackson Story*. New York: Dell, 1984.

Gillett, Charlie. *Sound of the City*. New York: Pantheon, 1983.

———. *Making Tracks*. New York: Dutton, 1974.

Guralnick, Peter. *Feel Like Going Home*. New York: Vintage, 1981.

Henderson, David. *'Scuse Me While I Kiss the Sky: The Life of Jimi Hendrix*. New York: Doubleday, 1978.

Haralambros, Michael. *Right On: From Blues to Soul in Black America*. New York: DaCapo, 1974.

James, C.L.R. *Beyond a Boundary*. New York: Pantheon, 1983.

Keil, Charles. *Urban Blues*. Chicago: University of Chicago, 1966.

Marcus, Greil. *Mystery Train*. New York: Dutton, 1976.

Miller, Jim, ed. *Rolling Stone Illustrated History of Rock*. New York: Random House, 1980.

Mills, Hillary. *Mailer: A Biography*. New York: McGraw-Hill, 1982.

Pareles, Jon, and Patricia Romanowski. *Rolling Stone Encyclopedia of Rock & Roll*. New York: Summit, 1983.

Quarles, Benjamin. *The Negro in the Making of America*. New York: Collier, 1969.

Sawyer, Charles. *The Arrival of B. B. King*. New York: Doubleday, 1980.

Shaw, Arnold. *Honkers and Shouters*. New York: Collier, 1978.

Tosches, Nick. *Unsung Heroes of Rock 'n' Roll*. New York: Schribners, 1984.

Toop, David. *Rap Attack*. Boston: South End, 1984.

Turner, Tina, with Kurt Loder. *I, Tina*. McGraw-Hill, 1986.

Westbrooks, Logan, and Lance Williams. *Anatomy of a Record Company*. Los Angeles: Westbrooks, 1981.

White, Charles. *Life and Times of Little Richard*. New York: Harmony, 1984.

INDEX

Aaron, Henry (Hank), 58, 61
ABC label, 71, 85, 102, 113–14, 135, 148–49
ABC-Paramount label, 82–83
Abner, Ewart, 166
Abramson, Herb, 27, 37–38
Abramson, Miriam, 37
Ace, Johnny, 32–33, 34, 50
Advance Motion Picture Company, 7
advertising: and black consumers, 53, 160, 183–84; black *vs.* white radio, 173; major labels and small retailers, 162
Age of Rock, The (Eisen), 107
"Ain't Nobody Here But Us Chickens," 19
Aladdin label, 26, 32
Alexander, James (Woody), 50,70–71, 79, 80–82
All Platinum label, 190–91
Allen, Bill (Hoss), 54, 126
Allen, Milton, 133

Allen, Rance, 196
A&M Records, 155
American Federation of Musicians (AFM), 23
Anderson, Eddie (Rochester), 20, 118
Anderson, Marion, 20
Andrews, Inez, 34
Anheuser Busch, 178–79
Annie Allen (Brooks), 39
Apollo Records, 27, 55
Apollo Theater (New York), 33–37, 50, 99, 101, 130–31, 148; amateur nights, 194; demise of, 162–63; revival of, 186
Arbitron ratings, 119, 184
Aretha Live at the Fillmore (album), 106
Arista Records, 151, 192
Aristocrat-Chess label, 27
Armstrong, Louis, 9, 12, 17, 25
Arnold, Larkin, 187
Ashburn, Benny, 177
Ashford, Nick, 148, 152, 159

assimilation philosophy, *xiv*, 3–4, 98, 121–22, 146; Jackson and Prince as symbols of, 174, 195–96; *vs.* self-sufficiency and racial identity, 3–8, 13, 19, 71–72, 96, 104, 187, 199–201
ATCO label, 110
Atlanta, and black radio, 45–47
Atlanta Braves, 58
Atlantic Records, 27, 55, 80, 86, 87, 88, 105, 125, 158, 194; and British rock, 110–11; and Ray Charles, 102; development of R&B, 37–39, 71; and Gamble and Huff, 143; Leiber and Stoller, 66; soul market and, 136–37; and Willis, 47
Avante, Clarence, 113–15, 126, 131, 166

"b-boys," 193
Baby, That Was Rock & Roll (Palmer), 66
Baker, Anita, 188
Baker, Ginger, 110
Baker, LaVern, 196
Baker, Ronnie, 142, 146
Ballantine Ale, 45–46
Band (the), 47
Banks, Homer, 138
Bar-Kays, 101, 133, 160, 177
Barker, Edwin, 7
Barnes, Nicky, 162
Barr, Fred, 117
Barry, Marion, 172
Bart, Jack, 98–99
Bartholomew, Dave, 53
baseball, 12–13: and integration, 57–58, 60–61
Basie, Count, 18, 24, 41; Orchestra, 99
Beach Boys, 92–93
Beastie Boys, 194
Beatles, 84, 92–93, 106, 195
bebop, 24–26, 35, 42, 156
Bee Gees, 110, 158, 160, 181
Bell, Al, 87, 88, 93, 111; and Davis at CBS, 141–42; and Jesse Jackson, 139–40
Bell, Cool Papa, 12
Bell, Thom, 143–44, 155, 180
Bell, William, 87
Belle, Regina, 188
Benson, Al, 41–42
Benson, George, 126, 148–49, 152, 155, 156, 159; cosmetic surgery, 173

Berlin, Irving, 8
Berman, Ike and Bess, 27
Berry, Chuck, 37, 107, 166; and rock & roll, 63, 68–69, 83, 181, 194; Freed and white audience, 69, 109; Beatles and Beach Boys and, 92–93
Beverly, Frankie, 186–87
big bands, *xii*, 11, 23–24, 37, 38, 67; and black music, 9, 200
Big Maybelle, 196
Bihari, Jules, Joe and Saul, 27
Bihari, Lester, 28
Billboard, 26, 101–2, 160, 174–75; charts, 157–58, 196, 200
Birth of a Nation (film), 6–7
Birth of a Race (film), 7
Bishop, Jimmy, 113
Black, J. D., 167
black elite, 5, 8–9. *See also* black middle class
Black Enterprise magazine, 126, 156, 176
"Black is beautiful" slogan, *xiv*, 185
Black Macho and the Myth of the Superwoman (Wallace), 104
black middle class, 153, 156, 160, 193: children of, 173; college-educated, 121, 129, 131–33, 153, 173
Black Music Association (BMA), 165–167
Black Muslims, xiii, 71–72, 166; Gamble and, 145
black nationalism, 96, 104
Black Panthers, 98, 118
Black Power, 96, 98, 103, 111, 140
black radio, *xv*, 11–12, 22–23, 147; beginnings, 18–19; black-owned stations, 126–30; black deejays and, 41–42, 47–51, 111–15; crossover hits and, 150–51; growth of, 28–29, 40–41; and reverse crossover, 158–59
Black Radio Exclusive magazine, 167
Black Swan Records, 10–11
black women, 104
black youth, *xi–xii*, 184–87, 193
blacks: in business, 29–36, 176–79; musical styles and creativity, 108; and voting rights, 4–5, 95
Blackwell, Bumps, 70–71, 79–80, 81
Blackwell, Otis, 63
Bland, Bobby (Blue), 32–34, 37, 107
Blavat, Jerry, 91
blaxploitation films, 123–24, 150, 158

Bledsoe, Gerry B., 91
Block, Martin, 17–18, 196
Blood, Sweat and Tears, 110
Bloods (Terry), 131
Bloomfield, Mike, 107
Blow, Kurtis, 189, 192
Blue Note Records, 149
Bluenotes, 145
blues, *xii*, 9, 25, 29–31, 93, 196; Berry and, 68; blacks' rejection of, 93, 107–8, 186, 200; Handy and, 10–11; Presley and, 62. *See also* gospel music.
Blues People (Leroi Jones), 200
BMI list, 26
Bogart, Neil, 129, 154
Booker T and the MGs, 138
booking agents, 89, 99, 163–64, 176. *See also* names of agencies and individuals
Boone, Pat, 31, 55
Bostic, Earl, 73
Bowen, Billy, 72–74
Bowen, Ruth, 72–74, 88–89, 93, 176
Bracken, Vivian and James, 83–85
Bradshaw, Tiny, 50
Brass Construction, 153
breakdancers, 193
Brides of Funkenstein, 155
British rock, 110, 137, 159. *See also* names of artists
Bootsy's Rubber Band, 155
Broadcast Music Inc. *See* BMI list
Bronze label, 27
Brooks, Gwendolyn, 39
Brotherhood of Sleeping Car Porters, 21
Brothers Johnson, 155
Brown, Charles, 25
Brown, Clarence (Gatemouth), 25, 32, 66
Brown, H. Rap, 104, 112, 114
Brown, James, 66, 78, 92, 109, 148, 160, 162, 188, 194–96; and King assassination, 102–3, 111; machismo of, 104; Nixon and black capitalism, 103–4; self-marketing of, 98–104; soul and funk, 101–2, 136, 157
Brown, Jim (football star), 122–23
Brown, Les, 24
Brown, Morrie, 181
Brown, Roy, 53
Brown, Ruth, 37, 66
Bruce, Jack, 110
Brunswick Records, 77–78, 151
Bryant, Willie, 48

Bryson, Peabo, 182–83
B.T. Express, 153
Buddah label, 148
Budweiser Superfest, 178–79
Buffalo, 89–90, 116–17, 127–28
Buffalo Booking Agency, 32–34, 163, 176
Bulleit, Jim, 27
Bunche, Ralph, 39
Burke, Solomon, 70
Burke, Spider, 43
Butler, Jerry, 79, 84, 125, 143, 144
Byrd, Gary, 43, 90–91, 116–19; on Drake format, 118

"Caledonia Boogie," 20, 25
California, 26, 28
"California Soul" concerts, 148–49
Calloway, Cab, 19–20
camel walk (dance), 92, 101
Cameo, 160, 177
Cameo-Parkway label, 75
Cameron, Hank, 116
Capitol Records, 23, 26, 148–49, 180; Beatles and, 84; and Bryson, 182; and Harvard Report, 135–37; Maze and, 186–87
Carlton, Carl, 196
Carmichael, Stokely, 82, 104
Carnegie, Andrew, 4
Carter, Benny, 24
Carter, Calvin, 83
Carter, Jimmy, 166
Casablanca Records, 154
Casey, Harry, 153
Cash, Fred, 85
Castleberry, Ed, 43
Cauldwell, Hank, 175–76
"Cause I Love You" (song title), 86
CBS, 110, 113–14, 161, 179–80; and black music, 134–35; crossover marketing and, 148–56; Harvard Report and, 135–38, 149–50; and 1979 recession, 167–69; and PIR, 142, 144–46; and Slaughter, 134–35. *See also* Columbia Records
Center for Study of Democratic Institutions, 113–14
Cerrone, 159
Chamblee, Eddie, 72–73
Chandler, Gene, 84–85

Charles, Ray, 66, 72, 83, 102, 105, 106; and soul, 70–71, 93, 105; economic independence of, 71
Checker, Chubby, 75
Cheeba, Eddie, 189
Chess, Leonard and Phil, 27, 32, 37, 64, 83, 144
Chess, Marshall, 144
Chess Records, 37, 55, 83, 85; and Gamble Records, 143–44
Chic, 157, 159, 169, 191
Chicago, 41, 183; and Martin Luther King, 96–97; and Regal Theater, 186; "soul" music, 82–85; South Side black community, xiii; Vee-Jay label and, 83–84
Chicago American Giants, 58
"Chicago soul" music, 82
"Chicago sound," 110
Children of the World (album), 158
chitlin circuit, 34, 50, 70, 88–89, 109, 152, 163, 177
CHR (contemporary hit radio), 183–84
Chudd, Lew, 27
Civil Rights Act (1964), 95–96
civil-rights movement, 5, 69, 83, 87, 97–98, 104, 160; and black nationalism, 106; losses under Reagan, 171–72; and Mayfield's music, 82, 85; and music business, 72
Clapton, Eric, 107, 108, 110
Clark, Dave, 17–20, 32–34, 89, 135, 139, 165; marketing of "real" black music, 196–97; and payola, 55–56
Clark, Dee, 84
Clark, Dick, 47, 75
Clay, Cassius. *See* Muhammad Ali
Cleaver, Eldridge, 104
Clemente, Roberto, 61
Cleveland, Rev. James, 180
Cleveland Buckeyes, 57
Cleveland Indians, 57
Clinton, George (Dr. Funkenstein), 101, 155–56, 180, 182
Clovers, 39
clubs: and rap beginnings, 189–90
Coasters, 64, 66
Cobbs, Arthur, 117
Cold Chillin', 194
Cole, Dick (Cane), 86
Cole, Nat King, 24–26, 45, 70, 73
Cole, Robert A., 58

"Cole Slaw," 39
Coleman, Ornette, 156
Collins, Bootsy, 156
Collins, Phil, 200
Coltrane, John, 116
Columbia Records, 23, 38, 76, 105, 111, 148, 180, 194; "In the Mood" and, 151–52; and Womack, 150–51. *See also* CBS
Commodores, 133, 149, 155, 177
concert promoters, 162–64, 166; black, and Budweiser Superfest, 176, 178–79
Congress of Racial Equality (CORE), 69
Constellation label, 84, 85
Cook, Bill, 47, 80
Cook, Ed, 43
Cooke, Sam, 70–71, 85, 93, 99, 102; Beverly and, 187; business sense, 80–81, 195; and crossover, 81, 150; musical importance of, 77; voice and talent, 79–80, 83
Coolidge, Rita, 138
Cooper, Gary (Mudbone), 156
Cooper, Jack, 18, 41
Cooper, Steve, 138
Cornelius, Don, 137–38, 165
Cosby, Bil, 112, 174, 193
cosmetic surgery, 173–74
Cotton Club, 11, 37
country music, 26, 30
Cream (rock group), 107, 110
Creatore, Luigi, 81
Crisis (Du Bois), 7
Crocker, Frankie, 91, 117, 134, 159, 160, 165; reverse crossover of, 159; and WBLS, 127–32, 160, 165, 183
Cropper, Steve, 109
crossover marketing, xi, xiv, 10, 81–82, 146, 176: black middle class and, 153, 156; and death of R&B, 147–56; decline of (1980s), 181–82; Jack Gibson's opposition, 184–86; and rap, 194
Crouch, Andrae, 166
Crudup, Arthur (Big Boy), 25, 63
Crusaders, 156
Crutcher, Bettye, 138
CTI label, 149
Culley, Frank, 39
cultural traditions, of blacks, xii–xv, 62, 199–201
Curtis, King, 34, 39, 125
Curtis, Wild Bill, 43

Curtom label, 125, 148
Cymone, Andre, 195

D. J. Lovebug Star-ski, 189
Daley, Mayor Richard, 96–97
dance music, 75; and disco, 153–55,
    180–81; and Hendrix, 109; and Jack-
    son and Prince, 195; and the JBs, 101;
    Philly sound and, 145–46; ragtime and
    jazz, 8–9; and rap, 188; and reverse
    crossover on black radio, 159; and *Soul
    Train*, 138
Davis, Benjamin O., 21
Davis, Bily, 155
Davis, Carl, 82–83, 110
Davis, Clive, 135, 137; and PIR, 144; and
    Stax, 141–42
Davis, Don, 138, 155
Davis, Miles, 93, 124, 129
Davis, Sammy, Jr., 45, 73, 81, 177
Davis, Tyrone, 150–52
Davis, Willie, 126
Day, Morris, 195
Dean, Larry, 43
Decca Records, 17, 19, 23, 25–26
Dee, Nat, 49, 51, 52
deejays, *xv*, 18, 29–30, 35; black, 40–52,
    84, 87–92; and BMA, 167; and James
    Brown, 99–100; and Davis at CBS,
    141; and disco, 154–55; and Drake
    format, 117–19; and king's assassina-
    tion, 111–12; and NARA, 112–15; and
    payola, 55–56, 75, 90–91; "personal-
    ity" jocks, 42, 116–19, 126–31, 189;
    women as, 132. *See also* names of
    deejays
Def Jam label, 191–92, 194
Dells, 84
Delsner, Ron, 148
Detroit, 82, 86
Deutsche Grammophon, 140–41
Diddley, Bo, 37, 83
disc jockeys. *See* deejays
"Disco Lady," 150–52, 157
disco music, *xii*, 150–55, 181, 188, 195;
    crossover and black radio, 157–59
"Disco 92"–WKTU, New York, 183
discotheques, 189; and crossover stars,
    176–77
Dissent magazine, 61
Dixie Hummingbirds, 32

Dixieland jazz, 93
Dixon, Thomas, 6
Dixon, Willie, 37
Dobey, Larry, 58
Dr. Daddy-O, 53
Dr. Jekyll and Mr. Hyde (rap act), 193
Domino, Fats, 53–54, 68
Dominoes, 77
"Don't Stop Til You Get Enough," 195
doo wop, 35–36, 93, 107
Dootones label, 36
Dorsey, Lee, 35
Dorsey, Rev. Thomas (Georgia Tom), 69
Dorsey, Tommy, 18, 24
Dot Records, 28, 54–55
Double Exposure, 146
Douglass, Frederick, 4
Down Home (album), 196
Dozier, Lamont, 148
Drake, Bill, 117–18
Drake format, 117–19
Dramatics, 138
Draper, Tom, 148–49
Drew, Dr. Charles, 21
Drifters, 39, 43, 66
drug use, 24, 40, 109, 124, 172, 193–94
Du Bois, W. E. B., 4–8, 96, 133, 173;
    segregation policy, 16
Duhe, Robin, 187
Duke Records, 28
Duke-Peacock Records, 31–33, 37, 55,
    88, 196
Durst, Lavada, 42
Dynasty, 179

Earth, Wind and Fire, 122–23, 136, 151,
    152, 155, 159, 165, 187; with CBS,
    180; and white management, 177
Eaves, Hubert, 181
Ebony magazine, *xiii*, 22–23, 41, 127, 177
Eckstine, Bily, 62, 138, 166
economic integration, 121, 156, 167,
    178–79
Economic Justice Movement, 178
economic self-sufficiency. *See* assimilation
    philosophy
Eisen, Jonathan, 107
Eldridge, Sheila, 133
electric bass guitars, *xii*, 38–39, 68, 109
electric blues, 26; revival of, 106–7

electric blues guitar: and rock artists, 109–10
Electric Flag, 107
Elektra-Asylum label, 110
Elektra Records, 180, 182, 191
Eley, Paris, 151–52
Ellington, Duke, 9, 11, 18, 24, 37
Ellis, Alfred (Pee Wee), 101
Ellison, Ralph, 15, 40
Enjoy label, 35, 190
Epic Records, 48, 110, 148–49, 151–52, 180
Errico, Greg, 109
Ertegun, Ahmet, 27, 110: and Atlantic, 37–38, 71; on black music, 93, 107; and soul, 70–71; as white Negro, 64. See also Atlantic Records
Ertegun, Nesuhi, 37
Eurodisco music, 153–55, 158. See also British rock
Evans, David, 173
Everett, Betty, 84
Everlast label, 35
Excelsior label (Exlusive), 27

Fair Deal Productions, 102
Fakaris, Dino, 152
Family Reunion (album), 145
Family Stone band, 109–10. See also Stone, Sly
Fat Boys, 192
FCC (Federal Communications Commission), 112, 115, 117, 141
Feld, Irving, 27
Fender, Leo, 38
Ferguson, Bert, 48–50, 51
Fields, Richard (Dimples), 164
Fillmore theaters, 106–7
film industry, 7, 121–26, 158
Fire label, 35
First Choice, 146, 148
First Priority (rap act), 194
Fitzgerald, Ella, 25
Fitzgerald, F. Scott, 9, 29
Five Blind Boys, 32, 34
Flack, Roberta, 125–26, 136, 182
Flamberg, Dan, 184
Floyd, Pink, 168
Foster, Andrew (Rube), 12, 58
Four Seasons, 84
Four Star label, 27

Four Tops, 124, 148
Fox, Ted, 163
Francis, Panama, 39, 73
Franklin, Aretha, xiv, 109–10, 124–25, 128, 153, 182; and Ruth Bowen, 74, 176; and soul recordings, 105–6; talent, 72
Franklin, Gwen, 133
Franklin, C. L., 105
Frazier, E. Franklin, 40
"free jazz," 156
Freed, Alan, 56, 66–69, 90–91, 106
Freedom label, 27
Fresh, Doug E., 193, 194
funk music, xii, 109, 124, 157, 188; Clinton's bands, 155–56; and JBs, 101–2; 1970s and disco, 153–56
Funkadelic (rock band), 149, 155
Fuqua, Harvey, 148
Furious Five (rap act), 35, 190–91, 193
Fury label, 35

Gabler, Milt, 19
Gabriel, Peter, 200
Gale, Moe, 17
Galuten, Albhy, 158
Gamble, Kenny, 142–45, 165, 167; and disco music, 155; return to independent status, 180
Gamble Rcords 43
Gant, Private Cecil, 25–26, 54
Gap Band, 180
Gardner, Robert, 186
Gaye, Marvin, 92, 124, 129, 157, 179
Gaynor, Gloria, 154
Gerry and the Pacemakers, 92
Gershwin, George, 64
"Ghetto, The," 125
Gibb, Robin, Maurice, and Barry, 158
Gibson, Jack, 43–46, 88, 112, 126, 130, 133, 167; on black radio, 160–61, 184–86
Gibson, Josh, 12
Gillespie, Dizzy, 24–25
Glaser, Joe, 17, 73–74
Glaser, Nathan, 199–201
Glover, Henry, 37
Goldberg, Whoopi, 173
Goldner, George, 36
"Good Rockin' Tonight," 26, 53
"Good Times," 157, 159, 169, 191

Gooden, Sam, 85
Goodman, Benny, 24, 38
Gordy, Berry, 32, 93, 98, 165; and black capitalism, 87; development of Motown, 83, 88–89; sale of Motown, 179
Gore, Lesley, 92
gospel music, *xii*, 25–26, 29, 31–32, 34, 62, 196; and Ray Charles, 70–71; and Sam Cooke, 79–81; and Aretha Franklin, 105; and R&B, 69
Gourse, Leslie, 72
Graham, Bill, 106–7
Graham, Larry, 109, 148
Graham Central Station, 148
Grandmaster Flash, 35, 189–91, 193
Graves, Earl, 126
Gray, Dobie, 116
Great Society programs, 104, 124
Green, Irving, 27
Greene, Al, 27, 38, 77
Greenlee, W. A. (Gus), 13, 58
Grein, Paul, 157
Grier, Pam, 123
Griffey, Dick, 164, 179–80
Griffith, D. W., 6–7
Grizzard, Herman, 54
Groce, Rocky, 117
guitars. *See* electric bass guitar
Gulf + Western, 138–41
Gulf-Gold Star label, 27
Gumbel, Bryant, 173
Gunn, Moses, 6
Guralnick, Peter, 33, 80, 87, 141
Gyra, Spyro, 156

hairstyles, 62, 93, 182
Haley, Alex, 40
Hall, Horace G., 58
Hall and Oates, 160, 194
Hamilton, Roy, 47–48, 80
Hampton, Lionel, 25, 39
Hampton, Mike, 156
Hancock, Herbie, 124
Handy, W. C., 10, 64
Hannusch, Jeff, 52
Hardy, John (Honey Boy), 43
Harlem, 11, 34–36, 127, 131; and bebop, 24; and Adam Clayton Powell, Jr., 96; and rap, 189. *See also* Apollo Theater; Cotton Club
Harris, Jimmy Jam, 195

Harris, Norman, 142, 146
Harris, R. H., 79
Harris, Wynonie, 26, 29–30, 54, 66
Harrison, Wilbert, 35, 66
Harvard Report, 135–38, 141, 149–50
Hathaway, Donny, 125–26, 129
Hawkins, Erskine, 25
Hawkins, Screamin' Jay, 47
Hayes, Isaac, 126, 129, 131, 133–34, 148, 181; arrangements by, 123–24, 138, 140, 157; and soul, 136
Haymon, Al, 178
heavy metal music, 110
Heller, Eddie, 36
Henderson, Fletcher, 10
Henderson, Jocko, 42–43
Hendrix, Jimi, 108–9, 194, 195
Henson, Matthew, 22
hep-cats: slang, 19, 24; and Presley, 62
Herman, Woody, 24
Hill, Z. Z., 150, 196
Hines, Earl (Fatha), 11
hip-hop, 189, 191–94
Hogan, Frank, 91
Holiday, Billie, 17, 45, 72
Holland, Brian, 148
Holland, Eddie, 148
Hollaway, Loleatta, 154
Holly, Buddy, 47
Hollywood, D. J., 163, 189–90
Hollywood film industry. *See* film industry
Hollywood Shuffle (film), 186
Homestead Grays (baseball team), 12–13
Hooker, John Lee, 26, 84
Horne, Lena, 113
Horny Horns, 155
Hot Buttered Soul (album), 138, 140
"Hound Dog," 63, 66
Houston, 32–34
Houston, Whitney, *xiv*
Howard, Miki, 188
Howard Theater (Washington), 50, 99, 162
Howard University, 125, 172; and WHUR, 127, 131–35
Howlin' Wolf, 107
Hudson, George, 48
Hudson, Ted, 162, 175
Huff, Leon, 142–45, 155; and Gamble, 180
Hughes, Langston, 64
Hulbert, Maurice (Hot Rod), 43, 49, 51

Humphrey, Hubert, 103, 114
Hunter, Ivory Joe, 25
Hurte, Leroy, 27
Hutch, Willie, 124
Hutson, Leroy, 125, 148
Hyman, Phyllis, 180

I Spy (television show), 112–13
"I'm So Proud," 85
Imperial label, 27
Impressions, 84–85, 125, 143, 148
"In the Mood," 151–52
independent record companies, *xi*, 79,
    154, 157; black and Jewish owners,
    28; demise of, 179–80; list of
    (1942–52), 27–28; "vs." major labels,
    147–49; and R&B artists, 26, 29–39;
    and rap, 188–92; record distribution,
    133–36
Indianapolis Clowns, 57
indies. *See* independent record companies
Ink Spots, 26, 72
Inner City Broadcasting, 127, 129–30
integration, 22, 29, 56, 59–50; and black
    acts downtown, 163; black radio
    speech and, 118–19; and blacks in
    suburbs, 131; consequences of, *xiv*,
    138, 199–200; crossover stars and
    black business class, 177; and Muslims,
    72; New York radio audiences and
    Crocker, 129–31; in R&B business
    world, 88–89; reverse, and Presley, 62.
    See also economic integration
International Creative Management, 163
Intruders, 143
Invisible Man (Ellison), 40
Isley Brothers, 66, 108, 136, 148, 150,
    180; protest songs, 187

Jack, Wolfman, 90
Jack the Rapper (radio tip sheet), 161,
    167, 184–85
Jackson, Miss., 29–30, 40
Jackson, Rev. Jesse, 138, 180; and An-
    heuser Busch boycott, 178; and presi-
    dential campaign, 178, 193; and
    Rainbow Coalition, 171–72
Jackson, Anthony, 144
Jackson, Bull Moose, 54, 66
Jackson, Hal, 43, 127

Jackson, Janet, 173
Jackson, Mahalia, 30
Jackson, Michael, 157, 180, 182; andro-
    gynous image, 174, 196; and *Off the
    Wall*, 168–69; retronuevo importance,
    194–96; and white management, 177
Jackson, Millie, 160
Jackson, Raymond, 138
Jackson, Walter, 85
Jackson Five, 148–49, 151, 157, 169
Jagger, Mick, 63–64, 92
James, Bob, 156
James, Elmore, 30
James, Harry, 24
James, Rick, 177, 182
Jan and Dean, 92
Jarreau, Al, 126, 148
jazz, 29, 93, 116, 188; and bebop, 25;
    Ertegun on, 93; Mailer and, 62; origin
    of term, 9; and R&B music, 124, 126
JBs, 101–2
Jefferson, Eddie, 194
Jenkins, Johnny, and the Pinetoppers, 87
Jim Crow, 15–16, 40, 97
Jive label, 192
Joel, Billy, 168
Johnson, Billy, 187
Johnson, Buddy, 25
Johnson, Evelyn, 33–34
Johnson, James P., 65
Johnson, James Weldon, 5
Johnson, Jesse, 195
Johnson, John, 22, 126–27
Johnson, Lyndon Baines, 95, 104
Johnson, Nicholas, 115
Johnson, Robert, 10
Jones, Grace, 154
Jones, Leroi, 200
Jones, Oran (Juice), 192, 194
Jones, Paul Laurence, 181
Jones, Pete (D. J.), 189
Jones, Quincy, 38, 155, 157, 195, 196
Joplin, Janis, 110
Joplin, Scott, 8
Jordan, Louis, 24, 26, 38, 39, 71, 99; in-
    fluence on artists, 68, 93, 101, 188,
    195; recordings, 25; and Tympany
    Five, 19–20
jubilee singing, 8
jukeboxes, 17, 20, 76–77, 134
jump blues, 25, 30
Junebug Star-ski, 189

Kags Music Publishing, 80–81

Karenga, Ron, 98, 118

Kashif, 181

Kaufman, Murray (Murray the K), 91

Kaul, Saul, 27

KC and the Sunshine Band, 153

Keen label, 80–1

Kelsy, Sonny Jim, 90

Kendricks, Eddie, 116, 153, 158

KGH, Los Angeles, 117–18

Khan, Chaka, 149

King, B. B., 34, 52, 196; as Pepticon Boy, 49–50; rediscovered, 107

King, Dr. Martin Luther, Jr., 46, 60, 69, 87, 98, 118, 122; assassination, 102, 111–12; and Chicago and Mayor Daley, 96–97

King, Evelyn, 166, 181

King, Riley B. *See* King, B. B.

"King Biscuit Time" (radio program), 12

King Records, 26, 27, 37, 55, 102

KISS radio stations, 160, 183, 190

Klotzman, Dick, 166

Klugh, Earl, 156

Knight, Gladys, 34, 35, 70, 106, 131

Knight, Gladys, and the Pips, 34–35, 148, 150, 182

Knight, Ken, 43

Kool and the Gang, 124, 153

Kragen, Ken, 177

Kramer, Billy, 92

Krasnow, Bob, 149

Krupa, Gene, 24

KUTE, Los Angeles, 187

KVIL and K104, Dallas, 183–84

KWEM, Memphis, 48–49

L. L. Cool J, 192

Labelle, Patti, 195

labels. *See* independent record companies; major record companies; names of individual labels; record industry

Laemmle, Carl, 7

Lakeside label, 180

Lance, Major, 85

Landis, John, 195

Lange, Arthur, 65

Laws, Ronnie, 156

Led Zeppelin, 110

Lee, Elliot, 176

Lee, Spike, 186

Leeds, Alan, 99

Leiber, Jerry, 64–66, 68, 85

Leonard, Sheldon, 113

"Let Yourself Go," 101

Levert, Eddie, 144

Lewis, Smiley, 54

Lewis, Terry, 195

Liberty Records, 149

Liggins, Kathy, 132

Lindsay, Melvin, 132, 172

"line syndrome," 31

Lipsyte, Robert, 58

Little Esther, 66

Little Richard, 54, 68, 86, 195; and Bumps Blackwell, 79, 81; and Don Robey, 31–32; sexuality of, 92, 174

Live at the Apollo (album), 102

Live in New Orleans (album), 187

Lockwood, Robert, 12

Long, Joe, 161–62

Lorenz, George (Hound Dog), 90, 116

Lorenz, Jack (the Bell Boy), 43

Los Angeles, 29, 140, 168; indies and, 26–28; radio stations, 28, 115, 117–18, 126, 128

Love Unlimited Orchestra, 131

Lowery, Roame, 187

Lubinsky, Herman, 27, 33

Lunceford, Jimmy, 9, 17, 18, 196

lynchings, 4–5, 9, 40, 61

Lynn, Gloria, 136

Maboya, 189

Mack, Richard, 135

Macy's label, 27

Magnificent Montague, 88

Mailer, Norman, 61–62, 63

major record companies: crossover marketing and, 147–56; and disco music, 155–56; and mom-and-pop retail stores, 161–63; and rap, 189, 191, 194; takeover of indies, 179–80; top-forty stations and, 128; and traditional acts, 152–53. *See also* Harvard Report; names of major labels

"Make Believe Ballroom," 17–18

Malaco Records, 196

Malcolm X, 71, 82

Malone, Deadric, 33

Mandrill, 124

Manhattans, 150

Mardin, Arif, 125–26, 158
Marie, Teena, 161
Markum, Pigmeat, 37
Marley, Bob, 162, 166
Marsh, Dave, 109
Marshall, Thurgood, 16, 20, 59, 95–96
Marsham, Viola, 27
Martin, Bobby, 143, 144
Martin, George, 92
Marvellettes, 89
Marvin, Junior, 84
mashed potato (dance), 101
Mathis, Johnny, 76, 136
Mattias, James, 28, 32
Maultsby, Portia, 18
Mayfield, Curtis, 84, 148, 153, 157; Chicago soul sound, 82; and films, 123–26; social philosophy songs, 85
Mayo, Barry, 183
Mayo, Buddy, 132
Mays, Willie, 36, 60–61
Maze band, 186–87
MCA Records, 135, 137, 148–49, 161; and Motown, 179–80
McCartney, Paul, 168
McCoo, Marilyn, 155
McCoy, Van, 146
McCrae, George, 153
McCrae, Gwen, 153
McDonald, Eugene, 22
McEwen, Joe, 78
McFerrin, Bobby, 194
McMurry, Lillian, 28–30, 83
McMurry, Willard, 28–30
McNeely, Big Jay, 26
McPhatter, Clyde, 69, 77
Meco, 157
Medina, Benny, 148
Melle Mel, 189, 193
Mellow Moods, 35
Melvin, Harold, and the Bluenotes, 144–45
Memphis, 50–51, 54, 82, 91, 140–42; Presley and, 62. *See also* Stax Records; WDIA, Memphis
Mercury Records, 27, 102, 143, 191
Mesner, Ed and Leo, 27
Meteor label, 28
MFSB, 144–46, 154, 180, 191
MGM Records, 26, 148
Michael, George, 200

Mighty Three Music, 144
Milburn, Amos, 26
Miller, Frank, 75
Miller, Rice, 12
Mills, Stephanie, 155, 177
Mills Brothers, 26
Mintz, Leo, 66
Miracles, 92
Modern label, 26–27, 66
Modern Sounds in Country and Western (album), 71
Moir, Monte, 195
mom-and-pop stores, xv, 29, 74–76, 138, 172; decline of, 174–76; and major record companies, 161–63
Monk, Thelonius, 24–25
Montana, Vince, 146
Montgomery, Monk, 38
Moore, Harry T., 40
Moore, Melba, 154
Moroder, Giorgio, 154
Morrison, Junie, 156
Motown label, 25, 82, 83, 84, 86, 99, 106, 109, 124, 142, 161, 168; demise of, 148, 179; and Gordy, 83, 87–89; and major record labels, 136–37; and PIR, 143; and Jackson Five, 149
Motown Revue, 74, 88–89
Mr. Magic, 190
Mtume, 182
MTV videos, 173–74, 192–93, 195
Muhammad, Elijah, 71
Muhammad Ali, 82
Murray, Albert, 9, 69
Murray, Donald, 16

NAACP, 5, 7, 16, 69, 96; and school desegregation case, 59
Nashboro–Ernie Y label, 28
Nathan, Syd, 27, 37, 102
National Association of Radio Announcers (NARA), 112–13
National Association of Black Promoters (NABP), 178–79
National Association of Retail Merchandisers (NARM), 169
National Negro Business League, 7
National Records, 27, 38
Native Son (Wright), 20
NATRA (National Association of Televi-

sion and Radio Announcers), 113–15, 119, 134, 165–67, 185; convention (1968), 127–28
NBC, 172–73
Negro Digest, 22
Negro Leagues, 12–13, 57–58
"Negro Radio" (Haley article), 40
Nelson, Richard, 27
Nevil, Robbie, 200
New Deal programs, 15–16
New Edition, 182
New Orleans, 28, 52–54
New York, 114; radio stations, 66–67, 90–91, 111–12, 116–17, 119, 127, 129; and urban radio, 183. *See also* WBLS-FM
New York Fresh Fest (revue), 192–93
Nixon, Richard Milhous, 103–4
Nobles, Gene, 28, 54–55
Novick, Harry, 127

Off the Wall (album), 157, 168–69
Ohio Players, 153
O'Jay, Eddie, 41, 93, 116, 126, 128, 130; in Buffalo, 89–91; on Freed, 66–67
O'Jays, 136, 145, 151
Okeh Records, 9, 46, 82–83, 85
O'Neal, Alexander, 195
Operation PUSH, 139–40, 178
Original 13 (deejays' organization), 43
Orioles, 35, 69
Osborne, Jeffrey, 175
Otis, Johnny, 29, 64, 65, 77
"Out of Sight," 102
"outcast" songs, 152–53
Oxley, Harold, 17

P-Funk, 162
Page, Gene, 155
Page, Satchell, 12
Page, Walter, 38
Paige, Sharon, 145
Paisley Park label, 195
Palmer, Robert, 64, 101–2
Paramount Pictures Music Division, 111
Paramount Records, 10–11, 140
Parker, Charlie, 24–25, 93
Parker, Maceo, 156
Parker, Ray, Jr., 155, 177

Parks, Gordon, 123
Parlet, 155
Parliament, 155
Parliament-Funkadelic, 187
Pate, Johnny, 82, 85, 182
Patton, Bob, 99
Paul, Billy, 145, 155
payola, 29, 75, 165; Freed and, 67; reasons for, 55; "white" and "black," 89
Peaches and Herb, 152
Peacock label, 27–28, 69. *See also* Duke-Peacock Records
Pendergrass, Teddy, 136, 144, 151, 152
Peoples, 180
Pepper, John R., 48, 51
Perren, Freddie, 152
Peretti, Hugo, 81
Perry, Andre, 132, 133
"personality" jocks, 42, 116–19, 126–31; and rap, 189–90
Petrillo, James C., 23
Pettiford, Oscar, 38
Philadelphia, 91, 99, 142–44, 162; and BMA conference, 166; radio stations, 88, 183; and Webb, 74–76
Philadelphia International Records (PIR), 142–46, 150; at CBS, 179–80
Philco-Aladdin label, 27
Phillips, Dewey, 52, 54, 91
Phillips, Sam, 28, 51, 52, 62, 65
Philly sound, 145–46, 155, 180, 195; and disco, 154
Pickett, Wilson, 128, 143, 144
Pilgrim Travelers, 79
Pips. *See* Knight, Gladys, and the Pips
PIR. *See* Philadelphia International Records
Pitts, Martha, 125
Pointer Sisters, 177
Poitier, Sidney, 118, 122–23
Polydor label, 148, 149, 152, 161
Polygram label, 180
pop music, 10, 143–44; charts and black artists, 181–82; corporate black, 155; major labels and crossover artists, 150–56; and radio, 23
pop radio stations, 128–29
Poppa Stoppa, 52–53
Porter, Cole, 38
Porter, David, 138, 181
Porter, Lew, 65

Possey, Cumberland, 12
Potts, Gene, 43
Powell, Adam Clayton, Jr., 59–60, 69, 96
Powell, Bill, 43
Powell, Teddy, 163
Presley, Elvis, 47, 52, 68, 78, 81, 194; and black culture, 62–64
Price, Lloyd, 53, 83
Prince, 181; retronuevo importance of, 194–95; sexuality and crossover image, 174, 196; and white management, 177
Profile label, 191, 192
Progress of Philadelphia, 74–75
Pryor, Ricahrd, 138–39
"psychedelic soul" recordings, 85, 124
Public Enemy, 192, 194
Pumpkin, 190
Purple Rain (film), 195–96

Queen Booking, 74, 88–89, 163
Queen (rock group), 159
"Quiet Storm" radio program and format, 132–33, 187–88
Quinn, Bill, 27

R&B (rhythm & blues), 188; beginnings, 23–29; and black radio, 29–30, 40–57; and civil-rights movement, 16; corporate control of, 133–38; and electric bass, 39; and films, 123–24; and gospel music, 80; and JBs, 99–102; Leiber and Stoller and, 64–66; musical and socioeconomic meanings of, *xii–xvi*; 1940s awards, 25; Presley and, 63–64; and recorded radio music, 18; and retronuevo, 186–88; *cf.* rock & roll, 68–69
race music, 9–12
racial identity, 199–201; Michael Jackson and Prince, 174
racism, *xiii*, 4, 59; in concert promotion, 163–65; 1980s resurgence of, 171; and payola investigation of 1976, 165
radio, *xv*, 11–12; and recorded music, 18, 23. *See also* black radio; urban radio
ragtime, 8, 9
Ragtime (film), 6
Rainbow Coalition, 171–72

Rainbow label, 36
Rainey, Ma. 9, 10, 73
Randolph, A. Philip, 21
rap, *xii*, 188–94
"Rapper's Delight," 169
Rapture (album), 188
Ravens, 26, 35
Rawls, Lou, 70, 79, 81, 155, 180
Raydio label, 155
RCA Records, 76, 81, 102, 135, 137, 149, 161, 179–80
RCA/Victor Records, 39
Reagan administration, 171, 176
Reconstruction period, 6
record industry, *xv*, 76, 119; black-owned labels, 10–11; and BMA, 166; distribution of race music, 11; and Howard graduates, 133; impact of WW II, 23; and 1979 recession, 167–68; in 1920s, 8–11; size of, in 1970, 136
Record World, 34, 129, 131
recordings. *See* independent record companies; major record companies; names of artists and groups
Red Robin label, 28, 35–36
Redding, Otis, 35, 47, 110–11, 115, 128, 138; and Bar-Kays, 100–101; and Sam Cooke, 79; death, 110–11; Stax and, 86–87, 138
Reed, Jimmy, 84
Reeves, Martha, 106
Regal Theater (Chicago), 162, 186
religious music. *See* Charles, Ray; gospel music
Rene, Leon and Otis, 27
REO Speedwagon, 168
retronuevo, 186–88; and rap/hip-hop scene, 189
Rhodes, Todd, 66
Rhythm Debs, 37
rhythm sections (bands), 38–39, 187
Ricco, Joe, 128
Rich, Charlie, 47
Richardson, Karl, 158
Richbourg, John R., 54, 86–87
Richie, Lionel, 155, 160, 175; and sales of singles, 182; and white management, 177
Righteous Brothers, 158
Ritchie Family, 154
RKO stations, 118
Robey, Don, 27–28, 56–57, 69, 176,

196; character and career, 31–34; and Joe Scott, 37

Robins, 66

Robinson, Bobby, 28, 34–35, 83, 115; and rap, 190

Robinson, Eugene, 172–73

Robinson, Frank, 58

Robinson, Jackie, 36, 57

Robinson, Smokey, 116, 128, 133, 158, 165, 166, 181, 188

Robinson, Sylvia and Joe, 190–91

rock & roll, *xii*, 137, 188; barnstorming shows, 192; and blacks, 92; evolution of, 106–11; Freed and, 66–68; impact on white teens and on blacks, 68–69; Jackson and Prince and, 195; and Presley, 63–64; as white music, after 1965, 93, 181

Rogers, Kenny, 160, 177

Rolling Stone, 32, 181, 194

Rolling Stone Illustrated History (Palmer), 101

Rolling Stones, 92, 110, 130, 159

Roosevelt, Franklin Delano, 15–16, 20–21

Roosevelt, Theodore, 4

Rosenberg, Michael, 178

Ross, Diana, 106, 130, 154, 179, 194

royalties, 80–81; and Atlantic Records, 37; and major labels, 149; and Don Robey, 31–33

RSO label, 158

Ruffin, David, 79, 158

Run-DMC, 192–93, 194

Rupe, Art, 27, 71, 79–80, 83

Rush Productions, 192

Salsoul Orchestra, 146, 154, 155

Sample, Joe, 156

San Francisco, 106, 108, 183

Santana, 136

SAR Records, 81, 102

Satellite. *See* Stax Records

Saturday Night Fever (film), 158–59

Savoy label, 11, 26–27, 33, 55

Scarlets, 35

School of Broadcast Science, NATRA, 114–15

Schriffen, Lalo, 113

Scorsese, Martin, 195

Scott, Emmett J., 7

Scott, Joe, 33, 37

Scott-Heron, Gil, 187

Sears, Zenas (Daddy), 46–47

Sehorn, Marshall, 115

self-sufficiency argument, 3, 6, 13, 71–72, 96

"sermon" songs (Mayfield), 85

sexuality, 8, 63; and Eurodisco, 154; and Presley, 62–63; of Prince, 174; of Wilson and Cooke, 78–80

Sgt. Pepper's Lonely Hearts Club Band, 158

Shaft (film), 123–24, 138

Shalamar, 179

sharecropping, 16, 40

sheet music, 8, 10

Sheila E., 195

Shider, Gary, 156

Shields, Del, 118; as deejay, 112–13, 126–27, 130; and NATRA, 113–15, 131, 166

Shiffman, Bobby, 131, 163

Sign "O" the Times (film), 195–96

Sill, Lester, 66

Silver Convention, 146, 154

Simmons, Joey, 192

Simmons, Lonnie, 180

Simmons, Russell, 189, 192, 194

Simon and Garfunkel, 110

Simpson, Donnie, 172

Simpson, Valerie, 148, 152, 159

Skyy, 177

Slaughter, Vernon, 133–35, 167–68

Sleeping Bag label, 191

Sly and the Family Stone, 136. *See also* Stone, Sly

Smalls, Tommy (Dr. Jive), 43

Smash label, 102

Smikle, Ken, 128

Smith, Bessie, 9, 10

Smith, Jim, 133–34, 141

Smith, Jimmy, 113

Smith, Mamie, 9, 83

Smith, O. C., 134

Smith, Trixie, 10

Soccio, Gino, 159

Solar Records, 179–80

songwriter-businessmen, 79–85

songwriter-producers, 180–81

Soul Children, 138, 148

soul music, *xii*, 18, 70–71, 93, 101, 106, 157, 182, 196; artists and crossover audiences, 150–53; and disco, 155–56; and Aretha Franklin, 105; and Harvard Report, 136; Hathaway and jazz orchestrations, 125; resurgence of, 186–88
Soul Stirrers, 70–71, 79, 81
Soul Survivor magazine, 47–48
Soul Train (dance program), 137–38, 165
Souls of Black Folk, The (Du Bois), 5
"Sound of Young America, The," 88, 106
Southern Christian Leadership Conference, 96–97
Spann, Hank (Dixie Drifter), 90–91
Spaulding, Norman, 18
Specialty Records, 27, 71, 79–80
Spielberg, Steven, 196
Spinners, 89, 155
spirituals, 9, 30
Spoonie Gee, 190
Staple Singers, 125, 133, 148
Starr, Edwin, 89
Staton, Candi, 152
Stax Records, 51, 82, 86–87, 109, 111, 133–34, 143, 148, 196; CBS and Harvard Report, 136–37; 146; and Gulf + Western, 138–41; and Jesse Jackson, 139–40
Stevenson, Adlai, 40
Stevenson, Mickey, 148
Stewart, Billy, 83
Stewart, Estelle, 86–87
Stewart, Jim, 86–87, 111, 139–41
Stewart, Rod, 159
Stigwood, Robert, 158
Stoller, Mike, 64–66, 85
Stomping the Blues (Murray), 9, 69
Stone, Freddie, 109
Stone, Henry, 153
Stone, Jesse, 37–39, 181
Stone, Sly (Sylvester Stewart), 101, 130, 134, 157, 188; gospel background and career, 108–11; song catalogues, 195
Stone, Toni, 57
stroll (dance), 47
Studio 54 (New York), 159, 189
Stylistics, 155
Sugar Hill Gang, 169, 191
Sugar Hill Records, 190–92
Summer, Donna, 154, 155, 177, 181–82
Sun label, 28, 51, 63

Super Disc label, 27
Superbreaks (rap album), 190
Superfly (film), 123–24
Supreme Court (U.S.), 59, 95–96, 171
Supremes, 88, 89, 92
Sutra label, 192
Sutton, Percy, 127, 186
Sweet Soul Music (Guralnick), 80–81
Sweet Sweetback's Badass Song (film), 122–23
swing music, 11, 24, 25, 67, 93; end of era, 200
Sykes, Roosevelt, 25
Sylvers, Leon, 179
synthesizers, 181, 187

Tangerine label, 71
Tarnopol, Nat, 77–78, 80, 165
Tarsia, Joe, 143
Tattersall, Marie, 137–38
Taylor, Johnnie, 79, 81, 138, 148, 150–52
Taylor, LeBaron, 88, 137, 150, 166; quits CBS, 167–68
Taylor, Sam (The Man), 39
Teagarden, Jack, 24
Teenage Awards Music International (TAMI), 92
teenagers: and electric music, 106–7; and Hendrix, 109; and rock & roll, 67, 92–93; and Sly Stone, 110
Teenchords, 35
Temperton, Rod, 168
Temptations, 89, 124, 153
Terry, Wallace, 131
Tex, Joe, 101, 136
Tharpe, Sister Rosetta, 30
That Nigger's Crazy (album), 139
Thomas, Carla, 86, 125
Thomas, Rufus, 50–52, 86, 133
Thornton, Willie Mae (Big Mama), 32, 63, 66
Three Degrees, 145–46
Thriller (album), 182
Time magazine, 105, 131
Time (musical group), 175, 195
TK Records, 153, 196
Tommy Boy label, 191, 194
Toop, David, 35
Tosches, Nick, 38

"Total Black Experience in Sound" (program), 129–30, 159
Total Experience label, 180
Toussaint, Allen, 34, 54
Townsend, Robert, 186
Tramps, 146, 158
Travolta, John, 158
Treacherous Three, 190
Trotter, William Monroe, 5
Trumpet label, 28, 30
Turner, Ike, 149
Turner, Joe, 39, 66
Turner, Tina, 106, 149
Tuskegee Institute, 4, 7–8, 21, 40
Tympany Five, 19, 39, 99
Tyrell, Jim, 166

Uncle Tom image, 4, 25, 72, 162; James Brown and, 103
United Artists label, 55, 150–51
Up from Slavery (Washington), 7
Uptown Theater (Philadelphia), 88, 99, 162
urban radio, 159–61, 183–84

Valentinos, 81
Valli, Frankie, 84
Van Peebles, Melvin, 122–23, 186
Van Walls, Harry, 39
Vanderpol, Sylvia. *See* Robinson, Sylvia and Joe
Vandross, Luther, 175, 177
Vanity, 175, 195
Vaughan, Sarah, 41
Vee-Jay label, 28, 82–85
Victor Records, 23, 26
Videos. *See* MTV videos
Vocaleers, 35–36

Walden, Phil, 115
Walker, Madame C. J., 60
Wallace, Michelle, 104
Walters, Norby, 176–77
Ware, George, 167
Warner Bros. Records, 135, 152, 155, 161, 194; and Atlantic, 110; "California Soul" concerts, 148–49
Warwick, Dionne, 106, 148

Washington, Booker T., 7–8, 21, 31, 60, 186. *See also* assimilation philosophy
Washington, Dinah, 26, 72–74, 188
Washington, Grover, Jr, 129, 156
Washington, D.C., 131–33, 135, 172–73
Waters, Ethel, 10
Waters, Muddy, 37, 83, 107
Watts Summer Festival (1972), 140
Wattstax, 139–40
WBLS-FM, New York, 129–30, 132, 159, 165, 190
WDIA, Memphis, 28, 40–41, 48–52, 62, 86
"We Are the World," 100, 186
WEA label, 110
Weather Report, 136
Weaver, Robert, 95
Webb, Bruce, 74–77, 133, 142, 162, 175
Webb, Chick, 11, 38
WERD, Atlanta, 28–29, 44–46
Wesley, Fred, 156
Westbound label, 149
Westbrooks, Logan, 134–35, 141
Wexler, Jerry, 37, 70, 80, 86–87, 115; and Aretha Franklin recordings, 105; and Stax, 110–11
Whispers, 179–80
White, Barry, 131, 146, 154–55
White, Granville (Granny), 134
White, Maurice, 155, 165
White, Skippy, 175
White, Sonny Joe, 160
"White Negro, The" (Mailer essay), 61–62
white Negroism, 29, 62–64, 177, 200; and CBS artists, 110; disco-crossover and black radio, 157–59; and rock & roll, 67
Whiteman, Paul, 9, 18
whites: and assimilation of black jazz, 9; and black-radio ownership, 183–84; and James Brown, 103; and Bryson, 182–83; love for black music, 200; musicians' creativity, 108; 1950s integration, 59–62; and Presley, 63; as R&B deejays, 51–52; and rock & roll, 106–10; and WBLS, New York, 130
Whitfield, Norman, 124, 157
Whodini (rap act), 189, 192–93
WHUR, Howard University, 127, 131–35, 172–73, 187
William, McKinnley, 187

William Morris Agency, 89, 163
Williams, Cootie, 25
Williams, Deniece, 152, 155, 180
Williams, Dootsie, 36
Williams, Dyanna, 132
Williams, James (D Train), 181
Williams, Paul, 26
Williams, Nat D., 49
Williams, Yancey, 21
Williamson, Sonny Boy, 12, 30, 48–50
Willis, Chuck, 46–47
Wills, Maury, 58
Wilson, August, 73
Wilson, Belinda, 164
Wilson, Brian, 93
Wilson, Jackie, 93, 99, 151, 165, 194; career and voice, 70, 77–79, 83
Wilson, Nancy, 134, 177
Winfrey, Oprah, 173
Winley, Paul, and Sound of New York, 190
WINS, New York, 66–67, 90
Winslow, Vernon, 52–54
Winter, Johnny, 108
Winwood, Stevie, 200
Witherspoon, Jimmy, 66
WKYS, Washington, 172–73
WLAC, Nashville, 29, 54, 62, 86, 126
WLIB, FM and AM, New York, 111–12, 127. *See also* WBLS-FM
WMAQ, Cleveland, 89–90

WMBM, Miami, 28, 45
WOKJ, Jackson, Mississippi, 40
Womack, Bobby, 79, 82, 150–51, 180
Wonder, Stevie, 89, 129, 168, 181; and BMA, 165–66; recordings, 124, 126, 130, 157, 168
Wood, Macy Lela, 27
Wood, Randy, 28, 54–55
Woods, Georgie, 88
Woods, Jimmy, 43
World War II, 13; and blacks, 20–22; and record industry, 23
Worrell, Bernie, 156
Wright, Ed, 113, 165–66, 167
Wright, Richard, 15, 20
WRKS, New York (aka KISS), 183
WUFO, Buffalo, 89–91, 116–17, 128
WWRL, New York, 116–17, 119, 127–28
WXLW, St. Louis (KXLW), 28, 40

Yarborough, 180
"You'll Never Walk Alone," 47–48
Young, Al, 102
Young, Early, 142, 146, 154
Young, Ernie, 28
Young, Paul, 200
Young Black Programmers Coalition, 167

Zenith Corporation, 22

FOR THE BEST IN PAPERBACKS, LOOK FOR THE

In every corner of the world, on every subject under the sun, Penguin represents quality and variety—the very best in publishing today.

For complete information about books available from Penguin—including Penguin Classics, Penguin Compass, and Puffins—and how to order them, write to us at the appropriate address below. Please note that for copyright reasons the selection of books varies from country to country.

In the United States: Please write to *Penguin Group (USA) Inc., P.O. Box 12289 Dept. B, Newark, New Jersey 07101-5289* or call 1-800-788-6262.

In the United Kingdom: Please write to *Dept. EP, Penguin Books Ltd, Bath Road, Harmondsworth, West Drayton, Middlesex UB7 0DA.*

In Canada: Please write to *Penguin Books Canada Ltd, 10 Alcorn Avenue, Suite 300, Toronto, Ontario M4V 3B2.*

In Australia: Please write to *Penguin Books Australia Ltd, P.O. Box 257, Ringwood, Victoria 3134.*

In New Zealand: Please write to *Penguin Books (NZ) Ltd, Private Bag 102902, North Shore Mail Centre, Auckland 10.*

In India: Please write to *Penguin Books India Pvt Ltd, 11 Panchsheel Shopping Centre, Panchsheel Park, New Delhi 110 017.*

In the Netherlands: Please write to *Penguin Books Netherlands bv, Postbus 3507, NL-1001 AH Amsterdam.*

In Germany: Please write to *Penguin Books Deutschland GmbH, Metzlerstrasse 26, 60594 Frankfurt am Main.*

In Spain: Please write to *Penguin Books S. A., Bravo Murillo 19, 1° B, 28015 Madrid.*

In Italy: Please write to *Penguin Italia s.r.l., Via Benedetto Croce 2, 20094 Corsico, Milano.*

In France: Please write to *Penguin France, Le Carré Wilson, 62 rue Benjamin Baillaud, 31500 Toulouse.*

In Japan: Please write to *Penguin Books Japan Ltd, Kaneko Building, 2-3-25 Koraku, Bunkyo-Ku, Tokyo 112.*

In South Africa: Please write to *Penguin Books South Africa (Pty) Ltd, Private Bag X14, Parkview, 2122 Johannesburg.*